TEACHING LANGUAGE IN CONTEXT

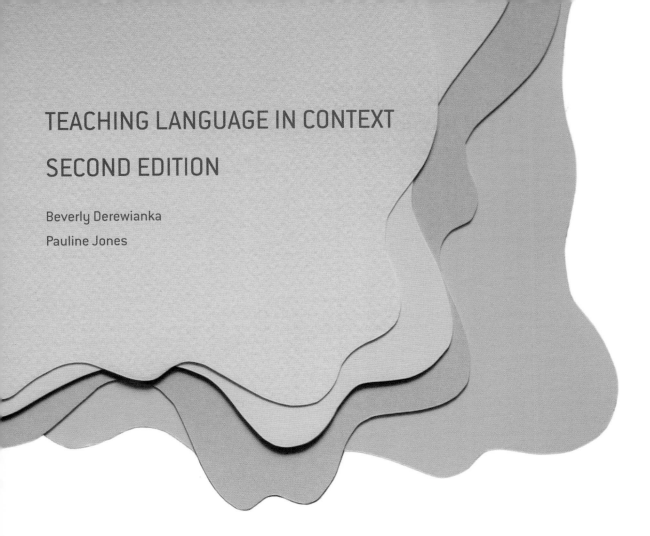

TEACHING LANGUAGE IN CONTEXT

SECOND EDITION

Beverly Derewianka

Pauline Jones

OXFORD

UNIVERSITY PRESS

AUSTRALIA & NEW ZEALAND

OXFORD
UNIVERSITY PRESS

Oxford University Press is a department of the University of Oxford.

It furthers the University's objective of excellence in research, scholarship, and education by publishing worldwide. Oxford is a registered trademark of Oxford University Press in the UK and in certain other countries.

Published in Australia by
Oxford University Press
253 Normanby Road, South Melbourne, Victoria 3205, Australia

© Beverly Derewianka and Pauline Jones 2016

The moral rights of the authors have been asserted.

First published 2012

Second edition published 2016

Reprinted 2018, 2019

National Library of Australia Cataloguing-in-Publication entry

Creator: Derewianka, Beverly, 1946- author.
Title: Teaching language in context / Beverly Derewianka, Pauline Jones.

Edition: Second edition.
ISBN: 9780190303686 (paperback)

Notes: Includes bibliographical references and index.

Subjects: English language—Study and teaching.
Literacy—Study and teaching.

Other Creators/Contributors:
Jones, Pauline, 1958- author.

Dewey Number: 372.6

Edited by Venetia Somerset
Cover design by Astred Hicks, Design Cherry
Text design by Rose Keevins
Typeset by diacriTech, Chennai, India
Indexed by Alisa Dodge
Printed in China by Golden Cup Printing Co. Ltd.

Links to third party websites are provided by Oxford in good faith and for information only. Oxford disclaims any responsibility for the materials contained in any third party website referenced in this work.

CONTENTS

LIST OF FIGURES

LIST OF TABLES

PREFACE: A LANGUAGE-BASED VIEW OF LEARNING

Language is at the heart of the learning process. We learn through language. Our knowledge about the world is constructed in language—the worlds of home and the community, the worlds of school subjects, the worlds of literature, the worlds of the workplace, and so on. It is through language that we interact with others and build our identities. Teachers' explanations, classroom discussions, assessment of student achievement, and students' understanding, composition, and evaluation of texts are all mediated through language. In this book, we will be exploring how an explicit understanding of how language works enables students to make informed choices in their use and understanding of texts.

The language of schooling differs from the language of everyday life. It involves increasingly complex, abstract, and detailed understandings of concepts. It requires students to interact with others in ways that extend, consolidate, and challenge their understanding. And it differs across the areas of the curriculum. The language of science is quite distinctive, as are the languages of history, geography, and the arts. This kind of language is not necessarily picked up. It needs to be taught in the context of regular teaching and learning activities.

As educators, our job is to make sure that all students have a good command of the language needed to succeed in school and beyond. In order to do this, teachers need to know about language and how it works. Our knowledge about language not only influences the conversations about language we foster in the classroom, it enables us to:

- plan units of work that are sensitive to the language demands placed on students
- design activities with a language focus
- select texts for reading at an appropriate level
- analyse texts to identify relevant language features
- create teaching materials that integrate an awareness of language
- help students to access meanings created through a variety of media (written, spoken, visual, multimodal)
- identify problems that students are having in reading academic texts
- assess students' written work
- extend students' ability to articulate what they are learning.

This book is intended as an introduction to the language that students encounter in the various curriculum areas as they move through the years of schooling. In this second edition, there is an increased emphasis on the multimodal nature of texts, particularly the relationship between image and language, and the place of visuals in supporting students to master the literacy demands of the curriculum. The book also recognises the increasingly elaborate texts found in the more complex literacy tasks of upper primary and lower secondary classrooms. We hope it will make visible the language challenges facing students and how we can support students in meeting these challenges.

HOW THIS BOOK IS ORGANISED

Part 1 introduces you to some general principles.

In *Chapter 1* we discuss the approach to language adopted in the book.

Chapter 2 provides a more detailed overview of the functional model of language. This is a chapter that you might need to keep referring back to as you work your way through the book as it outlines the whole model and how the different elements relate to each other.

Chapter 3 introduces a cycle of teaching and learning for implementing the approach to language taken in this book, identifying the importance of dialogue in learning to be literate and describing one classroom example in detail. Other examples of the teaching-learning cycle in action can be found in Part 2.

Part 2 goes into greater detail, focusing on the genres and associated language features encountered in school contexts. The chapters range across relevant areas of the curriculum and deal with the early years of schooling through to mid-secondary.

Chapter 4 explores the world of stories, looking at how narratives unfold and ways in which language builds up the characters and setting.

Chapter 5 deals with different kinds of recounts—from recounts of personal experience through to recounts of historical events.

Chapter 6 explores a number of different kinds of reports, the texts used for observing and describing the world.

Chapter 7 looks at the ways in which we use language to explain how things work and why things happen in areas such as science, technology, history, and geography

Chapter 8 examines the language of persuading, including arguments and discussions.

Chapter 9 focuses on the language of responses, including personal responses, reviews and critical analysis.

Chapter 10 is a new chapter that examines mixed texts or 'macrogenres' arising from the processes of inquiry in a range of curriculum fields. These texts include fair tests, lab reports, design reports, investigation reports, and problem-solution reports.

Your knowledge about the language system and how language functions to make different kinds of meaning will be systematically built up throughout the chapters (see Appendix 1 for an overview of the functional model of language and Appendix 2 for a map of how the model is dealt with across the chapters). For this reason, it might be preferable to work through the chapters in sequence, though to a certain extent the chapters can stand on their own.

In each chapter you will find activities that invite you to reflect on what you are learning ('Think about it') and activities that allow you to become familiar with the language feature in question ('Have a go!'). These activities can be done in collaboration with others or individually. We suggest that doing the activities will help to consolidate your understanding of the content.

GUIDED TOUR

1

AN APPROPRIATE MODEL OF LANGUAGE

Each chapter opens with clearly defined **Learning objectives** to help you focus on the key points of the chapter. Important **Key terms and concepts** in the chapter are also identified.

Language is at the heart of the learning process. In order to succeed in school, students need to use language for such purposes as explaining, arguing, recounting, and describing across a range of subject areas in a variety of media and modes. Such language does not come naturally to most students and generally requires explicit teaching. This means that teachers themselves need to have a solid understanding of how language operates in academic contexts. Unfortunately, however, this is not always the case. In an attempt to address this, the *Australian Curriculum: English* includes an explicit knowledge about language as a major focus. This chapter will begin to introduce the functional model of language that informs the national curriculum.

Learning objectives

In this chapter, you will:

- begin to become familiar with a functional model of language
- be introduced to the language system as a rich network of resources for making meaning
- understand how the context in which language is used impacts upon the kinds of choices made from the language system
- consider the implications of a functional model for your own understanding of how language works and for your classroom practice

Key terms and concepts

macrogenres
reports (descriptive, classifying, compositional, comparative, historical)
action verbs
relating verbs
auxiliary verbs

lexical cohesion
infographics
visual metalanguage
vectors
viewing angle

Margin notes provide definitions of key terms and cross-references to other chapters to help you navigate the text and aid your understanding as you read.

WHAT ARE THE MAJOR LANGUAGE RESOURCES FOR NARRATIVES?

Narratives draw on a wide range of language resources involving all three functions of language:

- representing various kinds of experience (the *Ideational* function)
- engaging the reader through, for example, the expression of emotion, the evaluation of qualities, and the judgment of human behaviour (the *Interpersonal* function)
- shaping the language into a cohesive text (the *Textual* function).
  Let's look at each of these in greater detail in relation to narrative.

See Chapters 1 and 2 to revise these functions.

Expressing and elaborating ideas: Developing control of field-related meanings

Narrative texts construct events and happenings through choices from the **Ideational function** of language:

- specific human and non-human Participants (*Andy's legs* started with a jolt; *his legs* started before *his brain* did, and *he* made after *Dave* and *Jim*. And *the dog* followed *Andy*.)

Ideational function: language resources for representing our experience of the world ('What's happening?', 'Who/ what's involved?', 'How? When? Where? Why?') and connecting ideas.

Think about it sections appear regularly throughout the text, encouraging you to reflect on what you are learning and think critically about the ideas addressed. These are also great for stimulating group discussions.

Think about it

The class was engaged in a unit of work on earthquakes. The teacher had asked the students to write a story about earthquakes, expecting that they would explain how an earthquake happens. One student wrote the following:

> Have you ever been in an earthquake? Well, I have. It was really scary. Our house started shaking and all my books fell off my bookcase and the cat ran under the house and we couldn't get her out so we had to get some food to get her to come out. There have been a lot of earthquakes in Japan and New Zealand. I hope we don't have another one here.

What does the text reveal about the student's understanding of the genre, field, tenor, and mode required? How could the teacher have provided better guidance?

Have a go!

Just by looking at the opening lines of a text, we can usually infer the genre being used. From the following, see if you can predict the likely genre. (Hint: Think about the likely purpose of the text.) What is it in the language choices that enable you to identify the genre?

- Once there were four children whose names were Peter, Susan, Edmund, and Lucy.
- The koala is an arboreal herbivorous marsupial native to Australia.
- Do this science experiment to learn about the chemical reaction that makes sherbet so fizzy when you put it in your mouth.
- There are many reasons why new laws should be introduced to make organic farming techniques compulsory for all Australian growers.
- The plants in our school vegetable garden are looking unhealthy.
- On Tuesday 3A went to the animal sanctuary to observe the wildlife.
- Erosion is the result of several factors.

Have a go! boxes give you the opportunity to try your hand at working with the language features discussed in each chapter, on your own or in group tutorials. They encourage you to consider the concepts and issues raised, and their importance in teaching.

In the classroom boxes present activities or scenarios taken from real classrooms, which will allow you to practise teaching methods and experiment with alternative practices.

In the classroom

Different diagrams offer different ways of explaining a phenomenon, but not all diagrams are equally effective. The following activity supports students in becoming critical interpreters of cycle diagrams.

1. Get students to look carefully at a collection of diagrams that attempt to explain the same phenomenon, such as the water-cycle diagrams below.
2. In pairs, ask the students to use each of the diagrams to orally explain the phenomenon (e.g. the water cycle).
3. Get them to choose which diagram they preferred in terms of how well it represented the phenomenon.
4. Ask them to explain why they chose that particular diagram. What did it offer that others didn't?

Do the above activity yourself with the diagrams in Figure 7.5. If you were scaffolding the students' understanding of the diagram, at which point of the diagram would you start? Could you have started elsewhere?

Figure 7.5   Diagrams of the water cycle

1. The sun heats the ocean.
2. Ocean water evaporates and rises into the air.
3. The water vapour cools and condenses to become droplets, which form clouds.
4. If enough water condenses, the drops become heavy enough to fall to the ground as rain and snow.
5. Some rain collects in groundwells. The rest flows through rivers back into the ocean.

CHAPTER SUMMARY

In this chapter we have examined how language is used to recount various kinds of personal experiences and historical events. We have seen how different recount genres are organised into significant stages. We have also investigated the characteristic language features of recounts, including various ways of talking about time, the past simple tense, and figurative language in literary recounts. We have focused on the mode continuum, moving from the exploratory spoken mode and working across to the more crafted, compact language of the written mode. We have also looked at how cohesion changes in the shift from oral to written language. Strategies for teaching and assessing these have been suggested.

FOR FURTHER DISCUSSION

1   What have you learnt from this chapter that you didn't know before? What provided useful insights? Which bits did you find challenging? What still needs clarification? How will you do this?

2   Design a series of lessons around recounts using the mode continuum as a guide.

3   How does the mode continuum map onto the teaching-learning cycle in Chapter 3?

REFERENCES

Lawson, H. (1970). *The Loaded Dog.* Sydney: Angus & Robertson.

South Australian Department of Education and Children's Services (2010). Engaging in and Exploring Writing. Literacy Secretariat Resource Paper, consultative draft, p. 2.

WEBSITES

The Learning Place
http://learningplace.com.au/deliver/content.asp?pid=36766

This website has been developed by and for Queensland teachers. It has suggestions for teaching a variety of genres as well as notes on functional grammar.

Teacher Moderation: Collaborative Assessment of Student Work
www.edu.gove.on.ca/literacynumeracy/inspire/research/Teacher_Moderation.pdf

This website from Ontario describes how teachers can use moderated assessment to evaluate recounts written by their students.

TeachFind
www.teachfind.com/primary-literacy-framework

This is a UK website that provides a very detailed lesson plan for teaching recounts.

100 Biographies & Memoirs to Read in a Lifetime: Readers' picks
www.goodreads.com/list/show/85102.100_Biographies_Memoirs_to_Read_in_a_Lifetime_Readers_Picks

A collection of outstanding memoirs, including several suitable for older students.

Chapter summaries consolidate your learning and highlight the significance of the issues discussed, and **For further discussion** questions let you apply what you have learned and stimulate your critical thinking.

Annotated **References** and **Websites** direct you to additional resources that will extend your thinking beyond the chapter.

ACKNOWLEDGMENTS

The authors and the publisher wish to thank the following copyright holders for reproduction of their material.

Alamy/© Pictorial Press Ltd, Fig 2.2; Australian Curriculum, Assessment and Reporting Authority (ACARA) for extract; Daniel DePierre for cover illustration from *The Loaded Dog* by Henry Lawson, Book Group Australia, 2010; Dogo News for extract from website www.dogonews.com; Harper Collins for use of cover from *The Loaded Dog* by Henry Lawson with illustration by Walter Cunningham, Young Australia Series: Angus & Robertson 1970; ILETS Buddy for report extract from website, www.ieltsbuddy.com/problem-solution-essays.htm; Macmillan Publishers Australia for use of cover image *The Loaded Dog* by Henry Lawson, illustration by Antony Elworthy, Macmillan Education, 2009; Michael Z Lewin for The Hand the Feeds Me. *In Rover's Tales*. New York: St Martins Press, 1998; National Library of Australia/ Gold Fields setting image; Oxford University Press for extracts from Oxford Reading Tree series; Salon for article *Dont Kill the Oxford Comma*! by Mary Elizabeth Williams, June 30, 2011 www.salon.com; Scholastic Press for extracts From the book *Wombat Stew* by Marcia Vaughan and Pamela Lofts. Text copyright © Marcia Vaughan 1984, illustrations copyright © Pamela Lofts 1984. First published by Scholastic Press, a division of Scholastic Australia Pty Limited 1984. Reproduced by permission of Scholastic Australia Pty Limited; Selah School for extract from website www.selah.k12.wa.us/; Shutterstock, Figs from Table 5.5, Fig 6.3, Tables 6.4, 6.14, 6.15; State of Queensland Library, Fig 6.8, John Oxley Library/Daintree, Richard 1832–1879; Supama Damany and Jack Bellis for figure from *It's Not Carpal Tunnel Syndrome!, RSI Theory and Therapy for Computer Professionals* by Supama Damany and Jack Bellis 1999; Terry Brew for extract from WW2 Peoples War, Lucky Me by Terry Brew, 2004 www.bbc.co.uk/history/ ww2peopleswar.

Every effort has been made to trace the original source of copyright material contained in this book. The publisher will be pleased to hear from copyright holders to rectify any errors or omissions.

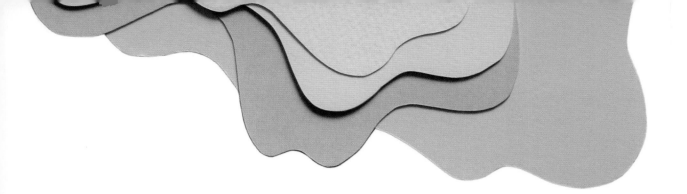

PART

LANGUAGE AND LEARNING

1

AN APPROPRIATE MODEL OF LANGUAGE

Language is at the heart of the learning process. In order to succeed in school, students need to use language for such purposes as explaining, arguing, recounting, and describing across a range of subject areas in a variety of media and modes. Such language does not come naturally to most students and generally requires explicit teaching. This means that teachers themselves need to have a solid understanding of how language operates in academic contexts. Unfortunately, however, this is not always the case. In an attempt to address this, the *Australian Curriculum: English* includes an explicit knowledge about language as a major focus. This chapter will begin to introduce the functional model of language that informs the national curriculum.

Learning objectives

In this chapter, you will:

- begin to become familiar with a functional model of language
- be introduced to the language system as a rich network of resources for making meaning
- understand how the context in which language is used impacts upon the kinds of choices made from the language system
- consider the implications of a functional model for your own understanding of how language works and for your classroom practice.

Key terms and concepts

functional model of language

context of culture

genres

context of situation

register (field, tenor, mode)

the language system

Note: throughout the chapters you will be invited to 'have a go' at certain activities. These can be done either by yourself or in pairs/groups.

INTRODUCTION

The *Australian Curriculum: English* places a major emphasis on 'knowledge about language', along with an appreciation of literature and expanding repertoires of literacy use. In the Framing Paper that guided the development of the national English curriculum, the following objectives were outlined:

> All students need to develop their understanding of how language functions to achieve a range of purposes that are critical to success in school. This includes reading, understanding, and writing texts that describe, narrate, analyse, explain, recount, argue, review, and so on. Such an approach aims to:
>
> - extend students' language resources in ways that support increasingly complex learning throughout the school years
>
> - help students deal with the language demands of the various curriculum areas
>
> - enable students to move from the interactive spontaneity of oral language towards the denser, more crafted language of the written mode
>
> - help students, in their speaking and writing, to move to and fro between the general and the specific, the abstract and the concrete, and the argument and the evidence
>
> - generally raise students' awareness of interpersonal issues, such as how to take and support a stand in an argument, how to express considered opinions, how to strengthen or soften statements, how to interact with a variety of audiences, and so on (DEEWR 2008, p. 10).

In Australia, teachers have been using a functional approach to language for the past couple of decades to address the above aspirations. Such an approach is concerned with how language functions to make the kinds of meanings that are important in our daily lives, in school learning, and in the wider community.

A functional model of language draws on the work of Professor Michael Halliday (see, for example, Halliday 2009), one of the leading linguists of modern times. Halliday sees language as a meaning-making system through which we interactively shape and interpret our world and ourselves. His interest is in language as 'a resource for making meaning'. Based on the work of Halliday, educational linguists such as Martin (1985) and Christie (2005) developed a 'genre-based approach' with the goal of making the language demands of the curriculum explicit so that all students have access to the linguistic resources needed for success in school and to the powerful ways of using language in our culture.

In this book, you will be learning about language and how it works from a functional perspective so that you can better support your students to learn language, to learn through language, and to learn about language.

LANGUAGE IN CONTEXT

A functional model describes how language varies from context to context. It shows, for example:

- how the language of science differs from the language of literature
- how the language we use when talking to close friends differs from that we use when giving a formal oral presentation
- how spoken language differs from written language.

In Figure 1.1, we can see the relationship between the language system and its context. According to Halliday (1985), the language system can be seen as a complex network of choices that have evolved to serve our needs. The context in which language is used has an influence on the kinds of choices we make from the language system.

In Chapter 2 you will be introduced more fully to the choices available in the language system.

Figure 1.1   The language system in a dynamic relationship with the context

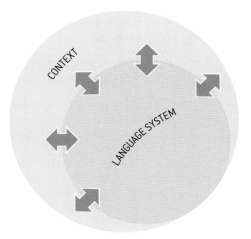

The relationship between the context and the language system is a dynamic one. We might enter a context with certain expectations regarding:

- the purpose of the interaction
- the topic to be discussed
- the nature of the relationship
- the channel of communication.

These factors in the context help us to predict the language choices we might make. As the interaction progresses, however, the context can also change as a result of the language choices being made. In an email exchange, for example, the initial purpose might be to complain about a faulty piece of equipment bought for the school. In a subsequent phone call, however, the purpose might change to an apology as you find out that in fact the equipment has been installed incorrectly. With the shift in context, the language choices will also change in terms of the purpose (complaint versus apology), the topic (the faulty equipment versus the faulty installation), the relationship (aggrieved versus contrite), and the mode of communication (email versus telephone).

Have a go!

From the above scenario, try to predict the kind of language choices made in the initial email exchange as opposed to the choices made in the telephone conversation. How do they differ?

Similarly, the language system as a whole is in a constant state of flux, impacted by the ways people use language in creative and unusual ways.

REGISTER

According to Halliday, in any particular situation there are three key factors in the context that affect the choices we make from the language system: the field, the tenor, and the mode.

The **field** refers to the content or subject matter. In a school context, our language choices will vary depending on such matters as the curriculum area and the topic being studied. The language choices we make in science, for example, will be quite different from those made in history. The topic of crystallisation will employ quite different language features from the topic of life in ancient Rome.

field: the subject matter or topic being developed in a particular situation.

The **tenor** refers to the roles we take up (student, parent, customer, employee) and our relationships with others in any particular situation. The tenor will be affected by such matters as the status, level of expertise, age, ethnic background, and gender of the participants. Language choices will vary according to such factors as how well people know each other, how frequently they meet, and how they feel about each other. If you are having a conversation with a close friend with whom you meet regularly, the choices will be quite different from a tutorial session with a senior lecturer and a group of students you hardly know.

tenor: the roles and relationships being enacted in a particular situation.

The **mode** refers to the channel of communication being used: the mode and the medium. Here, we are primarily concerned with the difference between the spoken mode and the written mode and the different roles these play in the learning process. This is an important consideration as students move from the oral language of the home and schoolyard to the increasingly dense and compact language of the written mode in academic contexts. Mode can also refer to visual and multimodal texts presented through a range of media.

mode: the channel of communication being used in a particular situation (e.g. oral, written, visual).

register: a combination of the field, tenor, and mode in a particular situation.

Any combination of these contextual features creates the **register** of a situation (see Figure 1.2). In one situation we might find a couple of old friends (tenor) discussing (oral mode) their holiday plans (field). In another situation, we might imagine a teacher and principal (tenor) corresponding through emails (written mode) about the agenda for the staff meeting (field). As you can imagine, the language choices will differ considerably depending on the register.

context of situation: a specific situation within a culture that gives rise to a particular register.

Figure 1.2   The register (field, tenor, and mode) of a particular situation

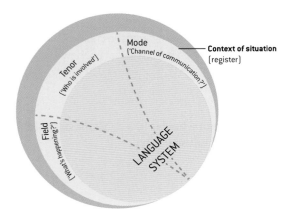

Have a go!

From the text below, see if you can infer the register (the field, the tenor, and the mode). What are some key language features that enabled you to do this?

> All students who have been sent to detention this week will meet me here after assembly. There has been an unacceptable increase in the number of students turning up late for class and disobeying school rules. If you break the rules, there will be consequences. And you all know what they are!

Part 2 of this book will introduce you more fully to a range of academic registers.

Being able to identify the register of a situation enables us to predict the kind of language our students will need to use in that situation. If we are planning a particular geography lesson, for example, our students might need support in using language to explain the movement of tectonic plates (field) to an unknown audience (tenor) in the written mode (mode).

GENRE

When we talk about register, we are considering the language choices made in response to a particular situation (the context of situation). At a more global level, we need to consider the relationship between language and the broader **context of culture**. The language system evolves within the context of a certain culture (including beliefs, values, and behaviours) to meet the needs of that culture. Our language choices will therefore be sensitive to the cultural context as well as the context of a particular situation within that culture. When we refer to 'culture', we don't necessarily mean national cultures (e.g. 'Australian', 'Asian', 'British'). Rather, we often think about cultures as a collection of discourse communities, subcultures, or social institutions such as sporting groups, theatre aficionados, book clubs, friends, and family. In this sense, we are thinking of the school as part of an educational discourse community.

context of culture: The broad cultural context within which we use language for purposes such as explaining, recounting, describing, and so on, depending on the discourse community—in our case, the discourse community of schooling.

Think about it

How many discourse communities have you engaged with over the past week or so?

How does your language change as you move between these communities?

In particular, following the work of Martin (Martin & Rose 2008), here we are concerned with the various purposes for which language is used in the culture. In our daily lives we use language to achieve a variety of social purposes: telling friends what we did on the weekend, instructing someone how to follow a recipe, explaining how a computer application works, persuading parents to buy a treat, completing tax forms, and so on. We can refer to these as **genres** (or text types)—goal-oriented social practices that have evolved in our culture to enable us to get things done. If our purpose was to obtain employment, for example, then a relevant genre to use would be a job application. If our purpose was to draw up a legally binding agreement, then an appropriate genre would be a contract. Or if we wanted to tell someone how to use a video camera, we might choose the genre of giving instructions.

genres: the ways in which we achieve our social purposes through language.

So in order to identify the genre of a particular text, we first ask what purpose the text is serving: describing, counselling, lobbying, instructing, recommending, informing, and so on. Rather than seeing genres simply as products or things, we will also be thinking of them as processes. We employ them to *do* things: to persuade someone to our point of view, to satirise, to share experiences, to complain about a service, and so on.

Genres evolve over time through social use. If social purposes change, then genres will modify themselves to accommodate these changes. Outmoded genres do not persist simply because of convention. If they are no longer functional, they will generally adapt or die out.

The study of genre has a long tradition. Some trace its history back to ancient Greece where the original categories of lyric, dramatic, and epic were developed. It was Aristotle who emphasised the role of rhetoric as a way of achieving various social purposes through spoken or written language.

For some time, the most widespread use of the term 'genre' has been in association with particular kinds of literature (later extended to include works of art and film). Thus works of literature of a particular style were referred to as genres of one variety or another: the elegy, the sonnet, the ballad, the romance genre, the pastoral genre, the gothic horror genre, the science fiction genre, and so on.

The meaning of the term has been extended these days to include non-literary texts—texts from the community (casual conversation, patient–doctor consultations, shopping lists), from the media (editorials, news bulletins, television documentaries), from the workplace (business reports, office memos, safety warnings), and from educational contexts (book reviews, classroom interaction, lab reports). As you can see, genres can be spoken, written, or multimodal (integrating visual elements with written text).

In this book, the terms 'genre' and 'text type' will be used interchangeably to refer to ways of achieving a specific social purpose through language within a particular cultural context.

In school contexts, we encounter a range of genres over which students need to gain control in order to succeed in their academic lives (see Table 1.1). In this book, we will be introducing some of the key genres of schooling.

Table 1.1   Examples of genres typically used in school contexts

Purpose	Genre (text type)	Examples
To entertain (Chapter 4)	Stories	Reading a narrative Sharing an Anecdote Innovating on a fable
To tell what happened (Chapter 5)	Recounts	Recounting the results of a science experiment Recounting an historical event Recounting how a maths problem was solved
To provide information about a general class of things (Chapter 6)	Information reports	Types of transport The feline family Rainforests
To explain how things work or why things happen (Chapter 7)	Explanations	How an electric circuit works What causes earthquakes How the Second World War began
To argue (Chapter 8)	Arguments/expositions	Essay developing a particular stance Discussion considering various sides of an issue Formal debate

Purpose	Genre (text type)	Examples
To respond (Chapter 9)	Responses	Responding personally to a text or artform Interpreting a text, artform, or body of work
To conduct an inquiry (Chapter 10)	Inquiry reports (macrogenre)	A science experiment A geography project A technology and design assignment A problem-solving inquiry

As we can see from Table 1.1, virtually all the activities in which students participate involve the use of particular genres. If we are clear about the purposes that students will be expected to achieve in a unit of work, then we can better support them in learning how to use relevant genres.

Have a go!

Just by looking at the opening lines of a text, we can usually infer the genre being used. From the following, see if you can predict the likely genre. (Hint: Think about the likely purpose of the text.) What is it in the language choices that enable you to identify the genre?

- Once there were four children whose names were Peter, Susan, Edmund, and Lucy.
- The koala is an arboreal herbivorous marsupial native to Australia.
- Do this science experiment to learn about the chemical reaction that makes sherbet so fizzy when you put it in your mouth.
- There are many reasons why new laws should be introduced to make organic farming techniques compulsory for all Australian growers.
- The plants in our school vegetable garden are looking unhealthy.
- On Tuesday 3A went to the animal sanctuary to observe the wildlife.
- Erosion is the result of several factors.

Each genre has a characteristic structure and goes through a number of stages to achieve its purpose. The various stages are generally ordered in a relatively predictable way (see Table 1.2). In a recount of an incident, for example, we typically find a stage at the beginning that lets us know who was involved, when and where it took place, and so on. This is generally followed by a description of the sequence of events. And finally, another stage might conclude the recount—a summarising comment, for example.

Interspersed through these broad *stages*, we might find a number of smaller *phases*. While the stages are relatively stable, the phases provide greater flexibility in terms of, for example, which to include, where to include them, how many to include, and even whether to include them. They allow for greater elaboration and for an element of creativity.

Table 1.2   Oral recount of visit to the dentist

Stages	Phases	
Orientation	Who? When? Why?	Did I tell you that um … when I went to the dentist last time I had to get this tooth pulled out? It was really badly stuck in and it was dead and it wouldn't come out. And … it wasn't really dead. It was still alive but it just got bad.
Record of events	Event 1	The dentist put … um … heaps … about ten needles in all round it 'cause it seems that it had heaps of pus in it.
	Event 2	And the dentist put in heaps of cloth. …
	Event 3	So he got the pliers … [Mimes pulling out tooth.]
	Comment	And then I didn't even realise that it was out. I said, 'Is it out yet?' and he goes 'It's already out.'
	Event 4	And then what happened was, after a while my … this gum puffed up really big.
	Evaluation	It felt really funny and numb.
	Event 5	And I bit my tongue 'cause I couldn't feel it!
Summarising comment		I hate going to the dentist.

In identifying the various stages, it is important to ask how each one contributes to achieving the overall purpose of the text. The terms used to describe the stages should be functional, that is, they should give an indication of the job the stage is doing within the text. Terms such as 'beginning', 'middle', and 'end', for example, are not really functional. They tell us about the structure, not about what role that stage is playing. Most genres have a beginning stage, a middle stage, and an ending stage, but they differ in terms of what these stages do. The beginning of an anecdote, for example, might make reference to a particular incident in someone's experience ('I'll never forget the day I ran into old Winston.'), whereas the beginning of a job application might identify the job being applied for ('I am writing in reference to the position of caretaker advertised in last Friday's *Gazette*.').

In analysing texts, students will come across stages that they may not have previously encountered. It is useful at these points to ask them to make up a term for this stage that indicates the function it has in the text.

Have a go!

What is the social purpose of the following text? What different stages can you identify in the text? What names could you give to each stage to indicate its role in achieving the overall purpose of the text?

For Auction

Piccadilly Gardens

Have you ever wanted to live in an apartment with old-world charm and yet have none of the worries of rising damp or dry rot? Then Piccadilly Gardens is the place for you. These apartments have been superbly renovated by expert craftspersons.

Choice of one or two bedrooms. Spacious lounge/dining room area. Modern kitchen and bathroom. Traditional open fireplaces and cornices. Original features include small-paned windows and picture rails.

Come and see for yourself. Phone us today and arrange for an inspection at your convenience.

Some genres are more predictable than others. Certain religious ceremonies, parliamentary question time, and formal meeting agendas, for example, go through very predictable stages. Other genres, such as casual conversations and certain literary texts, are much less predictable.

Have a go!

Identify the genres suggested by the titles below.

Write three brief texts about volcanoes, each using one of the genres. You can use your imagination if necessary.

- Explain how a volcano erupts
- The last days of Pompeii
- What are the common features of volcanoes?
- How to make a model volcano
- Problems caused by volcanic ash and what can be done about it
- My near death encounter with boiling magma!

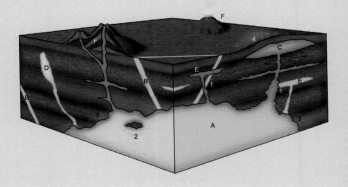

Did your texts involve more than one stage?

How might you label the stages of each text according to their function?

How do the stages differ between genres?

It is useful for students to be aware of how genres are organised differently according to their purpose. It is important, however, that genres are not taught as rigid formulae, but rather that knowledge about stages and phases can be used as tools for exploring how texts achieve their purposes in different ways. Ultimately, we might want students to play discerningly with the genre or even subvert it (as in spoofs), but before they can create the unexpected, they first need to be aware of what is the expected.

REGISTER AND GENRE IN PRACTICE

We can now extend our diagram to include the broader cultural context where we encounter the genres that we engage in. In Figure 1.3, we see that context can be viewed from the perspective of the overarching cultural context (genre) or from the perspective of specific situations that occur within the culture (register).

Figure 1.3   Context of culture and context of situation

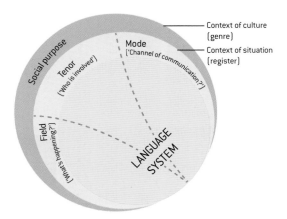

We might imagine an activity where students are debating the issue of global warming. At the level of the cultural context, the language choices will probably reflect a community in which argumentation is highly valued as intrinsic to the democratic process and where the social purpose of arguing has been formalised into the genre of the debate.

In this particular situational context, the *field* being developed by the debaters is concerned with the science of global warming and people's perceptions of the issues. The language choices will therefore express the kinds of happenings involved in global warming (increasing temperature, melting ice, rising sea levels), the kinds of participants in these processes (animate? human? physical? economic?), and the circumstances surrounding the activity (how quickly? to what extent? where? why?).

The *tenor* will probably be relatively formal, with students engaging with their peers in front of an audience, trying to persuade the adjudicator to their point of view. The language choices will therefore involve the use of rhetorical devices such as repetition, intensification, emotive vocabulary, rebuttals, and so on.

And while the *mode* is spoken, it will have features of the written mode in that the students will have had time to research, make notes, and prepare their arguments. The language choices will therefore reflect certain features of the oral mode (intonation, gesture, facial expression, pausing, volume, fluency) as well as features of the written mode (resources for organising the flow of the text, careful structuring of the points, and so on).

Have a go!

Comparing the two texts below, identify how they differ in terms of the genre and its stages, along with the field, tenor, and mode. Provide evidence from the text.

Text A:

Student 1:	*Okay. So we're making … Where's the diagram?*
	We've got magnets, two matchsticks … [checking off materials on the worksheet]
	You read, I'll count.
Student 2:	*OK, icy pole stick, 2 straws, 1 Blu-Tack, 4 wheels.*
Student 1:	*One, put the two matches through the straws.*
	Uh one and the other …
	Now, what's next? [picks up some wheels to attach]
Student 2:	*No, no, I want to do it here, here.*
	It's my turn, Dude. [reaches for the vehicle]
Student 1:	*Try the other one.* [hands over the vehicle]
	Cut the matchstick … I think we need a smaller one …
Student 2:	*That looks pretty schmick!*

Text B

Yesterday our class made a model of a Maglev train to test attraction and repulsion using magnets.

First we constructed the model in pairs using two matchsticks, four wheels, Blu-Tack, an icy pole stick, and a bar magnet.

Then we tested our vehicle to see if it ran smoothly. Ours got a bit stuck so we had to adjust the wheels.

After that, we used another bar magnet to test whether our model went faster or slower when the two magnets attracted or repelled each other.

We found that our vehicle moved faster over one metre when the magnets were attracting each other.

In the classroom

It is the teacher who creates the contexts for learning. Knowing about genre and register helps the teacher at the levels of planning, teaching, and assessing a unit of work. The following questions can be used as guidelines when you are required to plan or evaluate a unit of work or a series of lessons. In the remaining chapters, we support you to engage with such questions in further depth.

Planning

- Have you identified which genre/s your students will be dealing with in this unit of work?
- Have you selected texts that provide good models of the genre?
- Have you identified a relevant language focus?
- Have you planned activities that will help develop a sound understanding of the field and the language of the topic?
- Have you predicted the kinds of difficulties certain students might have (e.g. technicality, tense, relationship between ideas)?
- What different roles will you and the students take up during the unit of work (e.g. explainer, questioner, evaluator)?
- How will you support your students in the move from the oral–visual mode into the written mode?
- What roles will different media play in the learning process?

Teaching

- Have you made clear to students what the objectives of the unit of work are in terms of the purposes for which they will be reading and writing?
- Have you provided models of the genre so that they know what the target text will look like?
- Have you modelled to them the kinds of stages that the genre typically goes through in achieving its purpose?
- Have you ensured that students have control over the language features relevant to the genre and register of the unit?

Assessing

- Are you monitoring students' reading to see whether they can, for example, identify the purpose of the text, or predict how the text will unfold in stages?
- Does students' reading reflect a good grasp of the language constructing the field or topic?
- Does the students' writing successfully achieve the expected purpose?
- Does their writing demonstrate a confident control over the field?
- In their writing, do they engage effectively with the reader?
- Do they have sound command of the features of written language?

Think about it

The class was engaged in a unit of work on earthquakes. The teacher had asked the students to write a story about earthquakes, expecting that they would explain how an earthquake happens. One student wrote the following:

> Have you ever been in an earthquake? Well, I have. It was really scary. Our house started shaking and all my books fell off my bookcase and the cat ran under the house and we couldn't get her out so we had to get some food to get her to come out. There have been a lot of earthquakes in Japan and New Zealand. I hope we don't have another one here.

What does the text reveal about the student's understanding of the genre, field, tenor, and mode required? How could the teacher have provided better guidance?

From the discussion above, it is clear that an appropriate model of language for today's classrooms needs to go beyond what is offered by a traditional approach. We might conclude by considering, in Table 1.3, the differences between what a traditional model of language and a functional model offer.

Table 1.3   Differences between traditional and functional approaches

Traditional approach	Functional approach
Describes language in terms of grammatical classes (form), such as prepositions, pronouns, adverbs, conjunctions, and so on.	Describes language in terms of the relationship between the forms of language and their functions. An adverb, for example, can function to provide information about an action (*He ran swiftly*), to evaluate behaviour (*She sang beautifully*), to intensify a description (*very interesting*), to sharpen or blur (*exactly right* or *somewhat pleased*), to provide a comment (*Luckily he escaped*), and to structure a text (*First, …, second, …*).
Operates at the level of the sentence and below.	Deals with language from the level of the whole text through to the level of the word (and below), including the interaction between these levels.
Describes the grammar of written language.	Describes how written language differs from spoken language and offers a means of analysing visual and multimodal texts.
Sees language as a set of rules to be followed.	Sees language as a resource and seeks to extend students' potential to make meaning more effectively.
Focuses on grammatical accuracy.	Acknowledges the importance of accuracy, but goes beyond correct structure to focus on meaning-making.
Presents a decontextualised view of language.	Systematically describes how the choices we make in using language are influenced by factors in the context.
Uses a pedagogy that is typically concerned with labelling the parts of a sentence and manipulating these parts in exercises that are often inauthentic and unrelated to the classroom curriculum.	Draws on a scaffolding cycle that relates students' knowledge about language to the kinds of meanings they need to make in the various areas of the curriculum and in their daily lives.
Has little to say about students' language development over the years of schooling.	Describes language development from early childhood through to late adolescence in terms of the ways in which language is implicated in constructing increasingly complex meanings.

CHAPTER SUMMARY

In this chapter we have encouraged you to start thinking about the need for teachers to have a clear understanding about language and how their knowledge about language is significant in planning, teaching, assessing, and supporting students in achieving educational outcomes. We have explained how a functional approach provides us with an appropriate model of language for today's classrooms. In particular, we have focused on how a functional model describes the relationship between context and the choices we make from the language system. We have observed how the context can be seen in terms of the cultural context (and in particular, the notion of how genres enable us to achieve our social purposes) and the more specific context of a particular situation (i.e. the register—a particular combination of field, tenor, and mode).

FOR FURTHER DISCUSSION

1   How would you describe your current understanding of language? What kind of terminology do you use to talk about language? Do you feel it is sufficient to enable you to support students' language and literacy development?

2   Looking at Table 1.3, take each of the points listed, and see if you agree with how they distinguish between a traditional and a functional approach.

3   Identify three different classroom activities or tasks and describe how they differ in terms of the genre being focused on (refer to Table 1.1), their field (e.g. topic), the tenor (e.g. the relationship between writer and reader), and the mode (e.g. spoken or written) being used. Reflect on whether this helps you to clarify and predict the kind of language being used in such a context.

4   Write a brief recount of an experiment to see whether an object floats or sinks. Keeping the field the same, change the genre, the tenor, and the mode. What do you notice about how the language features change in relation to each of these factors?

5   Examine the details of one of your current assignments. What genre/s does the task require you to produce? Think about your previous experiences with texts of that type; for example, do you know how it should be structured? Is there a model available? What are the language demands in terms of field, tenor, and mode? If these are not clear, you might approach your lecturer and other sources of support. Many institutions have useful online resources to guide students as they complete assignments using different genres.

6   Download a copy of the *Australian Curriculum: English* (see websites list overleaf) so that you can refer to it as you work with this book.

REFERENCES

Christie, F. (2005). *Language Education in the Primary Years*. Sydney: University of NSW Press.

DEEWR (2008). *National English Curriculum—Framing Paper*. Sydney: ACARA.

Halliday, M.A.K. (2009). *The Essential Halliday*. London: Continuum.

Halliday, M.A.K. (with Hasan, R.) (1985). *Language, Context, and Text: Aspects of language in a social–semiotic perspective*. Melbourne: Deakin University Press. (Republished by Oxford University Press in 1989.)

Martin, J.R. (1985). *Factual Writing: Exploring and challenging social reality*. Geelong: Deakin University Press.

Martin, J.R., & Rose, D. (2008). *Genre Relations: Mapping culture*. London: Equinox.

WEBSITES

Australian Curriculum and Reporting Authority: The Australian Curriculum: English, version 8.1
www.australiancurriculum.edu.au/english/curriculum/f-10?layout=1

On this website you will find several documents relating to the *Australian Curriculum: English*, including the curriculum itself.

Grammar Online: Levels of delicacy
www.aisnsw.edu.au/services/_layouts/theseus/articulate/levelsofdelicacy/story.html

A website providing useful information on a functional approach and practical teaching ideas, from the Association of Independent Schools, NSW.

2

THE FUNCTIONS OF LANGUAGE

In the previous chapter we started to think about the relationship between the language choices we make and the context in which language is being used. In this chapter, we'll flesh out the functional model of language further, looking in greater detail at the language system and the functions that language serves in our lives.

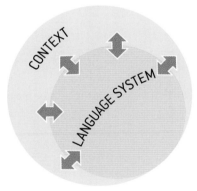

Learning objectives

In this chapter, you will:

- become familiar with the way that language functions to enable us to express ideas, to interact with others, and to shape coherent texts
- understand how these language functions become increasingly complex as learners move from early childhood through to adolescence
- examine the relationship between the register of the context (field, tenor, and mode) and related choices from the language system
- consider the role of the teacher in supporting students' language development.

Key terms and concepts

Ideational function ('expressing and developing ideas')

- expressing ideas (Processes, Participants, Circumstances)
- combining ideas

Interpersonal function ('interacting with others')

- Mood system
- Appraisal system (Attitude, Engagement, Graduation)

Textual function ('text structure and organisation')

- Theme and Rheme
- cohesion

INTRODUCTION

Student: You've written on my assignment 'Not clear. Could do better.' But I don't understand why it wasn't clear and how I could do better.

Teacher: Well, read it again. It just didn't sound right.

Student: But I've corrected all the spelling and punctuation—and you still say it isn't clear. Why did I only get a C and Steven got an A?

Teacher: Well, Steven wrote in a more lively way and organised his ideas better.

Student: But no one ever taught me how to do that.

This could be a typical conversation in many classrooms where students are confused about how to improve their use of language and teachers are unsure of how to help them. This book aims to provide you with tools to support your students with the academic language they need in order to deal with the demands of schooling. It might seem like a lot of theory at this stage but, as Halliday is fond of saying, there's nothing more practical than good theory. Without a sound theoretical foundation on which to base your decisions, you are prey to the latest fads. There are, of course, many theories you will need to draw on in your teaching—theories of phonics, theories of spelling, theories of learning, and so on. Here, we are concerned primarily with a theory of language and its role in learning.

Rather than regard language simply as a set of rules, we will be exploring how language functions, for example, to:

- express and combine ideas
- enable interaction with others
- organise increasingly complex texts.

Figure 2.1 represents how resources in the language system cluster into these three major functions. (Technically, these are called *metafunctions*.)

Figure 2.1   The functions of language

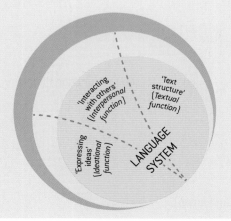

If you look at the *Australian Curriculum: English*, you will notice that these are key organisers in the Language strand.

In the next few sections, we will look briefly at each of these functions. They will be elaborated further in later chapters. Here, we are developing the big picture—a map to guide you through the book. We realise that this will be a fair bit to deal with and we don't expect you to take it in all at once. As you work through the following chapters the model will become more familiar. It takes time to develop a confident understanding of how language works—there is no quick fix—and it requires the support of sound, usable theory.

USING LANGUAGE TO EXPRESS AND DEVELOP IDEAS

A key function of language is to enable us to represent experience. We use language to develop and share our ideas about what is going on. In the school context, this might refer to what's going on in the curriculum—the fields of knowledge, understandings, concepts, and so on. Here, we are concerned with the **Ideational function** of language. (To 'ideate' means to reflect on and reason about something.)

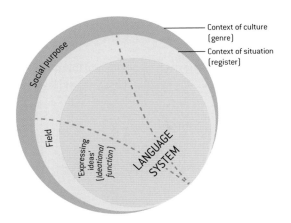

Context of culture (genre)

Context of situation (register)

Ideational function: language resources for representing our experience of the world ('What's happening?', 'Who/what's involved?', 'How? When? Where? Why?') and connecting ideas.

Note: Terms referring to the functions of language begin with a capital letter.

Our experience (and the experience represented in curriculum content) is made up of doings and happenings. In functional terms, we could refer to these as **Processes**.

These might represent activity in the physical world (e.g. sitting, driving, teaching, shopping), activity in the inner world of thinking, feeling, and perceiving (e.g. remembering, knowing, wanting, disliking, seeing), verbal activity (e.g. saying, spluttering, exclaiming), along with states of being and having (e.g. a koala *is* a marsupial. It *has* a pouch.).

These Processes involve a variety of **Participants**, such as doers and receivers of the actions, thinkers, sensers, sayers (along with what is thought, sensed, and said). Participants can be human or non-human.

Process: a doing, happening, or state.

Participants: people, animals, objects, and abstract things that participate in Processes.

Circumstance: the details surrounding an activity—Where? When? How? Why?, and so on.

And surrounding all this activity are various **Circumstances**: When? Where? How? Why? With whom? About what? (The technical term used by Halliday [1975] to refer to these three resources—Participants, Processes, and Circumstances—is the system of *transitivity*.)

Using these three terms, we are able to represent a particular field of activity, for example:

The Mole	had been working	very hard	all the morning.
Participant [who?]	Process [what's happening?]	Circumstance [how?]	Circumstance [how long?]

See Chapter 4 for greater detail about Processes, Participants, and Circumstances. This will be further consolidated in subsequent chapters.

Together, these three meanings create a clause. Traditionally, we refer to a clause as a group of words that contains a verb. This tells us about the structure of a clause. From a functional perspective, however, we could think of a clause as a 'slice of experience' representing what's going on.

Have a go!

Ask yourself (or your partner) the following questions in relation to the clauses below, and then identify each part of the clause. The first one has been done for you. Ask the questions in the following sequence:

- What's happening? (Process)
- Who or what's involved? (Participant)
- Are there any surrounding details (When? Where? How? etc.)? (Circumstance)

Once upon a time,	an old man	was walking	through the wood.
3. When? **Circumstance** [time]	2. Who's involved? **Participant**	1. What's happening? **Process**	4. Where? **Circumstance** [place]
clause			

His red woolly mitten	dropped	on the ground.

For a long time	the mitten	lay	in the snow.

Then one day	Munch-crunch Mouse	found	the old mitten.

The cold mouse	quickly	hopped	into it …

We are interested not only in how clauses are used to express ideas, but in how we might join clauses to link ideas together. In the following sentence, for example, two ideas are linked using the conjunction *and*.

The rat went away	and	he sat on the river bank in the sun.
clause	conjunction	clause

Or we might join clauses to express a contrast, using the conjunction *but*:

The rat came to help him,	but	their united efforts were not sufficient to right the cart.
clause	conjunction	clause

We could also connect two events in time by using a conjunction such as *when*.

They had not proceeded very far on their way	when	there was a pattering of feet behind them.
clause	conjunction	clause

Following chapters will consolidate your understanding of the Ideational function.

You will be introduced more fully to language for connecting ideas in Chapter 7.

USING LANGUAGE TO INTERACT WITH OTHERS

Interpersonal function: language resources for creating interpersonal meanings (interacting with others, expressing feelings, taking a stance, making judgments, etc.).

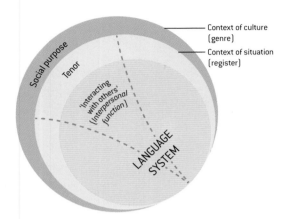

We saw above that language has an **Interpersonal function**. This enables interaction with others—taking on various roles, asking for information, providing information, requesting services, expressing feelings and opinions, engaging with other perspectives and possibilities, establishing and maintaining relationships. Here we will look at a couple of the major interpersonal resources: the Mood system and the Appraisal system (Attitude, Engagement, Graduation).

The Mood system

Mood system: the grammatical resources for making statements, asking questions, giving commands, and making offers.

One of the most basic ways of interacting is through the **Mood system**:

Table 2.1   Basic speech roles and functions

Speech role	Speech function	Typical examples
Asking for information	Question	*Where's the dog?*
Giving information	Statement	*He's in the shed.*
Asking someone to do or provide something	Command	*Give me the butter.*
Offering to give or do something	Offer	*Would you like a sandwich?*

These speech functions are significant in educational contexts in terms of the nature of classroom interaction.

- Who gets to ask the questions?
- What type of questions (closed or open-ended)?
- What roles do the various students take up in group work?
- Who dominates the interaction in pair work?
- How does the teacher use language to facilitate learning?
- How can speech functions be used in less direct ways (asking a question to get something done: *Have you finished?* instead of *Stop talking and get on with your work.*).

The Mood system will be dealt with in Chapter 8.

The Appraisal system

We don't interact simply by exchanging questions, statements, commands, and offers. Interpersonal meanings are also concerned with how we express attitudes, how we engage the listener or reader, and how we might adjust the strength of our feelings and opinions. Together, these form the **Appraisal system** (Martin & White 2005).

Attitude

One way in which we can provoke a reaction from the speaker or listener is to introduce an element of emotion or opinion:

- expressing a feeling (Affect)
- evaluating the qualities of a thing (Appreciation)
- assessing someone's character or behaviour (Judgment).

This is referred to as the system of **Attitude**. Attitudes can be positive or negative.

She enjoys the theatre. (positive)

She can't stand television sitcoms. (negative)

Attitudes can be expressed directly or indirectly:

He felt scared. (direct)

He huddled in the corner. (indirect)

Affect (pronounced with the stress on the 'A') expresses an emotional state or a surge of emotion. We might, for example, express feelings that relate to:

- matters of the heart (e.g. love, misery, excitement)
- satisfaction (e.g. curiosity, boredom, displeasure)
- security (e.g. feeling safe, anxious, angry, confident).

I felt *a spasm of panic* as I stared at her. (insecurity)

She *hugged me tightly* for a minute. (affection)

I hadn't made a secret of *my distaste for Forks*. (dissatisfaction)

He didn't need *to suffer* along with me. (unhappiness)

It made me *uncomfortable*. (insecurity)

Appraisal system: the ways in which we use language to express feelings and opinions, to engage with other voices and perspectives, and to adjust the strength of our utterances.

Attitude: using language to share feelings, express evaluations, and judge human behaviour.

Appreciation is concerned with evaluating the qualities of things (natural phenomena, literary works, architecture) or processes (performances, races). We can appreciate things (positively or negatively) in terms of such things as:

- the reaction they provoke (awesome, amazing, boring, repulsive)
- how well they are composed (harmonious, complex, balanced, disorganised, unclear, flawed)
- their social value (innovative, original, insignificant, authentic, everyday, dated).

I do a good job of blocking *painful, unnecessary* things from my memory. (reaction)

My skin could be *pretty*—it was *very clear, almost translucent-looking*. (composition)

I was glad to see that most of the cars were *older like mine, nothing flashy*. (social value)

Judgment relates to how we evaluate the behaviour of people. We can judge people's behaviour in terms of:

- the degree to which their behaviour is socially esteemed (how normal/extraordinary, how capable, how courageous, how tenacious, how resilient)
- the degree to which their behaviour is ethical or legal (how moral, how truthful).

How could I leave my loving, *erratic, hare-brained* mother to fend for herself? (negative capacity)

I tried to be diplomatic, but mostly I just *lied* a lot. (negative ethics)

Daughter of the Chief's *flighty ex-wife*, come home at last. (negative ethics)

They seemed impressed by *her bravery* in speaking to me. (positive esteem: courage)

I *didn't have the necessary hand–eye coordination* to play sports without humiliating myself. (negative capacity)

Have a go!

Interpersonal resources can be used to develop a particular 'tone' in a text (humorous, serious, maudlin, pompous, ironic, and so on). How would you characterise the tone of the following newspaper article? How is language being used to develop this tone? See if you can identify whether the underlined examples are of Affect, Appreciation, Judgment. Are they positive or negative? Are they directly stated or indirectly suggested? (The first paragraph has been done as a model.) Sometimes you might find more than one Appraisal resource being used in the same utterance.

Remember that when we look at language in terms of meaning, there aren't always clear-cut answers. Appraisal provides us with some tools to talk about different kinds of interpersonal meanings and their function in achieving certain effects. If possible, discuss your analysis with a partner and justify your decisions with reference to the Appraisal resources outlined above.

THURSDAY, JUN 30, 2011 11:14 ET

Don't kill the Oxford comma!
The university hands down a new edict about punctuation—but the world's grammar nerds will never back down
BY MARY ELIZABETH WILLIAMS
www.salon.com

Grammar lovers today were saddened, shocked, and mightily displeased at the news that the P.R. department of the University of Oxford has decided to drop the comma for which it is so justly famed. As GalleyCat reported, the university's new style guide advises writers, "As a general rule, do not use the serial/Oxford comma: so write 'a, b and c' not 'a, b, and c'." Cue the collective gasps of horror. The last time the nerd community was this cruelly betrayed, George Lucas was sitting at his desk, thinking, "I shall call him Jar Jar."

The serial comma is one of the sanest punctuation usages in the written language. So valuable is that serial comma that it's on frickin' Page 2 of Strunk and White, right after the possessive apostrophe. And it is good. I am, clearly, violently in favor of it, and have spent the better part of the last 15 years enduring the pain of watching our editors systematically remove it from my stories. Oh, how it burns! For clarity in list-making, for that sweet pause of breath before the final item in a group, the serial comma cannot be topped.

The prospect of the beloved Oxford comma being dumped by its own kin seems cruelly ominous. It's like Hugh Hefner saying he's no longer interested in blondes. And though you may think you've taken away our beloved little swipe of typeface this time, comma haters, the serial comma community is determined, tenacious, and resilient. We will keep sticking the comma into our sentences, and still sacrifice that one valuable character of our tweets in its service. We may still be reeling with denial, anger, bargaining, and depression, but you will never, ever have our acceptance.

Affect: insecurity (anxiety/anger), -ve, indirectly stated
Judgment: esteem (tenacious), +ve, indirectly stated

Affect: various feelings, -ve, directly stated
Appreciation: social value, +ve, directly stated

Appreciation: reaction, -ve, indirectly stated
Judgment: ethics, -ve, directly stated

Engagement

Engagement: using language to engage with others or with alternative perspectives and possibilities.

Another key feature of the Interpersonal function of language is the way in which it enables us to engage the reader or listener and open up spaces for the consideration of other possibilities, other voices, other points of view. This is referred to as the **Engagement** system. How can you grab your readers' attention? How can you draw them into your argument? How can you align them with your point of view? How can you create spaces for them to participate in the meaning-making? How can you bring in other perspectives? Such questions are important in considering, for example, your awareness of your audience and your sensitivity to their interests—a major skill in the art of persuasion.

We could take the following statement:

Gone with the Wind is the greatest movie ever.

This is what is called a 'bare assertion'. You have taken a stance and expressed an opinion (see Attitude above), so you might provoke a response. But have you opened up the interaction? To engage the reader or listener, we could invite them in by using a degree of modality:

Gone with the Wind **could be** the greatest movie ever.

Or we could indicate that this is simply our opinion, leaving open the possibility of a different perspective:

I think *Gone with the Wind* is the greatest movie ever.

Or we could explicitly introduce other voices into the conversation:

David and Margaret might not agree that *Gone with the Wind* is the greatest movie ever.

We might provide space for alternative points of view by using, for example, a clause of concession (*although*, *however*, *but*):

Gone with the Wind is the greatest movie ever, **though** *some believe it is too long.*

Anticipating the views and values of intended readers is important in establishing solidarity and aligning them with your stance.

Have a go!

How could you change this bare assertion to open it up to consider other possibilities, voices, and perspectives?

'She's a cheat and a liar.'

Graduation

And finally, as part of the Appraisal system, we can look at how we fine-tune, soften, or strengthen our Attitudes and Engagement strategies. This is referred to as **Graduation**.

We can make our feelings and opinions weaker or stronger by choosing a weaker or stronger vocabulary (lexical) item:

> I *like → enjoy → love → cherish → adore → long for* chocolate ice-cream.

or we can add an intensifier to increase the strength:

> I *really → very much → absolutely* like chocolate ice-cream.

or decrease the strength:

> I *kind of / somewhat / rather* like chocolate ice-cream.

We can intensify by repeating an item:

> I was *very, very* angry.

> I *fumed* and *fumed* and *fumed*.

We can also intensify through the use of quantification (how much? how many?):

> The play was a *huge* success.

> There is *vast* corruption in the government.

> There are *so many* problems with this essay.

And again, we can use quantification to downplay:

> He's just *a little* upset.

> I told only *a few* lies.

> There was only *a trickle* of complaints.

> **Graduation**: using language to adjust the strength and focus of our utterances.

You will find a fuller treatment of the Interpersonal function in Chapter 8, where we look at how it is used in argumentation.

Have a go!

If I said 'The movie was OK' I would be being fairly non-committal. How could you make this a much stronger statement? Take it up notch by notch. How many notches can you go up before you reach the strongest statement?

Now take it down to the most negative appraisal of the movie—again, notch by notch.

Now look back at the Oxford comma article on page 27. Can you find any examples of graduation? Are they 'boosting' or 'downplaying' the strength of the utterance? To what degree? With what effect?

USING LANGUAGE TO SHAPE TEXTS

Textual function: language resources for shaping texts that are coherent and cohesive.

The third main function of language is to create text. It is through the **Textual** resources of language that we are able to organise our ideas, attitudes, and so on into texts that coherently hang together and relate to the context. The choices we make will depend on the mode (oral, written, multimodal) and the medium (print, digital, sound, etc.).

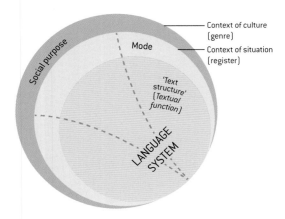

The textual function of language is concerned with how we use language in various modes and media to create texts that are coherent and cohesive, shaping the flow of information and guiding the reader or listener through the text.

Guiding the reader

As authors of texts grow in maturity and tackle longer, more complex texts, they take on the responsibility of helping the reader or viewer navigate their way through the text. In a multimodal or digital text, such as a website, the author will use a variety of strategies to guide the reader or viewer, such as icons, menus, buttons, colour, animations, and so on. Here, however, we will focus on written texts.

Theme: the first part of the clause that signals how the topic is being developed.

At the sentence level, the writer can use the beginning of the clause (or the **Theme**) to signal to the reader how the text is developing. To do this, the writer can use text connectives. Sequencers, such as *initially*, *second*, and *in conclusion*, for example, help to structure the flow of the text. Terms such as *however* or *on the other hand* would signal the beginning of an alternative proposition.

The writer could also introduce the clause with an interpersonal element, creating a certain tone. The writer might signal a tone of uncertainty by using a modal such as *perhaps*, or a tone of disappointment by using a comment such as *unfortunately*. Or the writer might flag to the reader the significance of the point being made with a comment such as *importantly*.

Alternatively, the writer might simply begin the clause with the topic being developed—what the clause is about—followed by new information about the topic.

	Theme	**Rheme** (new information)
'I'm telling you about lyrebirds'	Lyrebirds	are among Australia's best-known native birds.
'The topic is still lyrebirds'	A lyrebird	has a wonderful ability to mimic sounds from the environment.
'Now the topic is changing slightly'	The male lyrebird	has a huge tail when it is fanned out in display.
'Now I'm being more specific'	The Superb Lyrebird	is found along the east coast of Australia.

Rheme: the part of a clause that generally follows the Theme ('sentence opener') and introduces new information.

At the level of the paragraph, we guide the reader by using topic sentences to make links back to the overall topic of the text, to specify how this paragraph is contributing to the topic, and to predict how the paragraph will unfold.

And at the level of the whole text, the introduction to the text often performs the function of introducing the topic and foreshadowing the development of the text.

We will look at Theme and thematic patterns in further detail in Chapter 9.

Cohesion

The Textual function includes a range of devices to make **cohesive ties** between items as the text develops. In the excerpt in Figure 2.2, for example, we can see how various types of pronouns have been used to link back to a previous item, creating cohesive chains. This is called *pronoun reference*. Sometimes the item referred to is a Participant in the clause. Other times it can be a whole clause (or stretch of clauses). Towards the end of the text in Figure 2.2, 'this' refers back to 'Your hair wants cutting' and 'it' refers back to 'to make personal remarks'. This is referred to as *extended reference*.

Note also other cohesive devices apart from pronouns that have been used. When the table is introduced in the first line, it is referred to as 'a table'. When we meet the table again later, it becomes 'the table', thus establishing a link between new information that has now become old information and can be taken for granted.

Rather than repeating 'table' in *The table was a large one*, the word 'one' has been substituted for table. This is referred to as *substitution*, where a general word is substituted for a more specific word to avoid repetition. A similar device is an *ellipsis*, where a word is simply left out if its

cohesion: the ways in which language features are used to make links between items in a text.

Figure 2.2   The Mad Hatter's Tea Party

Source: Lewis Carroll, Alice's Adventures in Wonderland *(1865)*

There was a table set out under a tree in front of the house, and the March Hare and the Hatter were having tea at it. A Dormouse was sitting between them, fast asleep, and the other two were using it as a cushion, resting their elbows on it, and talking over its head. The table was a large one, but the three were all crowded together at one corner of it: *'No room! No room!'* they cried out when they saw Alice coming. *'There's PLENTY of room!'* said Alice indignantly, and she sat down in a large arm-chair at one end of the table. *'Have some wine,'* the March Hare said in an encouraging tone. Alice looked all round the table, but there was nothing on it but tea. *'I don't see any wine'*, she remarked. *'There isn't any'*, said the March Hare. *'Your hair wants cutting'*, said the Hatter. He had been looking at Alice for some time with great curiosity, and this was his first speech. *'You should learn not to make personal remarks,'* Alice said with some severity; *'it's very rude.'*

Source: Lewis Carroll, Alice's Adventures in Wonderland *(1865)*

meaning can be inferred from the surrounding text. In the following examples from Figure 2.2, we could go back into the preceding text to find the word in square brackets:

the other two [creatures]

the three [creatures] *were all crowded together*

'There isn't any [wine]*'*

The notion of cohesion has significant implications for young children learning to read and write. But more demanding cohesive devices can make the reading and writing of more complex texts quite challenging for older students as well.

We will return to cohesion and the Textual function in greater detail in Chapter 5.

Have a go!

Trace over the arrows in Figure 2.2, using a different colour for each cohesive chain. (This is an activity that children enjoy.)

A FUNCTIONAL MODEL

At this stage, let's bring together all the elements of the functional model we have been developing in these first two chapters.

Have a go!

As you read through the following section, keep referring to Figure 2.3 and see if you can make sense of the relationships between the parts of the model.

A functional approach sees language as a system of choices. The choices we make from the system vary according to the context:

- the social purpose for using language (genres of describing, recounting, explaining, arguing, narrating, instructing, and so on)
- the field being developed (everyday, concrete, specific subject matter through to specialised, abstract, and generalised meanings)
- the tenor (the roles being played by those involved in the interaction and the relationship between them in terms of such factors as age, power, status, experience, expertise, and familiarity)

- the mode (the extent to which the context involves the spontaneous, dynamic, exploratory, face-to-face use of the oral mode through to the more reflective, synoptic, dense use of the written mode; the way in which the choice of medium impacts on the way texts are organised).

You are no doubt becoming familiar with these concepts now. As we have seen in the previous chapter, the *social purpose* for using language is related to the *genre*. Any combination of *field*, *tenor*, and *mode* is referred to as the *register*. This chapter is concerned with how these features of the context in which language is used shape (and are shaped by) the choices speakers and writers make from the language system. Figure 2.3 shows the systematic relationship between these features of the context and the choices made from the language system.

Figure 2.3   The functions of language as they relate to the context

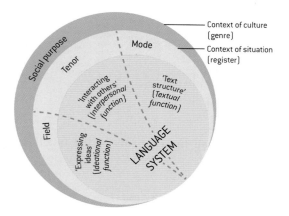

Looking at the diagram, we can see that in a particular context, the field (or subject matter) will be built up through certain choices from the resources for expressing ideas (the Ideational function) in the language system. If, for example, the field being developed is an explanation of how an ecosystem works, we might expect language choices involving action Processes in the present tense (*eat, grow, impact*), technical Participants (*producers, consumers, decomposers*), and Circumstances of place (*into the soil, from the sun*), along with relations of causality (*x because y*) and condition (*if a happens, then b might happen*). In a recipe for making a cake, it is likely that the field will involve a number of action Processes (*blend, mix, pour*). The Participants in these Processes are likely to represent concrete utensils and ingredients (*a bowl, the mixture, an egg*). The Circumstances will be critical to achieving the result (*carefully, for thirty minutes, in the oven, with a towel*).

The tenor will be developed through choices from the Interpersonal system. In the case of a student writing a book review for the school newsletter, for example, we might expect the use of persuasive language choices, including some expression of emotion regarding the writer's feelings about the story or characters, evaluative language appraising the qualities of the text, an element of judgment of the characters' behaviour in developing the moral theme of the story, and some use of modality (*might*, *perhaps*) to allow for other views.

And given a particular mode or medium, certain choices are likely to be made from the Textual system. A written historical recount, for example, will display a more prominent degree of crafting, greater density of information, more considered sequencing in time, and a higher level of internal cohesion than a spontaneous, oral recount of personal experience (as in the 'dentist' recount in Table 1.2 on page 10).

Taking it further

Finally, we can observe how the language system operates in terms of levels:

- the whole text (the way it unfolds in stages, the development of ideational meanings across the text, the build-up of interpersonal meanings throughout the text, the creation of cohesion)
- the paragraph (in the written mode, the use of topic sentences, the relation between paragraphs)
- the sentence (various combinations of clauses)
- the clause (its Ideational, Interpersonal, and Textual meanings realised through choices in grammar and vocabulary)
- the group or phrase (various kinds of meanings realised by noun groups, verb groups, adjective groups, adverb groups, prepositional phrases)
- the word and below the word.

We represent these levels as in Figure 2.4.

Figure 2.4   Levels in the language system

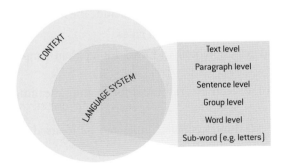

As you can see, a functional model enables us to work at a variety of levels from the word right through to the text (and even beyond to other texts) and to see the systematic relationships between these levels.

Have a go!

When we are planning, teaching, and assessing, it is useful to be aware of which aspect of language we are dealing with. Looking at the diagrams of the functional model above, see if you can identify which area of the model is being referred to in the questions below.

I am marking a test in terms of spelling. Which level am I likely to be interested in? In which mode?

I am concerned about a student's pronunciation of 'th'. Which level am I likely to be interested in? Which mode?

I am trying to make effective vocabulary choices in expressing my feelings about a film I've just watched. Which level am I concerned with? Which language function?

My students are having problems organising the information in their information reports. Which level should we focus on?

Sarah gets confused between using 'before' and 'after' to connect her ideas. Which function is this related to? At which level?

In summary, a functional model seeks to describe authentic language in use. It sees language as a resource for making various kinds of meanings, involving choices that are responsive to contextual factors. It provides teachers with tools for supporting students to investigate how language enables them to express their ideas about their world and to make connections between those ideas, to reflect on the relationships they are building with others and on how language shapes their own identity, and to explore the oral, written, and visual texts with which they engage in their daily lives. Because of this, the functional model is very useful for teachers of literacy in all curriculum fields at all stages of schooling.

In relation to education, the major principles of a functional approach include the following:

- Language is seen as a resource for meaning, not just a collection of rules.
- The role of the teacher is to extend the students' 'potential to mean' rather than simply correcting grammatical errors.
- Learning is a matter of the ongoing expansion of learners' resources for making meaning (primarily through language).
- Meaning is constructed at the level of the text, though smaller units can be focused on within the context of a text.
- Language is a system of choices.
- Our choices are responsive to the context in which the language is being used.
- Students need to be provided with tools to investigate and critique how language is involved in the construction of meaning.

- Emphasis is placed on using language to achieve real-life purposes and the language resources that are relevant to achieving those purposes.

In the following section we will revisit the functions of language and how they develop from early childhood through to adolescence.

LANGUAGE DEVELOPMENT IN EARLY CHILDHOOD

A functional approach to language grew out of observations of how children learn language—a useful starting point for our understanding of the theory. When we look at language development from a functional perspective, we are interested in how children use language to satisfy their needs (Halliday 1975; Painter 1984, 1989).

Right from the start, babies use language to *do* things. In the first few months, babies use relatively basic ways of communicating with others—grasping, crying, gurgling, gazing, and so on. But around nine months they start using sounds more deliberately to achieve specific outcomes. Each child initially develops his or her own individual system of meanings and expressions. They might use a certain expression systematically when they want to be given something: *yi*, for example, might mean 'I want that toy'. They might use another expression when getting someone to do something ('Pick me up'). Or they might use an expression that indicates pleasure in someone's company.

As the child grows, these first attempts at making meaning could be grouped into functions such as the following:

- obtaining material needs (a sound symbolising 'I want that')
- controlling the behaviour of others (a sound symbolising 'Come with me')
- close social contact with a person (a sound symbolising 'Let's look at this together')
- reflecting and asserting (a sound symbolising 'That's nice')
- finding out about the world (a sound symbolising 'What's that?')
- pretend play (a sound symbolising 'Let's pretend to be a lion')
- representing facts and information ('That's a pussycat').

Gradually the toddler starts to use language to go beyond the immediate context—the physical 'here and now'. The child can now share experiences with those who weren't physically present. When Daddy came home from work, Simon grabbed his hand, pointed to the wheelbarrow and rubbed his head, repeating *yay* in a mournful tone and with a sad expression. His mother co-constructed this recount for the father, explaining that Simon had fallen out of the wheelbarrow and hurt his head. Simon then proceeded to point to the barbed wire fence, holding up his finger and again intoning *yay*. His father was now able to interpret what had happened: 'Oh, you hurt your finger on the sharp fence, did you?'

By around 16 months, the child is starting to leave behind this idiosyncratic system of sounds and their associated functions (referred to as *protolanguage*) and is moving into the mother tongue. Between 18 and 24 months, the 'mini-functions' for which the toddler uses language converge into two key functions:

- language for reflecting on the world
- language for acting upon the world.

Expressing ideas in early childhood

The child can now use language to *reflect on experience* (the *Ideational function* of language). Language is used to represent the people, animals, and things in the child's life, the activities in which they participate, and the circumstances surrounding those activities ('Where?' 'When?' 'How?' 'With whom?', and the like).

Babies	go	in the prams	sometimes.
Who?	Do what?	Where?	When?

It is through the Ideational resources of language that they come to make sense of the world around them. Here, for example, a three-year-old is observing the similarities between babies. In a move that is critical to further learning, the child uses language to generalise about experience ('babies and what they do').

(S is watching a baby being strapped into its stroller by an adult)

S: Babies go in the prams sometimes.

M: What?

S: Babies go in the prams sometimes.

M: Yes, they do.

S: And babies go in the shops.

M: Oh yes, babies go in the shops.

S: And babies go to the Easter Show sometimes. (Painter 2005)

Now that the child can generalise, she or he is able to compare and contrast different categories of things, gradually forming taxonomies such as different types of vehicles or different types of animals—a critical step in moving from the everyday, familiar world of specific instances (*my puppy, Spot*) through to the more generalised world of school learning (*At preschool we have fishies and mouses and bunnies.*). Around this age, children are also beginning to use language to create connections between ideas. They start to make simple links using 'and', but eventually make basic cause-and-effect connections (*Don't touch 'cause it stings*), talk about conditional relationships (*If I go ching, you have to … you have to have your cart here.*), and infer consequences (*Helly pulled the string out of it, so it not … so it can't talk anymore.*). Again, this is the kind of language they will need in order to develop the kind of reasoning required for school learning.

Have a go!

Kylie is pretending to prepare and eat lunch with her mother. Using evidence from the transcript, how would you characterise the kind of experience being represented in language here? What Processes are represented? (Hint: are they action Processes like eating, doing, putting? Or are they linking information with words such as 'is' or 'has'? or perhaps feeling Processes such as 'would like?', 'want'?) Who/what are the Participants (human and non-human)? Are there any details of when and where?

Mother	Kylie
What's for lunch, Kyles?	Let's make pizza.
Okay. What would you like on your pizza?	Some of that. That's yummy!
This one?	Yeah. Put it on top. I love that.
You do it, honey.	Okay. What do you want?
I'll have mushrooms, please.	Here it is, mummy.
Thank you.	You can eat now.
What's this stuff?	That's pizza thing.
Pizza thing, eh?	Yeah. Eat now.

Interacting with others in early childhood

The child now also uses language to *act upon the world* (the *Interpersonal function* of language), interacting with others by asking for information (e.g. through questions), giving information (e.g. through statements), asking someone to do or provide something (e.g. commands) and offering to give or do something (offers). It is through the Interpersonal resources of language that toddlers negotiate meanings with others, constantly bombarding family members with questions, requests, and statements as they endeavour to make sense of the world and have their needs met.

In early childhood, children are learning to chain together the various speech functions to participate in extended conversations. They learn about initiating topics, taking turns, elaborating, challenging, agreeing, and disagreeing. These interpersonal skills evolve further with the ability to, for example, express positive and negative emotions and opinions, to create close relationships through the use of first and second person pronouns (I/we/you) and intimate terms of address (*Gramps, Bunnikins*), and to use facial expressions, gestures, and intonation with interpersonal force.

Have a go!

Look again at the transcript above (Kylie and mother). Now see if you can identify how the interaction draws on interpersonal resources: making statements, questions, commands, and offers; stating opinions; taking turns; using terms of address, politeness markers, personal pronouns, and so on.

Shaping texts in early childhood

As the child begins to make longer utterances, a third language function comes into play: language for organising text. This enables the child to *structure the flow of information* and to *make links* between different elements of the text and between a text and its context (the *Textual function* of language). Now the child can, for example, string words together that simultaneously represent an aspect of experience (the Ideational function) and that ask a question (the Interpersonal function): *Puss eat milk?*

In the spoken mode, meanings are typically made face to face in the here and now, with language linking to things in the immediate setting so there is no need to explicitly mention them as they can be seen, touched, pointed to, and heard by the interactants.

Have a go!

Look at the transcript above once more. This time, see if you can identify those instances where the interactants are referring to shared meanings in the setting without having to name them.

Now imagine that the mother is sight-impaired or that they are conversing over the phone. Rewrite the interaction filling in the gaps.

These three functions of language (the Ideational, the Interpersonal, and the Textual) are now all operating together in any utterance. The child at this stage has an unlimited linguistic potential for learning about the world in interaction with others, a resource that continues to develop rapidly throughout childhood.

Have a go!

There are many videos of babies and toddlers using protolanguage on sites such as YouTube. See if you can find one and observe how the child is using his or her protolanguage to achieve various functions.

Then find a video of a 2–4-year-old interacting. Identify how language is being used to represent 'what's going on' (Ideational meanings) and to build relationships (Interpersonal meanings) and how language is forming into extended text (Textual meanings).

LANGUAGE DEVELOPMENT IN LATER CHILDHOOD

As children grow, these three functions play an increasingly important role in their social and intellectual development.

Expressing ideas in later childhood

As they move through primary school, children use increasingly specific *Ideational* language resources to develop the fields of knowledge required in school contexts. Alongside the everyday, familiar topics of conversation, they begin to build an academic vocabulary, including Processes such as *classify, measure, summarise,* and *predict*; abstract Participants such as *concept, consequence,* and *problem*, and the occasional academic Circumstance such as *from our observations, frequently,* and *to some extent*. In school, their experience of the world is being shaped into different disciplines, each with their own way of using language. In Mathematics, for example, they will be demonstrating an understanding of the language of counting by naming numbers in sequences, and using language to solve simple addition and subtraction problems. In Health and Physical Education, on the other hand, they will be using language to describe ways to include others to make them feel they belong, and to discuss health information found in the media and on the internet.

Interacting with others in later childhood

As well as developing their *Ideational* resources to deal with the content of the primary curriculum, students will need to expand their *Interpersonal* language skills, learning new ways of interacting with a much wider range of people and taking on a greater variety of social roles: careful listener, group leader, activity partner, and so on. Rather than instantly initiating interactions around their own interests, they will need to attend to what others regard as significant. They will be learning new ways of relating to peers and adults and new routines for interacting. They will be expressing feelings and opinions and trying to persuade others in ways that are less direct.

Students' use of the mood system (statements, questions, commands, offers) is becoming more flexible, with the ability to use a range of grammatical forms for a particular function. Instead, for example, of getting someone to do something by using a command (*Give me that pencil!*) they might use a question (*Could you give me that pencil?*) or even more indirectly, a statement (*My pencil's broken.*) The English mood system can be a bit tricky for many EALD learners in terms of the subtle use of the speech functions by native speakers and how to form questions in English. For a more detailed explanation of the different structures of statements, questions, and commands see Derewianka (2011) and Humphrey, Droga, and Feez (2012).

Have a go!

Coming into primary school from the relatively free-flowing interactions of home, children benefit from being inducted into the language needed to take on new roles. To support effective participation in group work, for example, it is useful to explicitly teach students sentence starters to enable them to initiate moves. The roles and related sentence starters can be provided to students on laminated bookmarks for easy reference. Alternatively, each student can be given a selection of three sentence starters on a card and they have to use each sentence starter during the course of a particular activity.

In the following table, match the interaction role with a plausible sentence starter:

Role	Sentence starter
Initiate	I would disagree with that because ….
Affirm	So what we're saying is ….
Piggyback	What do you think?
Disagree	I think ….
Clarify	I agree with that because ….
Follow-up with evidence	What if … ?
Encourage participation	I like the way you explained ….
Speculate	But, if you look at p. 35, it says ….
Summarise	Can you explain what you mean by ….?

Shaping texts in later childhood

It is through the *Textual* resources of language that the Ideational and Interpersonal meanings are formed into coherent stretches of text. A major challenge as children enter school is the move from the spoken mode to the written mode. As we saw above, children in the early years are immersed in spoken language, supported by the surrounding setting and their conversation partners. In the written mode, however, they need to comprehend and create texts that are independent of the immediate setting and that make no assumptions about shared knowledge with the reader. As they engage with print in their environment, they are learning to understand the world not through direct experience but through an abstract representation of experience. They need to recognise and name abstract symbols: letters, words, numbers, and icons. It is this kind of abstract thinking that children will need as they become literate.

Primary students also need to deal with *multimodal* texts: relating the written text to surrounding images, interpreting and creating a variety of diagrams, and appreciating the illustrations in picturebooks. And, of course, they need to be able to navigate and design texts that combine a range of media. Even though we think of this generation as being adept at digital and visual literacy, we can't take this for granted.

Have a go!

Go back to the interaction between Kylie and her mother. Imagine that you are Kylie, now in primary school, and write a recount of what went on. As you write, think about what you need to do to make the written recount stand on its own for a distant reader. In what ways does your written text differ from the spoken one? What did you put in? What did you leave out? How did you fill in the gaps for the reader? How long did it take you? Did you have to do any revisions or did it just flow effortlessly onto the paper/screen?

LANGUAGE DEVELOPMENT IN ADOLESCENCE

It is often thought that learners' language and literacy are fully developed by the time they finish primary school, and that in secondary school they can just 'get on with learning subject knowledge'. In reality, however, the language demands of secondary school continue to expand considerably in each function and still require explicit teaching.

Expressing ideas in adolescence

Content and language are inseparable. A quick trawl through the 7–10 curriculum reveals the complexity of the language needed to deal with the increasingly abstract and technical fields of the different learning areas.

Students are now having to comprehend and use the Processes involved in higher-order thinking such as **developing** hypotheses, **analysing** data, **generating** viable options, **predicting** consequences, **deconstructing** real-world problems, **evaluating** alternative designs, **designing** and **validating** algorithms, and **identifying** risks.

The Participants in those Processes have become dense, abstract, and highly specialised:

Process	Participant
Identify	the key factors that influence major consumer and financial decisions.
Analyse	the short- and long-term consequences of these decisions.
Discuss	relevant thematic and intertextual connections with other texts.
Consider	a range of language features including nominalisations, clause combinations, technicality, and abstraction.
Describe	the constancy of the sine, cosine and tangent ratios.

And the Circumstances surrounding the Processes are more sophisticated and varied:

When? (duration in time)	The experiences of men, women and children *during the Industrial Revolution.*
When? (point in time)	Significant events and campaigns … such as the Jabiluka mine controversy *in 1998.*
Where? (extent in place)	The influence of the Industrial Revolution on the movement of peoples *throughout the world.*
Where? (specific place)	Reasons for, and effects of, international migration *in Australia.*
Where? (source)	Locate and share factual information about people, places and events *from a range of oral texts.*
How? (how much)	Students investigate wartime experiences through a study of World War II *in depth.*
How? (by what means)	Graph simple non-linear relations *with and without the use of digital technologies.*
How? (comparison)	The position of the Asian society *in relation to other nations in the world.*
Why? (purpose)	Process and synthesise information from a range of sources *for use as evidence in an historical argument.*
Why? (reason)	Propose individual and collective action *in response to a contemporary geographical challenge.*
For example?	Significant developments and/or cultural achievements, *such as the fall of Constantinople in 1453* AD.
About what? (matter)	Investigate community resources and ways to seek help *about health, safety and well-being.*

As before, we are also concerned with how connections are made between ideas. In secondary school those connections become more intricate, involving relationships of causality, justification, concession, contrast, condition, and so on.

Think about it

As you read the preceding section, you most likely found it daunting and started to tune out. And that's the point. The language of secondary school can be confronting for most students and, for many, impenetrable to the point where they become so frustrated they give up. As you can see, it's not just a matter of 'defining technical terms'. It's how a profusion of unfamiliar specialist and abstract terms are combined in complex and varied ways to represent the sophisticated thinking required in secondary education. Teachers can support students in 'unpacking' such language by asking questions such as:

- Which words tell us about the activity (the Process)?
- Which words tell us about who or what is involved (the Participants)?
- Which words provide extra information about the activity (the Circumstances)?

In secondary school, did you struggle with the language of the textbooks, of assignments, or of exam questions? Did you have teachers in secondary school who explicitly taught you the language needed to interpret, express, and connect the ideas involved in the various learning areas? Do you think this helped you to deal better with the subject matter? Whose responsibility is it to teach the language of the different curriculum areas?

Interacting with others in adolescence

Apart from dealing with the interpersonal challenges facing teenagers in their social lives, they also have to interpret and compose academic written texts that create subtle and nuanced relationships with the reader.

Have a go!

In the following excerpt from a persuasive text, see if you can identify examples of the following interpersonal features:

The use of logic to persuade	Who is the greatest hero: samurai or knight? I believe that the knight would be the greatest hero over samurai. The samurai have *of course* got advantages over knights, but I think that knights probably have greater advantages over samurais.
A plea to emotion	
Judgement of human qualities	
Alignment with the reader	
Taking a stance	When it comes to training, knights have to leave their families at a young age and spend their whole lives training. They learn the code of courtesy and strict behaviour expected of a knight. They risk their lives riding into battle with their master.
Recognition of an alternative point of view	
Rhetorical question to engage the reader's interest	With regard to mental training and academic skills, this is where the samurai have the advantage. They were extremely smart and were considered as an elite member of society. A samurai was willing to die and commit suicide if caught by the enemy. They would respect and protect women, children, and the weak.
Increasing the strength of a statement	
Use of modality	Knights had a larger range of weapons than samurai.
	Over all I believe that the knight would be the more heroic soldier. Over intense training, what they fight for etc.

Source: Amended from Year 8 Australian Curriculum: History www.acara.edu.au/ curriculum/worksamples/Year_8_History_Portfolio_Above.pdf

Overall, did you find the text persuasive?

Shaping texts in adolescence

Secondary students will be writing longer texts that need to be carefully crafted to make them coherent for the reader. Students need to draw on a range of Textual resources to make their texts flow well and hang together cohesively.

Have a go!

Have a look at the text above again. This time, consider how well the writer has organised the information in the text. In particular, think about:

- In the opening paragraph, does the writer foreshadow how the argument will be developed?
- Do the topic sentences of the subsequent paragraphs provide an effective framework to further the argument?
- Does each paragraph elaborate successfully on its topic sentence?
- Does the final paragraph pull together the main points into a convincing conclusion?
- How would you counsel this student?

THE REGISTER CONTINUUM

The continua in Tables 2.2, 2.3 and 2.4 (after Macken 1996; Derewianka 2003) provide a summary of how we might expect language to develop from early childhood through to adolescence in relation to these language functions.

Table 2.2   Using language to reflect on the world (Ideational function)

Early childhood	Later childhood	Adolescence
Uses language related to familiar, everyday, personal, concrete, non-specialised subject matter. Ideas are linked in a simple, spoken-like manner using connectors such as *and*, *but*, *so* and *when*.	Uses language to comprehend, interpret, and construct increasingly complex worlds. Ideas are connected in sentences using a variety of conjunctions reflecting more complex logical relationships such as cause and effect.	Uses language involving more abstract and technical subject matter relating to specific disciplines. Connects ideas in more sophisticated ways such as making concessions (*although, however*) and hypothesising (*if ... then*).

Table 2.3 Using language to act on the world (Interpersonal function)

Early childhood	Later childhood	Adolescence
Uses language to adopt a limited range of roles, interacting with family and friends in relatively informal ways. Feelings and opinions are expressed directly, with little self-regulation.	Uses language to construct a number of different roles and relationships drawing on a wider repertoire of interpersonal resources. Can deploy these resources to seek information, make requests, give opinions, persuade, deny, and so on, in increasingly subtle and indirect ways.	Uses language to negotiate relationships with familiar and unfamiliar adults and peers in a range of contexts, consciously attending to language choices depending on context. Employs more nuanced expression of emotion, more detached evaluation supported by evidence, an awareness of alternative perspectives and of how language can be used to position self and others.

Table 2.4 Using language to form coherent texts (Textual function)

Early childhood	Later childhood	Adolescence
Uses oral language that is spontaneous, exploratory, free-flowing, and closely tied to what's going on. Engages with relatively brief written and multimodal texts using a variety of media.	Moves into the more planned language of the written mode, comprehending and creating texts that are not dependent on the immediate context. Becomes more conscious of how different modes are combined in multimodal texts.	Interprets and crafts longer written and multimodal texts that are denser, more compact, more tightly organised, attending to a range of cohesive devices that make written texts flow coherently.

CHAPTER SUMMARY

In this chapter, we have observed language functioning in three important ways: to enable us to express and connect our ideas, to interact with others, and to create coherent texts. We have considered some language features of each of these functions, which will be further fleshed out in Part 2. The various elements of the functional model were then brought together, demonstrating how certain factors in the context (field, tenor, and mode) activate choices from corresponding functions in the language system (the Ideational, Interpersonal, and Textual). We have then looked at how these three functions increase in complexity as learners move from early childhood through to adolescence.

FOR FURTHER DISCUSSION

1   Look at the various figures in this chapter and see whether you can explain to a partner how the functional model works.

2   Have a look at the *Australian Curriculum: English* (see websites opposite). You will notice that three major substrands within the Language strand correspond to Halliday's three language functions. Now have a look through the content descriptions and elaborations for these substrands. Do you recognise any of the language features discussed in this chapter? Do you think you would be in a position to explicitly teach your students to achieve the content descriptions outlined in the Language strand?

3   Now have a look at the criteria used in marking the NAPLAN writing test (see websites opposite). Go through the marking guide in some detail and see if you can identify which of the specific criteria relate to the functions of language and the language features described in these first two chapters.

REFERENCES

Derewianka, B. (2003). Making grammar relevant to students' lives. In G. Bull & M. Anstey (eds), *The Literacy Lexicon*, 2nd edn. Sydney: Pearson, pp. 37–50.

Derewianka, B. (2011). *A New Grammar Companion*. Sydney: PETAA.

Halliday, M.A.K. (1975). *Learning How to Mean: Explorations in the development of language*. London: Edward Arnold.

Humphrey, S., Droga, L., & Feez, S. (2012). *Grammar and Meaning*. Sydney: PETAA.

Macken, M. (1996). Literacy and learning across the curriculum: Towards a model of register for secondary teachers. In R. Hasan & G. Williams (eds), *Literacy in Society*. London: Longman, pp. 232–78.

Martin, J.R., & White, P.R.R. (2005). *The Language of Evaluation: Appraisal in English*. London: Palgrave.

Painter, C. (1984). *Into the Mother Tongue: A case study in early language development*. London: Pinter.

Painter, C. (1989). *Learning the Mother Tongue*. Oxford: Oxford University Press.

Painter, C. (with Derewianka, B. & Torr, J.) (2005). From microfunction to metaphor: Learning language and learning through language. In R. Hasan, C. Matthiessen & J. Webster (eds), *Continuing Discourse on Language: A functional perspective*, vol. 2. London: Equinox, pp. 561–86.

WEBSITES

Australian Curriculum and Reporting Authority: The *Australian Curriculum: English*
www.australiancurriculum.edu.au/English/Curriculum/F-10

On this website you will find several documents relating to the *Australian Curriculum: English*, including the curriculum itself.

Australian Curriculum and Reporting Authority: *Writing Marking Guide*
www.nap.edu.au/naplan/about-each-domain/writing/writing.html

This site provides the writing guide used to mark NAPLAN tests. In future years the *Guide* might change, so you will need to locate the *Marking Guide* and criteria for the current year.

INTRODUCTION TO A TEACHING-LEARNING CYCLE

This chapter looks at how the functional model of language introduced in the previous chapters is used to inform classroom teaching. We introduce and describe in detail a cycle of teaching and learning used by many Australian teachers to extend their students' repertoires of literate practices and to develop their knowledge about language.

Learning objectives

In this chapter, you will:

- become familiar with a teaching-learning cycle designed to implement a functional approach to language
- develop understanding of the learning theory underpinning the teaching-learning cycle
- recognise the importance of teachers' knowledge about language in planning and teaching literacy
- begin to understand how this knowledge about language can be used in the classroom.

Key terms and concepts

the teaching-learning cycle (building knowledge of the field, supported reading, modelling/deconstructing the genre, joint construction, independent construction)

procedures

procedural recounts

scaffolding (designed-in, contingent/interactional)

metalanguage

Activities:

brainstorming/floorstorming

jigsaw task

bundling or categorising information

skim-reading

scanning

jumbled text

cloze exercise

differentiated writing

collaborative writing

think-pair-share

INTRODUCTION

The previous chapters have drawn on extensive research into language use in different social contexts to describe the nature of language and its central role in learning. This research has also been concerned with how to use such knowledge about language and learning in order to support teachers in school and tertiary classrooms to enhance their students' literacy outcomes in different curriculum fields and disciplines. In this chapter, we introduce a cycle of teaching and learning designed to help teachers plan and implement a sequence of carefully designed interactions around a particular topic and genre. Also known as 'genre-based pedagogy', the teaching-learning cycle takes the texts or genres associated with the different purposes for using language (e.g. persuading, arguing, informing) as the starting point for teaching literacy. While this cycle was originally designed by Rothery (1996) for the teaching of writing, it offers opportunities for extending students' oral language, and recent developments have placed a greater emphasis on reading. We introduce the model generally as we explain its theoretical underpinnings, then describe each stage before illustrating with a unit of work from a Year 4 classroom.

Theoretical underpinnings

Dialogue, because it is a process through which individuals construct understandings together, is at the heart of teaching and learning. In the previous chapter we saw how interactions between children and their parents and caregivers are crucial to the child's development; that is, to learning language and to making sense of the world. The teaching-learning cycle is inspired by this work, particularly that of Painter, who argues that when young children learn to speak, they:

- begin to learn the discourse patterns (including genres) of their culture
- learn language through engaging in everyday conversations
- demonstrate persistence in negotiating meanings with dialogue partners
- construct texts jointly with dialogue partners
- internalise models of the genres provided through repeated conversational encounters, and
- often copy the language patterns they hear in future monologues and conversations (1986, p. 81).

A number of these features are evident in the following extracts of dialogue from Halliday's research (cited in Painter 1986, p. 75). Here 2-year-old Nigel is recounting a meal shared with his mother to his father.

N:	Aunty Joan cook quack quack for you
F:	Aunty Joan cooked quack quack for you, didn't she?
N:	Aunty Joan cook greenpea
F:	And green peas

N:	Began shout
M:	Who began to shout?
N:	Nila began shout
M:	Did you? What did you shout?
N:	Greenpea!

(Later that day)

N: Aunty Joan cook quackquack for you …and greenpea … you began to shout GREENPEA

Notice how the initial encounter is dialogic; his father (who wasn't present) prompts Nigel for information and together the three speakers reconstruct a version of events. As a result of this conversational support, Nigel is able to produce the later complete monologue—evidence that he has internalised the jointly constructed version of events. The teaching-learning cycle is patterned on such early dialogic encounters in the home and community; its central tenet is 'guidance through interaction in the context of shared experience' (Rose & Martin 2012, p. 58).

THE TEACHING-LEARNING CYCLE

teaching-learning cycle: a framework for planning and teaching language and literacy in different curriculum fields. Based on the principle of 'guidance through interaction in the context of shared experience', the cycle scaffolds students as they gain increasing control of the curriculum topic as well as of language choices in the written mode. The teaching-learning cycle requires teachers to develop students' explicit knowledge about language.

Figure 3.1   The teaching-learning cycle

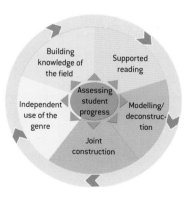

An overview

The **teaching-learning cycle** we describe here is a five-stage framework designed to develop students' knowledge in a particular curriculum field as well as enhance their language and literacy skills.

In contrast to the home and community where the events of everyday life usually form a shared context for learning, in formal learning institutions such as school and university the contexts for learning are curriculum and discipline topics—topics that students won't necessarily experience or encounter outside the classroom, and that usually require a different way of looking at the world. Thus, in the first stage, *building knowledge of the field*, the teacher designs and leads activities to begin to build shared understandings of the topic. Importantly, this field-building continues throughout the other stages of the teaching-learning cycle so that students' understanding of the field accumulates and becomes increasingly sophisticated.

The second stage, *supported reading*, involves intensive reading of carefully selected texts or text extracts in the topic area, focusing on developing students' appreciation of the topic at hand, their enjoyment of reading, and their comprehension and decoding skills as relevant to their needs.

The third stage, *modelling* or *deconstruction*, introduces students to the genre relevant to the topic under exploration. It may involve the teacher modelling the writing process but, more usually, deconstructing an example of the genre, considering its function or purpose, linking it to other texts, and explicitly pointing out how it is organised in terms of the typical stages and phases, and focusing on key language features. As we have seen with young children learning to speak, it often takes more than one encounter with models of the genre for learners to internalise the genre. So teachers frequently use a number of texts for this stage so that the students have multiple opportunities for encountering the patterns of language that are distinct to the focus genre.

In the fourth stage, *joint construction*, the teacher supports the students through the process of preparing and writing a text in the focus genre and related to the curriculum, providing them with demonstrations of how to organise their often spoken information into written language. This mirrors the way in which the parents we have read about earlier jointly constructed spoken texts with their young children. Once the students have been supported in the processes of gathering information, categorising the information, and jointly writing it up into a coherent text with the teacher, they are usually ready to independently go through the same process in the fifth and final stage. This stage is *independent construction* and involves students in researching a similar topic and writing their own texts. Through the repeated encounters with the focus genre throughout the teaching-learning cycle, the students are able to take over greater responsibility for constructing their texts.

Figure 3.2   Scaffolding as a gradual release of responsibility

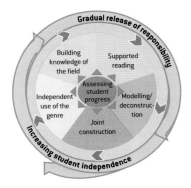

The role of the teacher

The changing role of the teacher is a particularly important aspect of the teaching-learning cycle. Initially, the role is deliberately interventionist as she or he leads instruction by providing models of important genres and explicitly teaching students about their use and patterns of language; and by extending students' language use into more written-like language during joint construction. This role parallels that of parents and caregivers who, according to Painter,

- provide models of language and genre as they respond to the young child's meanings
- assist the child's contributions through questioning and interpreting their utterances
- highlight salient features of genres and texts (1986, p. 82).

Such support is gradually reduced as the learners take increasing responsibility for independent use of the language. This handover of responsibility by the adult to the learner is often referred to as **scaffolding** or the process by which an adult or 'expert' helps someone who is less adult or less expert to complete a task that is initially beyond them (Wood, Bruner, & Ross 1976, p. 89). Scaffolding is a useful way of thinking about teachers' work.

Scaffolding is also strongly associated with the work of Vygotsky, in particular the Zone of Proximal Development (ZPD), a construct which refers to 'the distance between the actual development level as determined by independent problem solving and the level of potential development as determined by problem solving under adult guidance or in collaboration with more capable peers' (1978, p. 86). Vygotsky argued that learning was most effective when learners were assisted to work at challenging tasks that are ahead of their actual or current development; that is, in the uppermost limits of the ZPD. Scaffolding is just such assistance, designed to assist the learner so that she or he can independently complete the task successfully in new contexts. This notion of scaffolding as gradual release or handover of responsibility is captured in Figure 3.2.

However, because home and school are different contexts for learning, there are important differences between the scaffolding observed in early language learning environments and that in more formal educational settings. In home contexts, the young child frequently initiates interactions. In contrast, school interactions are often initiated by teachers who are accountable for the timely completion of curriculum goals. The young child is also likely to be interacting with fewer individuals than the school child, who is one of a number of children with one teacher in a classroom. And of course, the nature of the relationships between adults and children differs so that contexts are not always shared. For these reasons, it is useful to consider Hammond and Gibbons' well-known study (2005) of scaffolding practices in schools, in which they identified effective scaffolding as taking place on two levels: designed-in and contingent or interactional.

Designed-in (macro-level) **scaffolding** refers to the decisions teachers make as they design contexts for learning. The teaching-learning cycle may be thought of as a tool for 'designing-in' scaffolding. In using the cycle, teachers consider a range of factors such as curriculum outcomes; the relevant genre and example texts; students' prior knowledge, experience, and needs including their knowledge about genre and language; which tasks are suitable and how these will be sequenced; how different organisational patterns (pair, small group, whole class, individual) will be used and how the meaning-making resources available (language, image, colour, etc.) might be usefully deployed to support students to notice and remember aspects of text and its language features.

---

scaffolding: support provided to learners from a more experienced Other in order to achieve outcomes that they would otherwise not be able to achieve on their own.

designed-in scaffolding: the support consciously planned by teachers that takes into account students' prior knowledge and experience, the selection and sequencing of tasks, a range of student groupings, use of a focus text, use of multiple information systems such as image, colour, sound, etc., and metalinguistic and metacognitive awareness. Importantly, designed-in scaffolding provides the environment for interactional scaffolding.

Contingent or **interactional** (micro-level) **scaffolding** refers to the unplanned but responsive support that teachers provide to students during spontaneous unfolding of classroom events. We have presented a number of examples of interactional scaffolding in the parent and child dialogues in this and previous chapters. It is through this moment-by-moment scaffolding by the adults that children learn language and in doing so learn about the world. In school settings, the quality of contingent scaffolding rests upon the nature of the designed-in scaffolding; in other words, decisions teachers make at the macro-level shape the environment for micro-level scaffolding.

Different kinds of classroom dialogue

Research has revealed that while there is a good deal of talk in classrooms, unfortunately much of this talk is not of the type that engages students and scaffolds their understandings (Alexander 2008; Gibbons 2009). The most common kind of classroom talk is as follows:

Teacher:	What did the wolf say to the little pig?
Student:	I'll huff and I'll puff and I'll blow your house down.
Teacher:	Yes, good.

This dialogue structure was first identified by Sinclair and Coulthard in the 1970s and has proved an enduring feature of classrooms. It is commonly known as the IRF (Initiation, Response, Feedback) because of the distinctness of the contributions of teacher and student: typically, the teacher initiates the dialogue (*What did the wolf say to the little pig?*), the student responds (*I'll huff and I'll puff and I'll blow your house down*), and the teacher completes the interaction by providing feedback (*Yes, good*). It is also referred to as triadic dialogue, elicitation script, and the IRE (Initiation, Response, Evaluation). While there are times when such talk is useful for reviewing work and for sharing ideas among the whole class, students' responses tend to be restricted to brief utterances that simply report known facts. When it is the dominant pattern of dialogue in the classroom, the IRF offers little to students in terms of opportunities to use spoken language, to initiate interaction, to make tentative contributions, to provide extended responses, and to build on each other's ideas. In contrast, Hammond and Gibbons argue that teachers should exploit the potential of interactional scaffolding; that is, engage in talk that:

- listens to what students want to say and avoids 'scripted responses'
- engages students in lengthy exchanges so that turns are longer, ideas can be revisited, reworded, and refined
- builds on students' previous experiences
- recaps discussion at various stage and makes key points explicit
- appropriates students' contributions to provide a more technical or academic wording when necessary
- allows students more time to respond (perhaps by asking for further details) (Gibbons 2009, p. 158).

> **interactional scaffolding:** support provided by teachers to students in dialogue. It includes such strategies as recasting, recapping, making links to prior experience, and pointing forward. Interactional scaffolding is crucial to students' cognitive and linguistic development.

Have a go!

The following extract of talk is from a grammar lesson in a Year 2 classroom. The children have been learning to identify the parts of a simple sentence or clause that represent 'What's happening?', 'What state is being described?', 'Who or what is involved?' and 'What are the surrounding circumstances?' (ACARA 2015, p. 34). During a small-group reading activity, one of the students—in the belief that the Participant element of a clause must represent a human being—has queried whether 'nobody' could really be a Participant in the sentence from a picturebook: 'I started yelling for mum and nobody heard me'. The extract of talk is from the plenary or sharing time at the end of the lesson and his teacher has wanted to share the problem raised with the rest of the class. Note that the underlined words are spoken by the teacher with extra emphasis.

Identify the examples of designed-in and contingent scaffolding that are evident in the extract. What role is dialogue playing in this activity? How is it similar to or different from that occurring between young children and their parents or carers in settings prior to school?

1	Teacher:	*What was your point about that word here?* (pointing to the word 'nobody' in the clause highlighted on the interactive whiteboard: *'I started yelling for mum but nobody heard me'*)
2	Student:	*That um because nobody means that there's no person,*
3		*so how can it be a person*
4		*if nobody means there's no person?*
5	Teacher:	*So, 'who or what is involved?'*
6		*well nobody*
7		*does that really count as a person as a who or what?*
8		*I think in this clause it does*
9		*because it's who heard me?*
10		*Nobody heard me.*
11		*So it is,*
12		*we are still going to make it red**
13		*but I thought that was really a really interesting Participant, 'nobody'.*

*Many teachers have adopted the convention of colouring Participants red, Processes green, and Circumstances blue. What do you think the advantage of this colour coding is?

Think about it

The teacher in the extract above wanted to foster her students' interest in working closely with language as well as developing their knowledge of clause structure. The student's extended response to her initiating move may be seen as evidence of a developing interest. Note also the teacher's elaborated response in the dialogue. This short extract indicates a much richer talk between teacher and student/s than that often seen in the IRF. What factors enable this richer dialogue?

In terms of the teaching-learning cycle, the dialogue enabled by scaffolding that takes place throughout the stages is crucial to the success of the teachers' goals in terms of both curriculum content and language and literacy learning. Notice in Figures 3.1 and 3.2 that assessment is an important part of the teaching-learning cycle. At each stage of the cycle, teachers monitor students' progress by observing, listening, questioning, and analysing students' language use. As a result they can adjust the activities, the level of support, and their conversations with students.

So far, we have focused on the importance of dialogue in whole-class lessons. Students also need opportunities to participate in a range of different classroom organisational structures—individual work, pair work, and small-group work. Pair and small-group work offer particular opportunities for students to use language in a range of ways, provided it is well designed by the teacher and the students know how to participate.

Each stage of the teaching-learning cycle offers a range of different opportunities for dialogic talk; that is, dialogue that involves students and supports them to gain control over the language and literacy demands of the particular curriculum area. At times, the teacher loosely controls the dialogue so that the students have more freedom over how they complete the task and the language they use. At other times, the teacher exerts more control over the dialogue so that important language choices are made explicit to the students and their opportunities for misunderstanding or confusion are fewer. Such variations in freedom and control are important features of the teaching-learning cycle.

THE TEACHING-LEARNING CYCLE IN FURTHER DETAIL

In this section we consider the stages of the teaching-learning cycle in more detail, with particular emphases on the dialogic potential of each and the varying roles of teachers and students at different stages of the cycle. The cycle can involve a number of lessons over days, weeks, or even a term and there are multiple opportunities for talking, listening, reading, and writing around a range of texts and other artefacts.

Building knowledge of the field

This stage of the teaching-learning cycle is critical to engaging students in the curriculum topic and for beginning to build a shared context in preparation for working with the genre. The focus is on developing students' language related to the curriculum field; in other words, they

brainstorming: encourages students to make links between their previous learning and new information, for example, by listing features of a character or what they know about a topic.

floorstorming: an activity in which students respond to visual stimuli such as a montage of images related to the focus topic.

jigsaw task: an activity in which students are organised into groups and provided with information on a particular aspect of a topic. They become experts in that particular aspect, then form different groups comprising experts from each aspect to build common understandings of the topic.

bundling or categorising information: activities that require students to group or categorise information (images, sentences or parts of sentences, words, or even whole texts).

become experts in the topic whether it is to do with climate change, physical forces, or perhaps eighteenth-century London. Suitable activities for engaging students will vary across stages of schooling, but there are some common activities that help find out what students know. These include:

- discussions
- **brainstorming** (and its variation, **floorstorming**)
- think-pair-share activities.

Such activities are often used in combination with the following types to extend students' initial understandings of the field:

- hands-on activities such as experiments or problem-solving
- field trips and excursions
- guest speakers
- research activities such as **jigsaw tasks**.

Emphasis at this point is usually on students' spoken language, although the talk will frequently take place around written text, image, and other artefacts. Importantly, the activities are interactive so that students have opportunities to use, hear, and see the language associated with the topic. As Myhill, Jones, and Hopper (2006, p. 25) point out, two key features of dialogic talk are that it builds on participants' prior knowledge and that it is a process of constructing knowledge together. However, finding out what students know is only the first step in building students' field knowledge, as their knowledge will often be commonsense or everyday understandings and even misconceptions of the topic. Teachers need to extend these understandings into more abstract, subject-specific knowledge and associated language by helping to reorganise them through activities such as **bundling or categorising information** with genre-specific research proformas (see Figure 3.3), graphic organisers (see Chapter 7), shared reading or viewing of information texts, or interviews with prepared questions. While the activities develop students' expertise in the topic, they are usually designed with the focus genre in mind. As we have already pointed out, building the field does not occur only at this initial stage. It continues throughout the teaching-learning cycle as understandings are progressively developed to further depth and complexity.

Supported reading

The *supported reading* stage of the teaching-learning cycle is closely related to the field-building stage as it offers opportunities to extend students' knowledge of the curriculum topic by engaging in reading activities related to the curriculum field and to the general type of text (informative, persuasive, imaginative). Here the students are supported to read texts carefully selected by the teacher and related to the curriculum field, building reading skills such as comprehension and fluency as well as their understandings of the topic. In this way, teachers' regular reading focus can be closely aligned with language and literacy instruction across the curriculum areas. For example, teacher-led and shared reading lessons might focus on

Figure 3.3   Genre-specific research proformas for different writing tasks

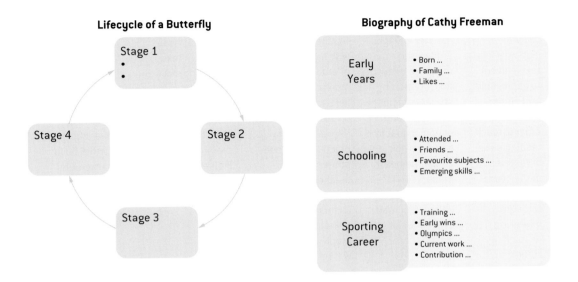

the contribution of images to the meaning of the text; guided reading provides opportunity for students to apply what they have learnt about images and their place in the text; and independent reading of related texts will provide practice in skills such as **skim-reading** and **scanning** for relevant information using images as well as written language. Alternatively, if the focus is on imaginative texts, teacher-led reading might focus on how mature writers describe settings and characters; collaborative reading will be an opportunity to prepare for innovating on the mature writer's patterns of language in preparation for later collaborative writing around settings and characters.

Activities suitable for the supported reading stage vary from teacher-led reading, to shared reading, guided, collaborative, and independent as indicated in Table 3.1.

While the activities described in the table are organised as a general shift from the teacher explicitly modelling aspects of the reading process to student independence, activities selected during the supported reading stage of the teaching-learning cycle do not necessarily follow this progression; rather, the teacher selects from such organisational patterns according to the identified student needs. These needs will vary in terms of the degree of support required and may involve specific areas such as research skills, text organisation, vocabulary, and sentence structure. Critically, supported reading should be related to the curriculum field; in this way a shared context is developed in which teacher and students have common understandings of the topic. Students should become increasingly familiar with the field as they revisit, reuse, and recycle subject-specific language such as vocabulary, discourse features, and genre.

skim-reading: designed for quickly gaining general information about a whole text. The reader skims over the surface to get a general sense of the content or its main points.

scanning: the reader looks through the text for particular pieces of information, paying close attention to sections. To do this, knowledge of the stages and phases of the genre is particularly useful.

Table 3.1   Supported reading within the curriculum field

Teacher-led ('I do')	Shared ('we do/I lead')	Guided ('you do/I help')	Collaborative ('you do together')	Independent ('you do')
Teacher selects a focus text relevant to genre, field and students' needs in order to teach reading skills or features of the genre explicitly through modelling or 'thinking aloud'.	Teacher engages students in reading a relevant text, supporting students to notice relevant features of text, to practise reading skills and strategies in preparation for writing. Might be enlarged or read over series of lessons.	Teacher works with small groups of students with similar reading levels. Emphasis is on students reading relevant texts to practise skills and strategies with teacher supporting as necessary. Could include guidance on note-taking in preparation for writing.	Students read a relevant text, practising skills and strategies introduced earlier. Might include completing genre-specific research proforma as in Figure 3.3.	Students select relevant texts within the field, reading for pleasure, to develop fluency, to further build background knowledge in preparation for writing. Might include genre-specific research proforma.
Whole class	Whole class	Small group	Pair or small group	Individual

Modelling or deconstruction

The *modelling*, or *deconstruction*, as it is often referred to, stage of the teaching-learning cycle is concerned with developing students' conscious knowledge about texts; that is, the focus shifts from field to genre. Students learn about the social purpose of the genre (why such texts are used, where they are found, who uses them). They learn about patterns of language and image from examining examples of the text (*What do texts of this genre always seem to have? What stages or features are optional?*). They learn about language at the levels of text, clause, group or phrase, and word, and about different kinds of images in order to answer such questions as *Why that choice in that text? What is the effect of that choice on meaning?* In this way students are learning that knowledge about language and image is useful for interpreting and constructing effective texts.

The teacher's knowledge about text comes to the forefront of this stage as the students are led through a number of activities designed to draw their attention to the salient patterns of meaning of the focus genre and to give practice in identifying and using these patterns before applying them further. Our research and that of many of our colleagues has indicated the importance of teachers' knowledge about text to the effectiveness of their modelling and deconstructing with students (Jones & Chen 2012; Myhill, Jones & Wilson 2016). The remaining chapters in this textbook are designed to build up your knowledge of the key genres of schooling and their associated patternings of language and image.

In the early years, this stage will involve the teacher modelling writing in multiple mini-lessons that arise from a particular curriculum field that is under focus in the classroom. While the teacher will have text patterns associated with the genre in mind, the emphasis is not always on whole texts but may be on aspects of writing such as text organisation, sentence structure, handwriting and punctuation, vocabulary, aspects of image, and cohesion.

In later years, the teacher may guide the students through an analysis of several texts in the target genre, asking such questions such as *Where have you seen texts like this before? What is the purpose of these texts? How are they similar? How are they different? What do they always/ usually/sometimes seem to have?* They might also look at individual examples of the text and discuss its register features; for example, *What is the text about (field)? Who is the intended reader or audience (tenor)? How is the information organised and communicated—language, image, or a combination (mode)?*

Once the students have developed an understanding of the purpose of the genre and the range of texts through which these are achieved, the teacher selects a good, clear model of the genre and, using an enlarged text (on an interactive whiteboard), identifies the typical stages and their functions with the students (*What are the functions of the stages?*). Students then annotate their own copies of the text using terminology appropriate to the genre. Once the students can readily recognise the stages of the text, it is important to point out phases, the patterns within its stages. Labelling these so that they make sense to the students is a useful strategy for reading because it enables students to predict the language to be encountered. At this point, it is useful to consider the contribution of image (if present) to how the text achieves its purpose. Activities for giving practice in recognising the salient features of genres and using functional terminology include **jumbled text**, labelling, bundling information under stage labels, and using relevant graphic organisers.

While students may use 'commonsense' labels initially, providing more accurate labels as appropriate to their needs is an important consideration. Many teachers, particularly those working with students in middle primary and upwards, adopt the functional terminology described in curriculum documents and this textbook because these terms tend to describe the contribution of the textual element to its overall purpose. Such a **metalanguage** provides continuity throughout school and across curriculum contexts as well as being meaningful to the students.

Modelling and deconstruction also involves examining the language patterns associated with different genres, and this stage of the cycle provides many opportunities for work with language at the level of sentence, paragraph, and whole text. Because this language work takes place within a particular curriculum context or field and within the context of a particular genre, the activities are meaningful and supportive to students. Activities include highlighting model texts, **cloze** passages focusing on the relevant language features, and labelling images with arrows and captions. Initially these activities may involve the whole class while students learn to identify the relevant language features, but they also lend themselves to small-group activities which foster students' talk about texts. We have also observed a number of interactive activities used effectively in this stage of the teaching-learning cycle (see, for example, Cochrane,

jumbled text: stages and phases of an example of the target genre are cut and mixed up, which students must reassemble using their knowledge of the stages of the genre. They can also be asked to label the stages and phases using functional labels.

metalanguage: a shared language for talking about language.

cloze exercise: a variation on traditional cloze exercises in that the teacher selects the particular language feature under focus to be deleted. For example, for a class studying procedures in an instructional text, it would be appropriate to delete the action verbs occurring at the beginning of the commands. Students must then supply the missing verb from either their own knowledge or a list.

Reece, Ahearn, & Jones 2012; Klingelhofer & Schleppegrell 2016; Rossbridge & Rushton 2015, pp. 31–56). In our experience, as students gain control over the metalanguage and have increasing confidence in seeing texts as objects of study, this stage of the cycle provides some very rich learning experiences in which teachers and students explore how texts make meaning.

Joint construction

Joint construction is a critical stage in the teaching-learning cycle, where the teacher leads the students to write a large-format text (in a topic similar but not identical to that which the students will later write independently) using the patterns and language features observed in the previous stage and in the curriculum field under focus. In preparation for joint construction, the teacher returns to building the field with the students, ensuring that they have sufficient background knowledge to contribute to the joint construction and that information gathered is organised visibly in a way that anticipates the genre to be jointly constructed. This may take the form of a brainstorming session in which students contribute their understandings (usually developed from previous research in the building the field stage), while the teacher scribes these in a way that supports the joint construction. For example, if the focus genre is a discussion (an examination of an issue with two sides), then the brainstormed notes will usually be scribed into two columns labelled 'For' and 'Against'.

Joint construction is a special kind of dialogue between teacher and students. Hunt (1994) describes joint construction as a four-phase activity in which the teacher first briefly reviews what students know about the genre, then orients the students to the writing task to be undertaken before moving into negotiating the joint text, and concluding with a reading of the complete text. Most work is done in the negotiating stage, the length of which varies according to the age and experience of the students. In upper primary and lower secondary years, texts are often too lengthy to be jointly constructed in one lesson; at times, only sections such as the opening paragraph are jointly constructed or the complete text is written over several sessions.

Joint construction is a strongly framed activity where the teacher takes a dominant role, leading by shaping the text as it unfolds (*Could we say that in fewer words?*), asking questions to solicit student responses (*What's a more technical term for that?*), making suggestions (*How about we move this sentence to here?*), recasting as necessary (*You mean …*) and reminding students of the stages, phases, and features of the deconstructed text (*What do we need in the opening stage of the text? Let's build some description into that noun group*). Rossbridge and Rushton (2015) have examined the nature of talk during joint construction and identified the following kinds of dialogic moves by teacher and students.

Teacher	Questions, paraphrases, recasts, thinks aloud (elaborating, restating), makes statements
Students	Compose content, make comments, question

Students' contributions during joint construction are usually oral, shaped by the teacher to approximate academic written-like language.

The focus for the joint construction will include choices about whole text, paragraph, or sentence structure. Although spelling and punctuation can be attended to as necessary, the emphasis is on the process of composing rather than creating a polished text. With some later editing, the text may be used for further modelling and deconstruction activities, but the jointly constructed text may also be used as a support to students writing independently in the next stage of the teaching-learning cycle. Teachers often provide further support to students in the joint construction stage by supporting small groups of students with similar needs to write together (**differentiated writing**), and by encouraging students to write together (**collaborative writing**).

Importantly, the distinction between the modelling or deconstruction stage of the teaching-learning cycle and the joint construction stage should be acknowledged. While we have stressed the place of the modelled text and the recurrent patterns of language choices identified in this stage of the cycle, joint construction—because of its emphasis on students' contribution to content—can also be an opportunity to guide students in constructing creative versions of the text under focus (see MacNaught, Maton, Martin, & Matruglio 2013).

Think about it

Is there anything that surprises you about joint construction? Does it resonate with your experiences of learning to write? What do you think are the benefits of this approach? What are some of the challenges? What demands does it make on the teacher?

Independent construction

In the *independent construction* stage students independently write a text on a different topic related to the field. This may require further research (independently or in small groups) or students may use an aspect of the topic that has been collaboratively researched. It will also involve drafting, editing, and publishing. A key scaffolding strategy for this stage of the curriculum cycle is the provision of explicit criteria to guide the students' work. Such criteria may be jointly constructed, but the important thing is that the criteria reflect the shared language and understandings about the genre and topic that the class has been working on. The criteria provide a useful tool for students to reflect upon their own work as they complete it. Teachers usually provide explicit feedback to students on their preparation, their drafts and final text in writing conversations with individuals and small groups of students as needs arise.

Of course, not every writing task will require this extended treatment. Students should have opportunities to write regularly in situations that foster creativity, pleasure, and fluency. However, short answer tests or 'quick writes' cannot provide the same learning opportunities as more extended writing tasks in which students must marshal their thoughts, consolidate understandings, fill in gaps in knowledge, and logically organise their thinking through processes of researching, drafting, editing, and polishing.

differentiated writing: here the teacher works with a small group of students with similar needs on a specific aspect of writing.

collaborative writing: students work together to construct a text, to provide feedback to each other such as they respond to the meanings of the text, or to edit according to the language focus of the task.

Think about it

What writing tasks have you witnessed or participated in? Were they 'one-shot' tasks? Were they longer term? Have you experienced the teaching-learning cycle (or part of it) in action? What are the advantages of it as a framework for teaching writing? What benefits are there for teachers? What benefits are there for students?

It is also important to note that independent control of a genre does not often happen in the course of just one teaching-learning cycle such as we have described here; much depends on the age of the learner, the level of English proficiency, and the degree of complexity in the genre or topic. A kindergarten class, for example, might complete the cycle with a collaboratively constructed text that then becomes the basis for further modelled reading and deconstruction activities. Nevertheless, throughout the cycle, emphasis is on supporting students while they are acquiring new knowledge and language skills, with a view to gradually handing over so that they can accomplish literacy tasks independently. While a single curriculum cycle might not include an independent construction stage, we would certainly be aiming to do so, if not in the next iteration of the cycle for that particular genre, then at a future time. With its basic principles of guided, dialogic interaction and shared understandings, the teaching-learning cycle offers a flexible framework for curriculum planning and assessment suitable for use in all learning settings, with different age groups and curriculum topics and with written, spoken, and multimodal texts. It makes considerable use of teachers' repertoires of scaffolding strategies and of their knowledge about language and the curriculum area. The designed-in scaffolding skills required include the selection of texts; identifying students' needs; designing, adapting, selecting, and sequencing activities; use of resources such as display boards, interactive whiteboards, and colour-coded cards; and different ways of grouping students.

Teachers' knowledge about language is called upon during designed-in and contingent scaffolding. The former includes recognising the language demands of each curriculum topic; assessing the suitability of texts for different tasks; designing assessment rubrics; and having a deep understanding of the genre and the patterns of meanings through which it achieves its purpose. All of this enables the teacher to maximise the opportunities for dialogic talk offered during the many contingent scaffolding opportunities that arise throughout the cycle and as students participate in a range of tasks that vary from teacher-led to collaborative small-group work.

Have a go!

Read the following description of an activity and match the activity with the teaching-learning cycle stage/s. You might like to add to this list of activities as you work through the book and have further experiences in classrooms. Note that while some activities might be used in more than one stage, it is important to be clear about why we select particular activities and how they fit with our instructional goals.

Activity	Stages of the teaching-learning cycle
Students work in pairs to edit each others' stories	Building knowledge of the field
Students reassemble a jumbled information report (one cut up into strips)	
Teacher and students write the orientation for a recount of a school excursion together	
Class goes for an excursion to a local wildlife park	Supported reading
Students use a proforma with guiding questions (*What does it look like? Where does it live?* etc.) to research Australian animals	
Students complete a cloze activity in which they have to add connectives (e.g. *First, In addition, Furthermore*) to an exposition	Modelling/deconstruction
Students sort bundles of information into paragraphs	
Teacher labels stages of a procedure with the students	
Students identify processes in a recipe	Joint construction
Students label a diagram of a kangaroo using factual noun groups e.g. *pointed ears* and *sharp claws*	
Students write their own texts recounting a class visit to the art gallery	
Students view a video about the human digestive system, while taking notes on a research proforma	Independent construction

THE TEACHING-LEARNING CYCLE IN A YEAR 4 CLASSROOM

The teaching-learning cycle was originally designed to be worked through over a period of time (a series of lessons or a unit of work) so that the students have opportunity for a sustained engagement with the field and with the genre under focus. However, some topics and texts can be addressed in a shorter period and adapted to fit into single literacy lessons or sessions. We conclude this chapter with an example of the teaching-learning cycle in action over two literacy sessions (approximately 90 minutes each) in a Year 4 classroom in an inner-city school. Most of the students in the class speak a language other than English at home and have been learning English for four years or less. Their teacher, Bianca, works closely with the specialist English language teacher, Catherine. During the reading lesson, Bianca and Catherine were joined by a student-teacher, Andy. At the time, the class was working on a Science and Technology unit on magnetism.

Procedures are the relevant genre in this instructional sequence. The focus for reading was a **procedural recount** (see Chapter 5) and the focus for writing was a simple procedure. Procedures include simple instructions that are often found in early reading classrooms because their structures and language patterns are highly predictable and lend themselves to concrete, physical tasks ('reading to do'). They are often also found in middle to upper primary Science classrooms as procedural recounts comprise instructions and a recount of the experiment or activity. The focus text for the lesson was an example of a procedural recount outlining the steps for making and testing a magnetic vehicle. It is reproduced in Table 3.2. The stages and phases of the genre and key language features are labelled.

Table 3.2   Focus text: A procedural recount (genre and language annotations added)

Stages and *phases*		Language features
Goal or title	Making a magnetic vehicle	
Materials	• two bar magnets • two matchsticks • one icy pole stick • 2 straws • 1 strip of Blu-Tack • 4 wheels	Noun groups are precise, containing adjectives of number and size (*2 small* pieces)
Method *Making the model*	1. Insert the two matchsticks through the straws. 2. Attach the 4 wheels to the end of each side of the matchstick (you may have to shave the end of the matchsticks to fit it on). 3. Join the wheels to the icy pole stick with two small pieces of Blu-Tack. 4. Attach a bar magnet to the top of the vehicle using Blu-Tack. 5. Test your vehicle. Does it run freely?	Commands Action verbs (*insert, attach, use, test*) Direct address to reader Low modality for suggestion (*You may have to* …) Adverbials of place (*through the straws, to the icy pole stick*) help make instructions explicit
Using the model in the test	**Use the other bar magnet to move your vehicle either by REPULSION or by ATTRACTION.**	
Results and discussion	What worked better, attraction or repulsion? Why? _____ _____ _____ _____	

Have a go!

Spend an hour or so collecting instructional texts from around your home, the community (including the workplace), and the university. Make a note of where you found each text. Try to sort them into different types (e.g. simple procedures, procedural recounts, directions, rules, and more complex flowcharts). Label them according to social purpose (enabling us to get around, to do something, to record the results of an activity, to encourage particular behaviours). Is there a link between the kind of instructional text and the place from where it was collected?

Which ones are suitable for using as models with school students? Remember that for modelling and deconstructing the genre, the students do not necessarily have to read every word. For many activities, examining the stages and elements (image, diagrams, subheading, fonts, hyperlinks, etc.) and just a few language features will suffice.

Building the field

To begin, Bianca led a brainstorming session focused on what the children already knew about magnets. The students contributed ideas such as *north-seeking pole, repel, attract, electromagnet, U-shaped magnet, south-seeking pole, horseshoe magnet*, etc. Many of the ideas had been developed during recent simple experiments with magnets so this stage was quite brief.

Supported reading

In the supported reading stage, Andy and Bianca read a PowerPoint text displayed on the whiteboard about the very fast, driverless maglev (electromagnetic levitation) trains. The presentation comprised texts and image organised around such questions as 'What is a maglev train?', 'Where are they found?', 'How do they work?', 'Are they environmentally friendly?'. The teachers led the students through the text, stopping at each slide to discuss diagrams, and to read and unpack abstract terms. Several of the students were familiar with such trains in overseas countries and were able to contribute information to the reading. Through these activities, the teachers were able to find out about and extend students' existing knowledge of the field to build a shared knowledge base, to stimulate interest in the topic and to highlight some of the key words that will be encountered during the reading. Such activities are designed to support students into successfully reading the text. The lesson provided many examples of designed-in and interactional scaffolding.

Have a go!

Identify the interactional scaffolding provided by Bianca as she read the PowerPoint text with the students during the supported reading stage. (… indicates a pause)

Teacher:	(reading) *TRAFFIC IS CONGESTED. What do you think congested could mean? Who knows? … when you have a bad cold … you are congested … because?*
Student:	*You're blocked up*
Teacher:	*Yes, so what about traffic?*
Student:	*It gets blocked up.*
Teacher:	*Let's go back and read that sentence together* (Teacher and students reread TRAFFIC and CONGESTED, with teacher stressing the pronunciation of the word 'congested')

Modelling or deconstruction

In the modelling or deconstruction stage of the teaching-learning cycle, Andy distributed copies of the worksheet (as per Table 3.2 without genre and language annotations) to each of the students, who read it silently for a few minutes. Because the students had encountered procedural texts previously, the teachers were confident that the children would be able to recognise the staging of the text and enough of the vocabulary to be able to complete this task.

Supported reading and deconstruction together

Next, Bianca led the students in a reading activity, here combining the supported reading and deconstruction stages of the teaching-learning cycle. The activity is similar to the detailed reading associated with scaffolding approaches to reading instruction (see Rose 2010) in which the teacher leads the students in a closely supported reading of a section of text. Here, Bianca focused on the materials and method stages of the text, drawing students' attention to these stages as well as to key grammatical features (e.g. the use of commands). As the students read the text, Andy acted out the commands. As a result of such support, the students were able to read the focus text confidently. Table 3.3 provides an extract of the talk during the activity; note the contingent or interactional scaffolding that Bianca provides and how these moves support her lesson goals.

The class worked through the remaining steps of the method stage in a similar way, Bianca supporting the students by telling them where to look in the clause, working between general cues (*Where? What?*), grammatical terms (*Underline the noun group. The first word is our action verb*), and sometimes the prompts and functional terms (*Is there any extra information? That's our Circumstance*). She also unpacked potentially challenging vocabulary such as *attach*, *shave*, *test*, and *freely*. Being able to see each step in detail as Andy (Mr Thomson) acted it out with slowed down and somewhat exaggerated gestures further assisted the students. In this way, students are learning grammar in a meaningful context. They understand the social purpose of the genre and the contribution that the grammar makes to the successful achievement of that purpose. They are also accumulating an explicit, coherent knowledge about language that will serve them in other curriculum contexts.

Table 3.3   Explicit talk about genre and grammar

Extract from classroom talk		Commentary
Bianca:	*Make sure you know what we need. We need …?*	Bianca reviews what children know about the genre so that they can predict how the stages will unfold and their contents. Note use of cued elicitation to scaffold students' responses (e.g. *We need …?, And then comes …?*).
Students:	*The materials.* [some students circle this]	
Bianca:	[holds up text and points to a relevant section] *And then comes …? What do we have to do? … the …?*	
Students:	*The method.*	
Bianca:	*The first step is the beginning of how to make the wheels. And it's a command because it is telling the reader what to do. Draw a circle around the whole command. We need two matchsticks and the straws. We'll read it together so that Mr Thomson can follow our instructions. The first word is our action verb, telling us what it is we have to do: 'insert', which means to put something into. Underline that word.*	Bianca explicitly labels the speech function and its purpose. Students circle the command. Bianca uses the grammatical label (*an action verb*), and its position in the clause. Bianca explains the meaning of *insert*.

Extract from classroom talk		Commentary
	[students underline *insert*]	Students physically locate the word.
Bianca:	*Now the text tells us what we have to insert—the two matchsticks. Underline that noun group: the two matchsticks.*	Bianca gives the Participant form (*that noun group*).
	[students underline *the two matchsticks*]	Students physically locate the group.
Bianca:	*Now, is there any extra information?*	Bianca uses probe for Circumstance (*is there any extra information?*).
Students:	*Through the straws.*	Students identify Circumstance.
Bianca:	*That's right, through the straws—that's our Circumstance: the extra bit of information that tells us what?*	Bianca confirms, using the function label (*Circumstance*) and links it with its probe (*the extra bit of information*).
Students:	*Where.*	Students identify the type of Circumstance.
Bianca:	*Terrific, underline that circumstance. Now let's read the whole command for Mr Thomson.*	Bianca confirms using a function label. Teacher and students read the command together.

Supported reading

In a move designed to support students to read collaboratively and to foster student–student dialogue, Bianca then returned to the supported reading stage of the teaching-learning cycle and asked the students to use the text to work in pairs to construct their vehicles. An extract of the dialogue from this activity was presented in Chapter 1.

This was an opportunity for students to see the social purpose of procedural texts in use, that is, they were reading for a purpose. They were also required to revisit the worksheet several times during the activity as they checked steps and clarified finer details of the task.

The testing of the vehicles proved particularly interesting for the students as they discovered some minor construction faults. Each pair of students then joined with another pair and took their vehicles to different places in the room where the teachers had marked tracks with chalk. This variation on the **think-pair-share** strategy is designed to foster student talk immediately. Students work initially in pairs on a task, then join with another pair to form a small group for a further stage of the task. In this lesson, the new larger group of students undertook the experiment; that is, they had to measure distance covered by the vehicle in 5 seconds and the speed of the vehicle over 1 metre.

This part of the lesson led to a good deal of lively discussion about how to improve performance of the vehicles. One group, with the assistance of the ESL teacher, used a wooden ruler as a guide rail, similar to one they had seen on the initial PowerPoint presentation. The experiments were recorded on the worksheet and discussed by the whole class at the end of the lesson.

think-pair-share: a strategy designed to foster student talk. Students are given a short period of time to marshal their thoughts individually before working with another on a task, then the results are shared with a larger group. **Pair-share** is a variation in which students work in pairs initially to talk through a problem before sharing with a larger group.

Joint construction

In this stage, in preparation for writing together, the children played a teacher-made 'Go Fish' game using magnets attached to wooden rods and focused on the vocabulary associated with the field of magnetism. The goal was to match terminology such as *attract* and *repel* with definitions and collect as many pairs as possible. This provided a shared experience from which to jointly construct the instructions for playing the game (an approximation is provided in Figure 3.4). The resultant text enabled Bianca to remind students of the stages of a procedure (the Goal or Title, Materials, and Steps for the game) as well as some of the salient language features (use of commands, precise noun groups, action verbs at the beginning of the steps, extra information such as circumstances for explicitness).

Independent construction

In this stage of the teaching-learning cycle, the children designed and made their own fishing games using magnets as preparation for writing individual instructions. After they had written their instructions, they swapped them so that other students could 'test' the accuracy and explicitness of these texts.

Figure 3.5 provides an overview of the activities described in Bianca's class according to the stages of the teaching-learning cycle. It summarises the shift from teacher dependence towards student independence evident in the classroom. It also highlights the range of different activities and participation structures that are possible throughout the cycle, providing opportunities for students to see, hear, and use language associated with the topic as well as the metalanguage.

Figure 3.4   Jointly constructed instructions for playing 'Go Fish'

How to Play 'Magneto Go Fish!'

You need:
1 magnetic rod for each player
one pond
fish

Play:
1. Decide who goes first.
2. The first player catches one fish, turns it over and reads the information on the back.
3. She has another go and if the second card matches the first, she keeps it and has one more go. If it does not match, she puts the fish back.
4. Player 2 has a turn.
5. Play continues like this until all the fish are gone.
6. The person with most pairs is declared the winner.

Figure 3.5   The teaching-learning cycle in Bianca's classroom

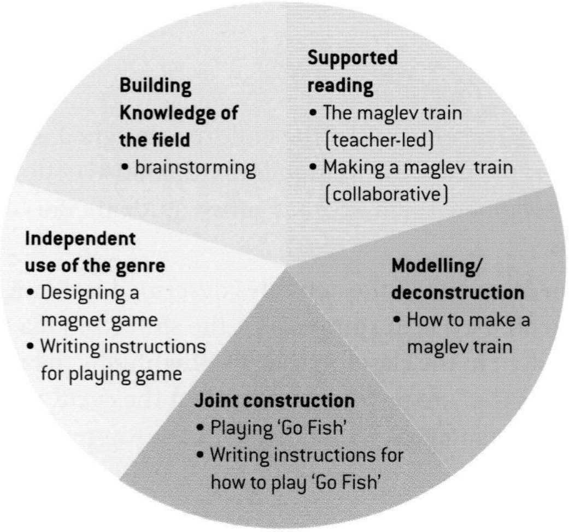

Building Knowledge of the field
• brainstorming

Supported reading
• The maglev train (teacher-led)
• Making a maglev train (collaborative)

Modelling/ deconstruction
• How to make a maglev train

Joint construction
• Playing 'Go Fish'
• Writing instructions for how to play 'Go Fish'

Independent use of the genre
• Designing a magnet game
• Writing instructions for playing game

Have a go!

How confident are you to try lessons such as this? What skills and knowledge are needed?

Revisit one of your instructional texts and select a short passage such as that described above in the supportive reading stage of Bianca's practice. Locate one command and identify the Process, Participant, and Circumstance/s (if any). Write three or four key questions that you would use to draw students' attention to these features. Remember to mention the position, the meaning cue, the example, and a functional and/or grammatical label.

CHAPTER SUMMARY

We have introduced a version of the teaching-learning cycle that we will elaborate in the remaining chapters of the book. While the model is fairly straightforward here, it is evident that teaching is not a simple activity. In order to design effective literacy pedagogy, teachers need to know about how language works as well as what the curriculum requires of students. They also need to know how to convert this knowledge into classroom activities that support students' developing literacy repertoires. Our intent in this book is to assist you to develop your expertise to do the same.

FOR FURTHER DISCUSSION

1   Revisit the stages of the teaching-learning cycle and think about possible opportunities for assessing students' learning. How might you adapt activities for assessment purposes? What are some principles for assessment? (Hint: Consider the difference between a student learning to do an activity and being assessed on how well they can do it.)

2   Scaffolding, as we have described, is support provided to students to enable them to do something that they would not otherwise have been able to do. 'Handover' is an important associated concept that refers to points at which responsibility is passed over to students to enable them to become increasingly independent. At what points in the case study do you think handover occurs?

3   How suitable is the teaching-learning cycle for different groups of learners? How might it be adapted for use with different age groups? For different genres? For teaching mixed genres? For teaching spoken texts?

REFERENCES

Alexander, R. (2008). *Essays on Pedagogy*. London: Routledge.

Australian Curriculum, Assessment and Reporting Authority (ACARA) (2015). *The Australian Curriculum: English, version 8.1.* Sydney: ACARA.

Cochrane, I., Reece, A., Ahearn, K., & Jones, P. (2013). Grammar in the Early Years: A games-based approach. In P. Paper (ed.), (Vol. 192). Sydney: PETAA.

Gibbons, P. (2009). *English Learners, Academic Literacy and Thinking: Learning in the challenge zone.* London: Heinemann.

Hammond, J., & Gibbons, P. (2005). Putting scaffolding to work: The contribution of scaffolding in articulating ESL education. *Prospect, 20*(1), 7–30.

Hunt, I. (1994). Successful joint construction. *Primary English Notes, 96.*

Jones, P.T., & Chen, H. (2012). Teachers' knowledge about language: Issues of pedagogy and expertise. *Australian Journal of Language and Literacy, 35*(2).

Klingelhofer, R., & Schleppegrell, M. (2016). Functional grammar analysis in support of dialogic instruction with text: Scaffolding purposeful, cumulative dialogue with English learners. *Research Papers in Education, 31*(1), 70–88.

Macnaught, L., Maton, K., Martin, J. R., & Matruglio, E. (2013). Jointly constructing semantic waves: Implications for teacher training. *Linguistics in Education, 24*(1), 50–63.

Myhill, D., Jones, S., & Hopper, R. (2006). *Talking, Listening, Learning: Effective talk in the primary classroom*. Maidenhead, Berkshire: Open University Press.

Myhill, D., Jones, S., & Wilson, A. (2016). Writing conversations: Fostering metalinguistic discussion about writing. *Research Papers in Education, 31*(1), 23–44.

Painter, C. (1986). The role of interaction in learning to speak and learning to write. Paper presented at the 'Writing to Mean: Teaching Genres across the Curriculum' conference, University of Sydney.

Rose, D. (2010). *The Reading to Learn Teacher Resource Package*. Sydney: Reading to Learn.

Rose, D., & Martin, J. R. (2012). Knowledge about Language. In *Learning to Write, Reading to Learn: Genre, knowledge and pedagogy in the Sydney School* (pp. 206–64). London: Equinox.

Rossbridge, J., & Rushton, K. (2015). *Put it in Writing: Context, text and writing*. Sydney: PETAA.

Rothery, J. (1996). Making Changes: Developing an educational linguistics. In R. Hasan & G. Williams (eds), *Literacy in Society*. Essex, UK: Addison Wesley Longman.

Vygotsky, L. (1978). *Mind in Society: The development of higher psychological processes*. Cambridge, MA: Harvard University Press.

Wood, D., Bruner, J., & Ross, G. (1976). The role of tutoring in problem-solving. *Journal of Child Psychology and Psychiatry, 17*, 89–100.

WEBSITES

Teaching Learning Cycle—Ross
www.youtube.com/watch?feature=endscreen&NR=1&v=kq2tr1ELNmw

This YouTube video captures a unit of work on instructional genres in an early primary classroom. Each stage of the teaching and learning cycle is exemplified and a range of strategies is demonstrated.

Joanne Rossbridge—Jointly constructing a text in class
https://youtu.be/WByszvdMWm4

This video captures the joint construction stage of the teaching and learning cycle with Joanne and an upper primary class. As she jointly constructs an historical recount with the students, Joanne is working on concepts such as point of view and characterisation in the context of the History curriculum.

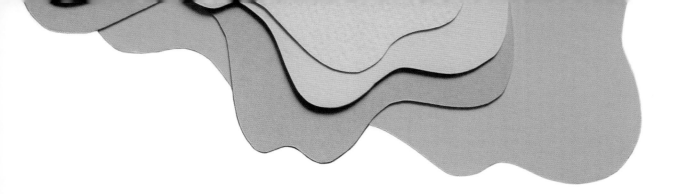

PART

LEARNING ABOUT LANGUAGE

LANGUAGE FOR APPRECIATING AND CREATING STORY WORLDS

This chapter introduces one of the major functions of language: to represent our experience of the world—in this case through stories.

Learning objectives

In this chapter you will:

- learn about the major genres for storytelling
- identify how they are structured to achieve their purposes
- observe how students learn to read and write stories across the years of schooling
- become familiar with the major language resources for creating story worlds
- explore curriculum contexts for appreciating and composing stories
- discover some useful classroom strategies for teaching the language of stories.

Key terms and concepts

narrative genre (Orientation, Complication, Resolution)

Processes (expressed through such resources as action, sensing, saying, and relating verbs)

Participants (expressed through such resources as noun groups)

Circumstances (expressed through such resources as adverbials)

Ideational function

Interpersonal function

Textual function

clause

past simple tense

verb group

embedded clause

INTRODUCTION

Novels such as Markus Zusak's *The Book Thief* (2005), which is narrated by Death, inspire readers to share what they have enjoyed about the story, such as the following comments from the Goodreads website:

> Occasionally, you will read a novel that offers you new ideas about what a novel can actually do, how point of view and voice can be used differently but powerfully, and how characters can be developed to such an extent that they seem more human than those we come into contact with each day. This seems to be the case with *The Book Thief*. If you love to read and if you love to care about the characters you read about and if you love to eat words like they're ice cream and if you love to have your heart broken and mended on the same page, this book is for you.

What is it about good stories that makes them so engaging and thought-provoking? Here are just a few of the many reasons:

- They enable us to experience worlds different from our own by inviting us to imagine other possibilities and perspectives.
- They introduce us to people and places that we might never come across in our own world.
- They provoke us to reflect on issues and situations that arise in our lives and to sort through moral dilemmas about human nature.

And stories do this by creating entertaining scenarios that engross us with their suspense, making us want to read on.

Think about it

How many stories have you immersed yourself in over the past few weeks? How many of these were movies or television stories? How many were in print form? How was the experience of the multimodal stories different from the print stories? How many children's or adolescents' stories have you read recently? How would you select a story to share with learners in your class? What criteria would you use in choosing a story for more intensive study?

Stories have always been highly valued in the curriculum, stimulating learners' reading enjoyment and extending their composing abilities. In this chapter we will explore a variety of stories for ages ranging from the early years through to adolescence. There are many different story genres, but here we will focus on one particular type—narrative.

Narrative stories are classified in a number of different ways. Here, we will characterise them in the first instance in terms of their social purpose: to provide entertainment by introducing a problem that needs to be resolved. In the process of entertaining, they might pass on cultural traditions and values or they might provide insights into the human condition or they might simply captivate, comfort, distract, or amuse. The social purpose helps us to predict the way in which the story will unfold, passing through a number of stages and phases in achieving its goal of entertaining.

Beyond their basic social purpose, we can categorise narratives in terms of their field, tenor, and mode. The field might be reflected in the subject matter of the story: adventure, horror, romance, and so on. The tenor relates to the audience to whom the story is directed (such as adolescents, reluctant readers, or boys), the relationship between the author and the reader (e.g. parent and child, teacher and students), and between the characters in the story. And the mode refers to the particular medium employed or form that the story takes: oral, animated, illustrated, and the like.

Table 4.1 Categorising narratives by field, tenor, and mode

Genre: narrative Social purpose: to entertain (determines overall structure)		
Field (subject matter)	Tenor (audience)	Mode (form and medium)
<ul><li>traditional or contemporary</li><li>classic or popular culture</li><li>fiction, factual, faction</li><li>detective</li><li>adventure</li><li>science fiction</li><li>horror</li><li>romance</li><li>quest</li><li>soap opera</li><li>fairy tale</li><li>espionage</li><li>thriller</li><li>western</li><li>fantasy</li></ul>	<ul><li>children</li><li>juniors</li><li>adolescents</li><li>girls or boys</li><li>adults</li><li>unknown audience</li><li>peers</li><li>parents</li><li>reluctant readers</li><li>readers of sophisticated literature</li></ul>	<ul><li>print (book, magazine, lift-the-flap books)</li><li>oral (scripted, improvised, read aloud)</li><li>visual: still and moving (comics, manga, picturebooks, feature films, short films, animation)</li><li>digital (interactive storybooks, e-books, e-zines, immersive environments, hyperfiction)</li><li>forms typically taken by stories: novel, graphic novel, novella, short story, chapter book, narrative poem</li></ul>

When considering the field, we might also include texts from diverse cultural perspectives, written either in the native language or English (e.g. Indigenous Australian ancestral stories or Dreaming stories, contemporary Indigenous literature, literature of the Asia–Pacific region, British literature, US literature, Australian literature). It is important not to impose assumptions and values from our own culture on stories from other cultures that have their own way of seeing the world: different ties to the land, different histories and traditions, different concepts of time, different kinship values, different ways of organising society, and different views on the nature and purpose of stories.

Have a go!

Identify a variety of narratives that you are familiar with and try to characterise them in terms of their field, tenor, and mode. Consider, for example, a multimodal picturebook (mode) for young children (tenor) about a naughty rabbit (field). Try to describe as many different combinations of field, tenor, and mode as you can.

While we will be focusing on the language features of narratives, remember that this is only one aspect of a good literature program. The focus on language should not be at the expense of students' enjoyment of literature. Here we are providing students (and yourself) with tools for exploring how narratives work, with a metalanguage for discussing the language features of literary texts, and with resources for appreciating the choices made by authors and for creating students' own stories.

HOW NARRATIVES UNFOLD

Most narratives begin by introducing the characters and providing some context to orient the reader, such as the setting in time and place. The key characteristic of a narrative is that it involves a complication that needs to be resolved. It is the complication that creates suspense and entices the reader to read on.

Not all narratives follow the pattern we are suggesting of Orientation, Complication, and Resolution. Literary texts like to play around with patterns. You might, for example, have a story that begins with a Complication, such as the one below. Or it might start with the Resolution and work backwards. Or there might be multiple Complications and pseudo-Resolutions. There might also be other stages that are optional, such as the moral stage of a fable or the coda, which makes a comment.

There are many different types of stories. Not all of them involve a Complication. We usually reserve the term 'narrative' for those stories that have a strong Complication stage. Many short stories, for example, often don't follow the pattern of narratives. Some are written as a slice of life—a brief vignette that illustrates a moral issue with a quick brush stroke. (Such a story is often referred to as an 'exemplum'.) Some might simply present a multilayered scenario for the reader to make of it what they will. Or it might be an amusing anecdote or a literary recount. Some picturebooks have a cumulative, repetitive structure, without a problem to be solved. In order to decide what type of story we're dealing with, we need to identify the stages it goes through.

Remember that the stages of a genre are not straitjackets to be taught as formulae, but are tools to help us reflect on how texts are structured in ways that achieve their purposes.

NARRATIVES FOR YOUNG CHILDREN

These days young children have access to narratives in a multitude of media and formats: picturebooks, lift-the-flap books, videos, computer games, animations, and interactive stories on DVDs. Here, we will look at a picturebook, *Wombat Stew*, an Australian classic written by Marcia Vaughan and illustrated by Pamela Lofts.

Have a go!

Why not read out aloud the 'Emu' excerpt from the story in Table 4.2 to practise your storytelling skills? Think about:

- When would you pause for effect?
- How would you raise and lower your voice, using effective intonation?
- Are there points where you might use louder and softer volume?
- How would you say the dialogue in ways that capture the mood, the situation, and the personality of the character?
- Where might you inject some emotional tone?
- When might you change the pace?
- How might you involve students in the reading? (repeating the refrain, asking questions, getting them to predict, drawing their attention to the pictures).

Wombat Stew

Here we will summarise the story, but we encourage you to find a copy of the book from your library or bookstore.

The story starts almost immediately with a Complication: a dingo catches a wombat beside a billabong and decides to make a pot of tasty wombat stew. How will the wombat's dilemma be resolved?

Before he pops the wombat into the boiling water, there are a number of Events, with other animals coming by and offering suggestions of ingredients to make it a particularly 'crunchy, munchy, gooey, chewy, brewy, hot and spicy' stew. Although not directly stated, it is implied that their suggestions are in fact a plot to save Wombat.

Platypus scoops up 'big blops of billabong mud' to make the stew gooey.

Emu contributes some of her finest feathers to make it chewy.

Old Bluetongue the Lizard snaps up a hundred flies to make it crunchy.

To make the stew munchy, Echidna digs up all sorts of slugs and bugs and creepy crawlies.

And Koala adds gumnuts to make it spicy.

Just as the dingo is about to add the wombat to the stew, the other animals insist that he tastes the brew beforehand. He takes a slurp of the stew and grasps his throat, howling that he has been poisoned. As Dingo flees into the bush, Wombat does a jig of jubilation.

The following excerpt from *Wombat Stew* gives a sense of the careful language choices made by the author.

Table 4.2 *Wombat Stew* (excerpt)

Phases	Wombat Stew
Introduction of character Interaction	Waltzing out from the shade of the ironbarks came Emu. She arched her graceful neck over the brew. 'Oh ho, Dingo,' she fluttered. 'What have we here?' 'Gooey, chewy wombat stew,' boasted Dingo. 'If only it were a bit more chewy,' she sighed. 'But don't worry. A few feathers will set it right.' 'Feathers?' Dingo smiled. 'That would be chewy! Righto, in they go!'
Event	So into the gooey brew Emu dropped her finest feathers. Around and around the bubbling billy, Dingo danced and sang … 'Wombat stew, Wombat stew, Crunchy, munchy, For my lunchy, Wombat stew!'

'If only it were a bit more chewy,' she sighed. 'But don't worry. A few feathers will set it right.'

'Feathers?' Dingo smiled. 'That would be chewy! Righto, in they go!'

Waltzing out from the shade of the ironbarks came Emu. She arched her graceful neck over the brew.

'Oh ho, Dingo,' she fluttered. 'What have we here?'

'Gooey, chewy wombat stew,' boasted Dingo.

So into the gooey brew Emu dropped her finest feathers.

Think about it

What would you say is the theme (message) of the story? What do you think the Complication is in *Wombat Stew*? How was it resolved? How would you discuss the Complication and its Resolution with young children? How would you relate it to their own experience ('text to self')? What links could you make to similar stories such as 'Stone Soup' or to 'Waltzing Matilda' with the reference to Emu 'waltzing out from the shade of the ironbarks' ('text to text')? What connections could you make beyond the story to the broader world ('text to world')?

In the classroom

Wombat Stew lends itself well to Reader's Theatre, where students perform a story by reading aloud a script adapted from a written work. This provides practice in fluency, with no need for memorisation, props, or costumes.

Students can be guided to create a procedure by jointly constructing a recipe from *Wombat Stew*. The recipe can then be contrasted with the original narrative in terms of such features as the purpose and structure of the genre and the choice of language features.

The illustrations in children's picturebooks do a number of jobs. They can, for example,

- simply replicate what is in the verbal text—very useful when young children are making links between the words and the pictures to understand the meaning of the story
- extend what is in the verbal text, enhancing the meaning of the story and provoking the imagination
- contradict what is in the verbal text, setting up alternative interpretations and multilayered meanings
- make a link to the following page to help children predict what is coming
- contribute to the emotional impact of the story.

In *Wombat Stew*, the illustrations extend the verbal text by adding to the suspense—depicting the increasing concern felt by the other animals as the time comes closer to add Wombat to the stew. In contrast, Dingo is seen dancing joyously as he contemplates his 'delicious' meal. In the final scene, it is Wombat who is doing a joyous dance as he escapes his terrible fate. The animals' complicity in tricking Dingo is suggested by the sly smiles as they add their ingredient to the stew. Although not mentioned in the story, a kookaburra appears on nearly every page, playing the role of commentator—pulling disgusted faces as each ingredient is added and poking fun at Dingo.

Have a go!

Look at the pictures accompanying the story in Table 4.2. What kinds of jobs do you think they are doing? Which one/s simply provide a visual representation of what is in the text? Which one/s provide an interpretation that isn't directly stated in the text?

NARRATIVES FOR OLDER CHILDREN

Older children are, these days, blessed with an abundance of rich narratives to enjoy and stimulate their imaginations. Aside from contemporary stories, there are also narratives of enduring value that are part of their literary heritage. Here, we will look at one such story, *The Loaded Dog* by Henry Lawson, which is set in the Gold Rush era. *The Loaded Dog* tells the story of three mates mining for gold who decide to use their explosives to catch fish by blowing up the water-hole. But when the stick of dynamite has been prepared and left unattended, it is picked up by their mongrel retriever, who drags the fuse through the fire and bounds after the fleeing men, who scatter in all directions.

This is a rollicking Australian yarn, based on a true story involving Lawson's father. Here, we will provide an abridged version of the story, but it is worth reading in its full length.

Read through the story first for enjoyment (preferably out loud, enjoying the rhythms in a bushman's drawl), and then we'll discuss how it is structured to achieve its purpose of entertaining.

Table 4.3 *The Loaded Dog*

Stages and phases	The Loaded Dog
Orientation *Introduction of characters* *Setting*	Dave Regan, Jim Bently, and Andy Page were sinking a shaft at Stony Creek in search of a rich gold quartz reef, which was supposed to exist in the vicinity. There is always a rich reef supposed to exist in the vicinity; the only questions are whether it is ten feet or hundreds beneath the surface, and in which direction …
Context for complication *Problem* *Response to problem* *Event*	There was plenty of fish in the creek, fresh-water bream, cod, catfish, and tailers. The party were fond of fish, and Andy and Dave of fishing … But now it was winter, and these fish wouldn't bite … Dave got an idea. 'Why not blow the fish up in the big water-hole with a cartridge?' he said. 'I'll try it.' … Andy made a cartridge about three times the size of those they used in the rock. Jim Bently said it was big enough to blow the bottom out of the river. The inner skin was of stout calico;

(continued)

Table 4.3 *The Loaded Dog (continued)*

Stages and phases	The Loaded Dog
Event *Event*	Andy stuck the end of a six-foot piece of fuse well down in the powder and bound the mouth of the bag firmly to it with whipcord. The idea was to sink the cartridge in the water with the open end of the fuse attached to a float on the surface, ready for lighting… Then he went to the campfire to try some potatoes, which were boiling in their jackets in a billy, and to see about frying some chops for dinner…
Introduction of character Description *Anecdote*	They had a big black young retriever dog—or rather an overgrown pup, a big foolish, four-footed mate called Tommy, who was always slobbering round them and lashing their legs with his heavy tail that swung round like a stock-whip. Most of his head was usually a red, idiotic, slobbering grin of appreciation of his own silliness. He seemed to take life, the world, his two-legged mates, and his own instinct as a huge joke. He'd retrieve anything: he carted back most of the camp rubbish that Andy threw away. They had a cat that died in hot weather, and Andy threw it a good distance away in the scrub; and early one morning the dog found the cat, after it had been dead a week or so, and carried it back to camp, and laid it just inside the tent flaps, where it could best make its presence known when the mates should rise and begin to sniff suspiciously in the sickly smothering atmosphere of the summer sunrise.
Event	Andy was cook today; Dave and Jim stood with their backs to the fire, as Bushmen do in all weathers, waiting till dinner should be ready. The retriever went nosing round after something he seemed to have missed… Dave glanced over his shoulder to see how the chops were doing and bolted… Jim Bently looked behind and bolted after Dave. Andy stood stock still, staring after them.
Complication *Response to complication*	'Run, Andy! Run!' they shouted back at him. 'Run ! ! ! Look behind you, you fool!' Andy turned slowly and looked, and there, close behind him, was the retriever with the cartridge in his mouth wedged into his broadest and silliest grin. And that wasn't all. The dog had come round the fire to Andy, and the loose end of the fuse had trailed and waggled over the burning sticks into the blaze; Andy had slit and nicked the firing end of the fuse well, and now it was hissing and spitting properly. Andy's legs started with a jolt; his legs started before his brain did, and he made after Dave and Jim. And the dog followed Andy. Dave and Jim were good runners—Jim the best—for a short distance; Andy was slow and heavy, but he had the strength and the wind and could last. The dog leapt and capered round him, delighted as a dog could be to find his mates, as he thought, on for a frolic. Dave and Jim kept shouting back, 'Don't foller us! Don't foller us, you coloured fool!' but Andy kept on, no matter how they dodged.
Response to complication	They could never explain, any more than the dog, why they followed each other, but so they ran, Dave keeping in Jim's track in all its turnings, Andy after Dave, and the dog circling round Andy, the live fuse swishing in all directions and hissing and spluttering and stinking; Jim yelling to Dave not to follow him, Dave shouting to Andy to go in another direction, to 'spread', and Andy roaring at the dog to go home. Then Andy's brain began to work, stimulated by the crisis: he tried to get a running kick at the dog, but the dog dodged; he snatched up sticks and stones and threw them at the dog and ran on again.

Stages and phases	The Loaded Dog
Response to complication Reflection	The retriever saw that he'd made a mistake about Andy, and left him and bounded after Dave. Dave, who had the presence of mind to think that the fuse's time wasn't up yet, made a dive and a grab for the dog, caught him by the tail, and as he swung round snatched the cartridge out of his mouth and flung it as far as he could: the dog immediately bounded after it and retrieved it. Dave roared and cursed at the dog, who, seeing that Dave was offended, left him and went after Jim, who was well ahead. Jim swung to a sapling and went up it like a native bear; it was a young sapling, and Jim couldn't safely get more than ten or twelve feet from the ground. The dog laid the cartridge, as carefully as if it was a kitten, at the foot of the sapling, and capered and leaped and whooped joyously round under Jim. The big pup reckoned that this was part of the lark.
Event Setting Extension of complication	The dog bounded off after Dave, who was the only one in sight now ... There was a small hotel or shanty on the creek, on the main road, not far from the claim. Dave was desperate; the time flew much faster in his stimulated imagination than it did in reality, so he made for the shanty. There were several casual Bushmen on the verandah and in the bar; Dave rushed into the bar, banging the door to behind him. 'My dog!' he gasped, in reply to the astonished stare of the publican, 'the blanky retriever—he's got a live cartridge in his mouth.'
Response to complication	The retriever, finding the front door shut against him, had bounded round and in by the back way, and now stood smiling in the doorway leading from the passage, the cartridge still in his mouth and the fuse spluttering. They burst out of that bar. Tommy bounded first after one and then after another, for, being a young dog, he tried to make friends with everybody.
Setting Introducing character Description Problem Reaction to problem Introduction of characters Description	The retriever went in under the kitchen, amongst the piles, but, luckily for those inside, there was a vicious yellow mongrel cattle dog sulking and nursing his nastiness under there—a sneaking, fighting, thieving canine whom neighbours had tried for years to shoot or poison. Tommy saw his danger—he'd had experience from this dog—and started out and across the yard, still sticking to the cartridge. Halfway across the yard the yellow dog caught him and nipped him. Tommy dropped the cartridge, gave one terrified yell, and took to the bush. The yellow dog followed him to the fence and then ran back to see what he had dropped. Nearly a dozen other dogs came from round all the corners and under the buildings, spidery, thievish, cold-blooded kangaroo-dogs, mongrel sheep and cattle dogs, vicious black and yellow dogs that slip after you in the dark, nip your heels, and vanish without explaining, and yapping, yelping small fry. They kept at a respectable distance round the nasty yellow dog, for it was dangerous to go near him when he thought he had found something which might be good for a dog to eat.
Resolution	He sniffed at the cartridge twice, and was just taking a third cautious sniff when ... It was a very good blasting-powder—a new brand that Dave had recently got up from Sydney; and the cartridge had been excellently well made ...
Reflection	Bushmen say that that kitchen jumped off its piles and on again. When the smoke and dust cleared away, the remains of the nasty yellow dog were lying against the paling fence of the yard looking as if he had been kicked into a fire by a horse and afterwards rolled in the dust under a barrow, and finally thrown against the fence from a distance ...

(continued)

Table 4.3   *The Loaded Dog (continued)*

Stages and *phases*	*The Loaded Dog*
Dénouement	For half an hour or so after the explosion there were several Bushmen round behind the stable who crouched, doubled up, against the wall, or rolled gently on the dust, trying to laugh without shrieking … Dave decided to apologise later on, 'when things had settled a bit', and went back to camp. And the dog that had done it all, Tommy, the great, idiotic mongrel retriever, came slobbering round Dave and lashing his legs with his tail, and trotted home after him, smiling his broadest, longest, and reddest smile of amiability, and apparently satisfied for one afternoon with the fun he'd had. Andy chained the dog up securely, and cooked some more chops.
Coda	And most of this is why, for years afterwards, lanky, easy going Bushmen, riding lazily past Dave's camp, would cry, in a lazy drawl and with just a hint of the nasal twang: 'El-lo, Da-a-ve! How's the fishin' getting on, Da-a-ve?'

Source: Lawson 1970

Think about it

As you read the interpretation below of how the story is structured, keep referring back to the stages and phases (in italics) indicated in the left-hand column above. Do you agree with the analysis? Are there parts that you would have labelled differently? Remember that descriptions of stages and phases don't represent a recipe for writing; they simply try to capture the way in which this particular story developed to achieve its purpose.

The narrative follows the characteristic stages of:

1 Orientation

2 Complication

3 Resolution.

Within these main *stages*, you will notice that the story includes a number of minor *phases*. While the stages are common to most narratives, the phases tend to vary depending on the particular story. It is the phases that give us flexibility in developing texts.

In the Orientation, we are introduced to the three gold-miners and are given some *background context*, to let us know that they are excavating for gold in the bush country. During the Orientation stage, a narrative usually starts to develop the *context for a complication* to arise. Here, for example, we find that the miners were fond of fish. But there was a *problem* that set the stage for the later Complication: the fish wouldn't bite because it was winter. In *response* to that problem, they had the idea of using explosives to blow the fish out of the water, so Andy prepared the stick of dynamite before going back to cooking dinner—significantly, on an open fire.

In the next phase of the Orientation, we are *introduced to Tommy*, their retriever dog. We have phases where he is *described* and then an *anecdote* is told, pointing out that it is in the nature of such dogs to retrieve things—however unpleasant or dangerous. The following phase is an *event* that sets the scene for the Complication: the men were standing with their backs to the fire, not noticing that the dog had picked up the stick of dynamite and dragged the fuse through the flames. The Complication sets off a train of *responses*. As they ran to escape, Andy tried kicking the dog and threw sticks and stones; Dave made a grab for the dog's tail, snatched the cartridge from its mouth and flung it away—but the dog retrieved it, and Jim scrambled up a tree.

At this point there is a *change of setting* where the Complication continues to play out. They all end up in the nearby hotel, the dog bounding around and scattering the patrons. With another *change of setting*, the dog finds himself under the kitchen, where we are *introduced to another key character*—the vicious yellow mongrel—who creates a *problem* by nipping the retriever, who drops the cartridge *in response*. In the following *event*, the mongrel picks up the cartridge. He is surrounded by a number of other dogs, who are *introduced* and *described*. As they crowd around, we have an *event* that signals the Resolution of the Complication—the dynamite finally explodes, taking with it the mongrel that the townsfolk had been trying to get rid of for years.

You will notice that the narrative doesn't end there. There are a couple of optional stages—a Dénouement, which is the aftermath of the action, unravelling the tension and returning to normalcy, and a Coda, which makes a general comment on the story.

Usually, you can identify the phases within the stages by using common sense and developing labels that reflect the function of the stage—its role in developing the story. It's also useful to look for the Process type: *events* are usually signalled by action Processes; *descriptions* often involve relating Processes; a *reflection* phase typically involves a thinking or saying Process; a *reaction* phase will probably contain a 'feeling' Process. Table 4.4 provides a few suggestions for phase labels (adapted from Rose 2006):

Table 4.4 Phases within narratives

Phase type	Function
Setting	Locates the story in a particular physical context or time period and establishes a mood. The setting can change during the story.
Introduction of characters	Introduces main and subordinate characters at various points in the story.
Description	Where the action is slowed to describe the physical setting or characters.
Response to Complication	Events that occur in direct response to the Complication.
Event	Other events that continue the tension of the story ('and then').
Problem	Minor problems that arise along the way, usually related to the overarching Complication. These create tensions and sustain the suspense.
Solution, attempted solution	Some problems might be solved, but others might result in an attempted (or pseudo) solution, which often makes things worse.
Reaction	Characters' feelings in reaction to an event or situation ('he felt').

(continued)

Table 4.4   Phases within narratives *(continued)*

Phase type	Function
Reflection	Characters' thoughts reflecting on the situation and/or evaluating its significance ('he thought/said').
Comment	Intrusion of the narrator's comments, explanations, or summarising (for example, of a moral point).

We will return to *The Loaded Dog* later on to appreciate Lawson's use of language.

IMAGES IN NARRATIVES

We can use the categories of field, tenor, and mode to explore the illustrations in narrative genres.

Field: Characters

- Identify the main characters and minor characters in the story. Which Participants appear in the illustrations?
- Ask students to visualise a character (e.g. Tommy or the yellow dog) from a description in the text before seeing an illustration of the character. (They might even draw the character as you read the description.) See how their visualisation relates to the illustration. How

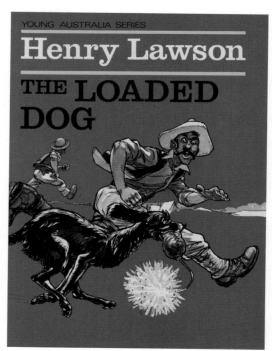

do illustrations impact on the freedom of your imagination? Or do they help create richer descriptions of the characters than you can visualise?

- Develop a character network to describe the relationships between the Participants (maybe including minor characters).
- What are the visual characteristics of each main character? e.g.:
  - How has the illustrator captured the personality/qualities of the character?
  - Is the character a human or animal (representing a human)? If animal, which animal? Why has the author/illustrator chosen that particular animal? Is it a stock character (e.g. sly fox, sensible hen) or a specific individual?
  - What is the character wearing? How does the clothing help develop the character?
- How has the illustrator made you respond to the character? (empathy? fear? admiration?)
- How realistic are the character illustrations? (photographs? detailed and lifelike? sketchy? fanciful? caricatures?) What difference does this make?
- What Processes are the characters engaged in? How does this help to develop the character and their relationships (e.g. actions, reflecting, interacting, initiating, reacting, feeling)?
- Does the portrayal of the character change throughout the story? How? Why?
- How do the illustrations relate to the description in the written text? Do they mirror the written text? Do they add more than is in the written text? Do they contradict the written text? Look at the picture without reading the text. What do you notice? Now read the words. Do you notice more things/details than you did before?

Field: Setting

- What role does the setting play in the story?
- What is the physical setting of the story as represented visually? (natural, e.g. the bush, the seaside, the desert? built, e.g. the city, a village, inside a home? real or imaginary?)
- What is the setting in time? What time of day do you think it is? What clues are given by the illustrator? Is the time of day important? Do the illustrations portray a particular historical period? How?
- Does the illustration suggest a particular social or cultural setting? How?
- What items/fixtures (e.g. furniture, implements, furnishings, toys) has the illustrator included in the setting?
- How are the characters positioned in the setting? Are they interacting with items in the setting?
- Has the illustrator included any indication of the weather? What does this add to the story?
- Does the setting change during the story? How? Why? (e.g. in *Where the Wild Things Are*, the size and colour change as the story drama develops and then become smaller and less colourful as Max returns to his mundane life.)
- Why do you think the illustrator has made these choices? What is the effect of these choices? What alternative choices could have been made? How would this affect the meaning?

Tenor: Creating relationships between image and reader

- How does the image invite you to interact by directing your gaze in a particular way (e.g. face-to-face eye contact, averted gaze, free choice of gaze)?

- How does the image construct a social distance (e.g. by using a close, mid-, or long shot)?

- How does an image in a narrative create a relationship between the characters (e.g. in books by Anthony Browne such as *Gorilla*)?

- How does the realism of the image affect the degree of interpretation involved? For example, what is the difference between a photo, a blurred image, a cartoon, a painting in terms of how much information/detail is provided and how much the viewer has to infer/imagine?

- How do the various colours create a particular mood, e.g. 'Hot' colours—excitement, happiness, anger; 'Cool' colours—harmony, peace, sadness; 'Dark colours'—mystery, gloominess, scaryness.

Mode: Composition

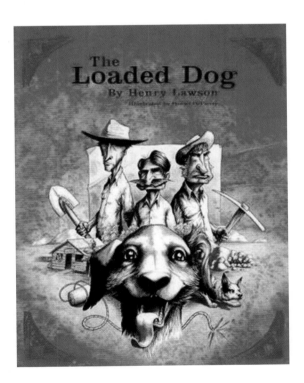

- How has the illustrator made certain features more prominent/drawn attention to a particular element of the illustration (e.g. size, colour, position)?

- What medium has been used (e.g. pencil, water colour, oils, chalk, charcoal, ink, collage, mixed media)? What effect does this have?

- Has the illustrator used any unusual layout features? What is the effect (e.g. space to create isolation, busyness to create energy, chaos)?

- What is the ratio of written text to image?
- What typography/lettering style has been used? Does this change at certain points in the story (e.g. size, colour, shape [smooth, wavy, jagged], font)? With what effect?
- When comparing two images, how could you guide your students to discuss such composition choices as:
  - Colour?
  - Medium?
  - Prominence/focus?
  - Symmetry/balance?
  - Framing?
  - Horizontal and vertical planes?
  - Contrast?
  - Movement?
  - Complexity?
  - Relationship between the elements?
  - Relative sizes?
- What is the effect of these choices?

NARRATIVES FOR YOUNG ADOLESCENTS

In Table 4.5 we have another story about a dog, this time in a more serious vein. It is written in the style of crime fiction by Michael Z. Lewin, a writer of detective novels. Try reading it aloud with the voice of the narrator of a 1950s detective movie.

Table 4.5   *The Hand That Feeds Me*

Stages and phases	*The Hand That Feeds Me*
	It was one of those sultry summer evenings, warm and humid and hardly any wind. The sun was just going down and I was grazing the alleys downtown, not doing badly. It never ceases to amaze me the quantity of food that human beings throw away. Especially in warm weather. The only real problem about getting a decent meal is the competition.
	When I saw the man poking in a barrel I said to myself, 'Here's trouble'. I was wrong. But I was right.
	The old guy was grazing too and at first he didn't notice me. But when he did, though I couldn't make out the words, he was obviously friendly. And then he threw me a piece of meat.
	It's not always smart to take meat from strange men, but this guy seemed genuine enough. I checked the meat out carefully, and then I ate it. It was good. Topped me up nicely.

Stages and *phases*	*The Hand That Feeds Me*
	I stayed with the old guy for a while, and we got along. I'd root a bit. He'd root a bit. And we'd move elsewhere.
	Then he settled down to go to sleep. He patted the sacking, inviting me to sleep too, but it was kind of early so I moved on.
	A couple of hours later it was semi-dark, like it gets in the town … I could tell immediately that something was wrong. I approached cautiously, but nothing happened. Nothing could happen. The old guy was dead.
	There was blood on his face. There was blood on his clothes. Someone had given him a terrible beating. Beatings are something I know about.
	I licked one of the wounds. The blood was dry on top, but still runny under the crust. The old guy's body was pretty warm. Whatever had happened wasn't long over.
	Nosing around, I picked up the scents of three different men. They were all fresh, hanging in the tepid air. Three men together, three against one. One old man. That could not be right.
	I set out after them.
	They had headed away from downtown. Curiously, they had stuck to the alleys, these three men, though they hadn't stopped at any of the places I would have. The places my dead acquaintance would have …
	After another block I began to find beer cans they had handled.
	At first I picked each can up, carefully, and I put it where I could find it again. But once I had one can from each of the men, I ignored the rest. I followed the trail with increasing confidence. I figured I knew where they were going.
	The long, narrow park by the river is popular on a summer's night. I could tell immediately that it was teeming with life, and not just because so many scents crossed that of the trio I was following. All you have to do is listen. A dozen human beings, not to mention the other creatures.
	But my trio made it easy again. They were down by the riverside, whooping and hollering and throwing things into the water.
	I was extremely cautious as I drew close. I wasn't quite sure what I would do. I only knew that I would do something.
	I saw them clearly enough. Young, boisterous men, rough with each other and loud. They picked up stones and swung thick sticks to hit the stones into the river. Already drunk and unsteady, most of the time they missed, but when one connected they would all make a terrible din to celebrate the crack of the stick on stone.
	Lying on the grass behind them were more cans of beer and a pile of jackets. There was also a fire. A fire! On a hot night like this.
	It wasn't until I crept near that I realised that in the fire they had been burning something belonging to the old man. The old man who gave me meat. The old man they had beaten to death.

(continued)

Table 4.5   *The Hand That Feeds Me (continued)*

Stages and phases	*The Hand That Feeds Me*
	I was sorely tempted to sink my teeth into the nearest one, maybe push him over the bank and into the water. But I was self-disciplined. A ducking was too good for these three, these murderers.
	I edged close to the fire, to the beer cans. To the jackets.
	The idea was to grab all three garments, but just as I made my move, one of the louts happened to turn around and see me in the light from the embers.
	He yelled ugly things to his friends, and they reeled back towards me. I am not a coward but they did have sticks. And I am considerably bigger than a stone.
	I grabbed the top jacket and ran for it.
	They chased for a while, but they were no match for me running full out, even lugging the flapping jacket…
	I went straight back to the body of the old man. I laid the jacket down by one of his hands and pushed a sleeve as best I could into its forceless grip. I spread the jacket out.
	I left the old man three more times. After each trip I returned with a beer can. Each can reeked of a killer. Other men might be able to track them from the smell, but each of the cans bore a murderer's finger marks.
	Then I sat and rested. I didn't know what it would look like from higher up, but from where I sat the scene looked as if the old man had grabbed the jacket of one of the men who had attacked him. Beer-drunk men. The old man had grasped and wouldn't let go. They, cowards that they were, ran off.
	Cowards that they were, if one of them was brought to justice from his jacket, he would squeal on the other two from his pack.
	I was pleased with my justice.
	I raised my eyes to the moon, and I cried for the dead man. I cried and cried until I heard living men near the alley open their doors. Until I heard them come out into the still summer night. Until I heard them make their way to the alley to see what the fuss was.
	Once I was sure they were doing that, I set off into the darkness.

Source: Lewin 1998

Have a go!

When you've read the story in Table 4.5, go back and see if you can identify the main stages of Orientation, Complication, and Resolution. Are there any other optional stages?

Now see if you can identify any phases within the stages and insert them in the left-hand column. Were the phase labels introduced earlier helpful? Did you have to make up any other labels to indicate the function of a particular phase? Share your analysis with a partner and discuss whether your analyses agree.

We will return to this narrative when we consider the language choices made by the author.

DEVELOPING CONTROL OVER NARRATIVES

Ideally, children initially learn about narrative by being immersed in stories from early childhood—read aloud by adults or older siblings who engage them with questions about the story and pictures. This kind of interaction around stories is continued into the early years of schooling, with daily shared reading sessions and opportunities to read favourite stories independently.

As students progress into upper primary and even secondary, they should still enjoy the pleasure of hearing stories being read aloud. Now, however, they should be increasingly guided towards an explicit awareness of how the story works—its structure and language features. They need support in developing an informed appreciation of the literary qualities of narrative and of the skill of the author. This is best done in the context of collaboratively participating in the reading, discussion, and composition of stories in a variety of media: multimodal, animated, digital stories, videoed dramatisations, graphic novels, as well as traditional written stories.

WHAT ARE THE MAJOR LANGUAGE RESOURCES FOR NARRATIVES?

Narratives draw on a wide range of language resources involving all three functions of language:

- representing various kinds of experience (the *Ideational* function)
- engaging the reader through, for example, the expression of emotion, the evaluation of qualities, and the judgment of human behaviour (the *Interpersonal* function)
- shaping the language into a cohesive text (the *Textual* function).

Let's look at each of these in greater detail in relation to narrative.

Expressing and elaborating ideas: Developing control of field-related meanings

Narrative texts construct events and happenings through choices from the **Ideational function** of language:

- specific human and non-human Participants (*Andy's legs* started with a jolt; *his legs* started before *his brain* did, and *he* made after *Dave* and *Jim*. And *the dog* followed *Andy*.)

See Chapters 1 and 2 to revise these functions.

Ideational function: language resources for representing our experience of the world ('What's happening?', 'Who/what's involved?', 'How? When? Where? Why?') and connecting ideas.

- a variety of Processes (see section below), for example:
  - action (He *snatched up* sticks and stones and *threw* them at the dog and *ran on* again.)
  - thinking (The big pup *reckoned* that this was part of the lark.)
  - perceiving (Tommy *saw* his danger.)
  - saying ('Run, Andy! Run!' they *shouted*.)
  - relating (It *was* a very good blasting-powder.)
- various Circumstances, for example:
  - place (Then he went *to the campfire* to try some potatoes, which were boiling *in their jackets in a billy* …)
  - purpose (… and to see about frying some chops *for dinner*.)
  - time (*Early one morning* the dog found the cat.)
  - manner (begin to sniff *suspiciously* …).

See Chapter 2 (and later in this chapter) for an introduction to Participants, Processes, and Circumstances.

Fostering interaction: Developing control of tenor-related meanings

Narratives draw on the **Interpersonal function** of language to enact relationships between characters in story worlds as well as between the reader and the author:

Interpersonal function: language resources for creating interpersonal meanings (interacting with others, expressing feelings, taking a stance, making judgments, etc.).

- enabling interaction between the characters: questions ('Why not blow the fish up in the big water-hole with a cartridge?'), statements ('I'll try it.'), commands ('Run, Andy! Run!')
- expressing attitudes
  - sharing feelings (both directly and indirectly): 'Dingo wagged his tail', 'Dingo laughed and licked his whiskers', 'with a toothy grin', 'They were fond of fish', 'trying to laugh without shrieking'
  - evaluating qualities positively or negatively: '*Gooey, brewy, yummy, chewy*, Wombat stew!', 'She arched her *graceful* neck', 'What a *good* idea', 'it was *dangerous* to go near him', 'a third *cautious* sniff'
  - judging people's (or animals-as-people's) character and behaviour positively or negatively in terms of such attributes as their capacity, their braveness, their social esteem, their morality, and so on ('that *very clever* dingo', 'this guy seemed *genuine enough*', 'Dave and Jim were *good runners*', 'I was pleased with *my justice*', 'Most of his head was usually a red, idiotic, slobbering grin of appreciation of his own *silliness*', 'Look behind you, *you fool*!', 'a *sneaking, fighting, thieving* canine', 'They, *cowards* that they were, ran off.')
- adjusting the strength and focus
  - increasing and decreasing the force ('the *best* thing for a gooey stew is mud', 'There was *plenty* of fish in the creek', 'I was *extremely* cautious', 'the cartridge had been *excellently* well made.', 'I'd root *a bit*', 'The old guy's body was *pretty* warm.')
  - focus: pinpointing ('My stew is missing *only* one thing', 'Dave was the *only* one in sight now', 'The *only real* problem about getting a decent meal is the competition.', '*Especially* in warm weather.') and blurring ('it was *kind of* early')

- engaging with other voices, possibilities, and perspectives
  - attribution ('*Bushmen say* that that kitchen jumped off its piles and on again.')
  - modality in order to create space for other possibilities ('I *should* have thought of that', 'a rich gold quartz reef, which was *supposed* to exist in the vicinity', 'He had found something which *might* be good for a dog to eat.', 'I *wasn't quite sure* what I *would* do', '*maybe* push him over the bank')
  - negatives ('*Don't* worry.', 'you *can't* make a spicy stew without gumnuts', 'You *can't* put that wombat into the stew yet.', 'Three against one. One old man. That *could not* be right.').

Tenor-related meanings will be dealt with in greater depth in Chapter 9.

Have a go!

In the narratives above, see how many more examples you can find of each of these interpersonal resources.

Discuss how they contribute to the impact and meaning of the narrative. Why, for example, is judgment of behaviour important in *The Hand That Feeds Me*?

When we explore interpersonal meanings and how the author engages with the reader, we can look at the way different points of view are created. *The Loaded Dog*, for example, is told by an omniscient third person narrator, seeing and knowing everything that happens within the world of the story. *The Hand That Feeds Me*, on the other hand, is told in the first person, from the point of view of the stray dog.

Think about it

As the reader, did the point of view in each of the narratives affect how you engaged with the story? Did you notice the different voices that the authors had adopted? How does point of view affect how the story is told? What can the first person narrator do that the third person one can't? And vice-versa?

At what point did you recognise that the narrator was a dog in *The Hand That Feeds Me*?

Creating cohesive texts: Developing control of mode-related meanings

The **Textual function** of language refers to how well the text hangs together. When we deal with narratives we need to be able to track the various participants through the text. To do this, we use a range of cohesive devices that create chains to link bits of the text together. In the excerpt following, you can see how pronouns have been used to create cohesive ties.

Textual function: language resources for shaping texts that are coherent and cohesive.

The retriever saw that *he*'d made a mistake about Andy, and left *him* and bounded after Dave. Dave, who had the presence of mind to think that the fuse's time wasn't up yet, made a dive and a grab for the dog, caught *him* by the tail, and as *he* swung round snatched the cartridge out of *his* mouth and flung *it* as far as *he* could: the dog immediately bounded after *it* and retrieved *it*. Dave roared and cursed at the dog, who, seeing that Dave was offended, left *him* and went after Jim, who was well ahead. Jim swung to a sapling and went up *it* like a native bear; *it* was a young sapling, and Jim couldn't safely get more then ten or twelve feet from the ground. The dog laid the cartridge, as carefully as if *it* was a kitten, at the food of the sapling, and capered and leaped and whooped joyously round under Jim. The big pup reckoned that *this* was part of the lark.

In the last sentence of the text above, you will notice that 'this' refers back to a whole stretch of text (extended reference).

Have a go!

See if you can track the Participants in the excerpt below, preferably using different colours for each Participant.

Underline the Participant being referred to and circle the referring word. (Note that the first reference to the narrator points outside the text.)

The old guy was grazing too and at first he didn't notice me. But when he did, though I couldn't make out the words, he was obviously friendly. And then he threw me a piece of meat.

I don't usually take meat from strange men, but this guy seemed genuine enough. I checked the meat out carefully, and then I ate it. It was good. Topped me up nicely.

I stayed with the old guy for a while, and we got along. I'd root a bit. He'd root a bit. And we'd move elsewhere.

Then he settled down to go to sleep. He patted the sacking, inviting me to sleep too, but it was kind of early so I moved on.

Refer to Chapter 2 for an introduction to cohesion.

This is a good activity to try with students—particularly with a text involving a number of Participants, human and non-human.

Another way in which we create cohesive patterns in text is to use repeated expressions (sometimes referred to as 'parallelism'). Notice the way that the author of *The Hand That Feeds Me* does this:

- I was wrong. But I was right.
- I was grazing the alleys … The old guy was grazing too.
- I approached cautiously, but nothing happened. Nothing could happen. The old guy was dead.
- There was blood on his face. There was blood on his clothes.
- They hadn't stopped at any of the places I would have. The places my dead acquaintance would have.
- … something belonging to the old man. The old man who gave me meat. The old man they had beaten to death.
- I edged close to the fire, to the beer cans. To the jackets.
- They, cowards that they were, ran off. Cowards that they were, if one of them was brought to justice from his jacket, he would squeal on the other two from his pack.
- I raised my eyes to the moon, and I cried for the dead man. I cried and cried until I heard living men near the alley open their doors. Until I heard them come out into the still summer night. Until I heard them make their way to the alley to see what the fuss was.

In *Wombat Stew*, there is also a rhythm set up by the repetition of such refrains as 'Righto, in they go!' and 'Around and around the bubbling billy, Dingo danced and sang.' and of the following ditty, tying the events together:

'Wombat stew, Wombat stew, gooey, brewy, yummy, chewy, Wombat stew!'

Alliteration also has a cohesive effect, creating a connection between words that form a 'bundle of meaning' as in *Wombat Stew*:

big blops of billabong mud

around the bubbling billy

the Lizard came sliding off his sun-soaked stone

This careful crafting of a text is characteristic of literary texts, including poetry. Apart from creating cohesive patterns, such repetition contributes to the build-up of interpersonal meanings in the text.

Mode-related meanings will also be explored in Chapter 5.

clause: in terms of its grammatical form, a clause can be described as a group of words containing a verb. In terms of its meaning, however, one way of thinking about a clause is that it represents a slice of experience involving a Process, Participant/s in that Process, and any Circumstances surrounding the Process.

Process: a doing, happening, or state.

Participants: people, animals, objects, and abstract things that participate in processes.

Circumstance: the details surrounding an activity— Where? When? How? Why?, and so on.

Think about it

In *The Hand That Feeds Me*, what is the significance of *I said to myself, 'Here's trouble'. I was wrong. But I was right.*?

How do some of the repetitions above create a bond between the dog and the old man?

FOCUS ON FIELD

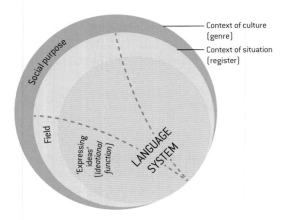

Towards the end of each chapter we will be focusing on a specific area of language. While it might be related to the particular genre being explored in the chapter, it will also relate to other genres. In this chapter our focus will be on the language choices available to build up a particular field. By the end of the book, you will have covered most of the knowledge about language outlined in the *Australian Curriculum: English*.

In looking at how ideas in a story are developed, we can investigate the language choices made by the author. As a starting point, we can look at how **clauses** work to represent a slice of experience. To do this, we can simply ask three questions:

- What's happening?
- Who or what is involved in the activity?
- What are the surrounding Circumstances: when?, where?, how?, and so on.

By answering these questions, we end up with a clause consisting of a **Process**, the **Participant/s** in the Process, and any **Circumstances** surrounding the Process.

In the classroom

A good starting point when introducing the idea of a clause is to use a well-chosen image that represents something happening. The image opposite is from a children's reader, *Coco's Puppies*. Ask the students what they can see in the image. This might elicit sentences such as:

Coco is watching her puppies.

Ethan is looking after the puppies.

The black puppy is drinking some water from the bowl.

Three puppies are playing in the basket.

Some puppies are chasing the ball.

The grandmother is smiling.

Then ask the questions above to probe further the parts of a clause:

- What's happening? 'is drinking'
- Who or what is involved? 'the black dog' and 'some water'
- When? Where? How? etc.: 'from the bowl'

As you write each clause on the board, you could use colour coding:

- green for the Processes
- red for the Participants
- blue for the Circumstances.

You might then get the students to ask each other these three questions about a range of images, gradually introducing the terms 'Process', 'Participant', and 'Circumstance'.

This is a very easy way of introducing to students the notion of a clause and what it does. The colour coding helps students to easily identify the parts of the clause and can assist with reading as they highlight the meaningful chunks.

WHAT'S HAPPENING?

Because narratives deal with human experience, they represent the full range of doings and happenings in which human beings engage: physical, mental, emotional, and saying Processes. The main Processes are summed up in Table 4.6, indicating the kinds of meanings being made and the grammatical choices that express those meanings.

Table 4.6   Process types: Relationship between meaning and form

Meaning	Form
Material Processes	action verbs
Thinking Processes	
Feeling Processes	sensing verbs
Perceiving Processes	
Verbal Processes	saying verbs
Relational Processes	relating verbs
'Existing' Processes	'existing' verbs

In the *Australian Curriculum: English*, the terms in the right-hand column of Table 4.6 are used as an attempt to capture both function and form in the one term.

Action verbs

action verb: a verb or verb group expressing a material Process of doing or happening.

Careful choice of **action verbs** helps to make a story vivid and memorable, as in these examples from the stories in this chapter.

Wombat Stew

- Platypus *came ambling* up the bank.
- Dingo *danced* and *sang*.
- Up through the red dust *popped* Echidna.
- He *dashed* away.

The Loaded Dog

- Tommy, who was always *slobbering* round them and *lashing* their legs with his heavy tail that *swung round* like a stock-whip …
- The dog *leapt* and *capered* round him.
- … and the dog *circling* round Andy, the live fuse *swishing* in all directions and *hissing* and *spluttering* and *stinking*.
- The dog *laid* the cartridge at the foot of the sapling, and *capered* and *leaped* and *whooped* joyously round.

The Hand That Feeds Me

- I *was grazing* the alleys.
- They *were whooping* and *hollering* and *throwing* things into the water.
- Each can *reeked* of a killer.

In the classroom

Focusing on the action verbs in *The Loaded Dog*, act out some of the action sequences.

This is a good activity to do with students. First, they might be guided to identify some of the vivid action verbs in a carefully selected story. Second, as the teacher reads aloud part of the story containing several of these action verbs, selected students improvise the characters, listening for the action verbs as they act out the scene.

This activity is particularly motivating when students dramatise their own stories. After they have written a first draft, the teacher might model some powerful action verbs from a similar story. These verbs can be added to a wall chart listing different types of verbs in columns. The students then revise their stories, focusing on their choice of action verbs. When they have conferenced with a peer about their action verbs, they might read aloud their story as some of their classmates act it out as above.

Sensing verbs

Stories often make reference to what the characters are thinking, feeling, or perceiving through their senses (seeing, hearing, and so on). Unlike action verbs, **sensing verbs** refer to inner processes. A rule of thumb in how to identify a sensing verb is to check whether it can potentially be followed by 'that' (he thought that …, we saw that …).

> **sensing verb:** a verb or verb group expressing an inner mental process of feeling, thinking, or perceiving.

The following are a selection of thinking verbs from our narratives. Notice how they give us insight into the characters.

Wombat Stew

- [The dingo] *decided* to make wombat stew.
- 'I *should have thought* of that!'
- 'Any bush cook *knows* you can't make a spicy stew without gumnuts.'

The Loaded Dog

- Dave, who had the presence of mind *to think* that the fuse's time wasn't up yet …
- The retriever *saw* that he'd made a mistake about Andy.
- The dog, who, *seeing* that Dave was offended, left him.
- Tommy *saw* his danger.

- The big pup *reckoned* that this was part of the lark.
- Dave *decided* to apologise later on.

  The Hand That Feeds Me
- I *couldn't make out* the words.
- I *could tell* immediately that something was wrong.
- Beatings are something I *know* about.
- I *ignored* the rest.
- I *figured* I *knew* where they were going.
- I *could tell* immediately that it was teeming with life.
- I only *knew* that I would do something.
- I *realised* that they had been burning something belonging to the old man.
- I *didn't know* what it would look like from higher up.

Notice that the meaning of verbs such as 'saw' and 'tell' above depends on the context of use. Here, they have the meaning of thinking (e.g. 'realise').

In the stories above, there are also some other sensing verbs representing feelings and perception:

- 'You *need* slugs and bugs and creepy crawlies.'
- When I *saw* the man poking in a barrel.
- At first he *didn't notice* me.
- I *saw* them clearly enough.
- I cried and cried until I *heard* living men near the alley open their doors.
- It never ceases to *amaze* me.

Think about it

Looking at the examples above, discuss the contribution to the story of opportunities for characters to engage in Processes of thinking, perceiving, expressing feelings, and evaluating provided by the sensing verbs.

Saying verbs

saying verb: a verb or verb group expressing a Process of saying (e.g. reporting or quoting).

In stories, the characters interact, typically indicated by **saying verbs**. Authors often choose a saying verb that captures the way in which the dialogue is being spoken, the personality of the speaker, or the emotions involved in the situation at the time.

Wombat Stew

- 'Blops of mud?' Dingo *laughed*.
- 'Oh ho, Dingo,' Emu *fluttered*. 'What have we here?'
- 'Gooey, chewy wombat stew,' *boasted* Dingo.

- 'If only it were a bit more chewy,' she *sighed*.
- 'Feathers?' Dingo *smiled*.
- 'Sssilly Dingo,' Lizard *hissed*.
- 'Wait a bit. Not so fast,' Echidna *bristled*,
- 'Look here,' Koala *yawned*,
- 'I'm poisoned!' he *howled*. 'You've all tricked me!'
  The Loaded Dog
- Jim Bently *said* it was big enough to blow the bottom out of the river.
- 'Run, Andy! Run!' they *shouted* back at him.
- They *could never explain* why they followed each other.
- 'My dog!' he *gasped*.
- Lanky, easy going Bushmen *would cry*: 'El-lo, Da-a-ve! How's the fishin' getting on, Da-a-ve?'

In the classroom

Although it is fine to use neutral verbs such as 'said', 'replied', and 'stated', every so often it is very effective to choose a saying verb that provides an insight into the character ('he whined') or indicates the emotion behind what is being said ('she growled').

When reading stories with students, get them to identify any unusual saying verbs and add these to a wall chart divided into different types of verbs.

Ask them to think about how the choice of saying verb can contribute to the development of the story and the characters.

Get them to say the dialogue in the manner suggested by the saying verbs. Have a go at this yourself with the bits of dialogue above from *Wombat Stew*.

As they write their own stories, get them to think about opportunities to use well-selected saying verbs, perhaps chosen from the wall chart.

Relating verbs

Relating verbs are quite different in meaning from the other types of verbs above. They don't represent any kind of activity. When we use relating verbs we create a process of relating one bit of information to another, typically using verbs of being and having. In the examples below, the thing being described is being related to its description by the verb 'was':

The old guy	was	dead.
Thing being described		Description

relating verb: a verb or verb group expressing a process of creating a relationship between two pieces of information (e.g. between a thing being described and its description).

Wombat Stew

- 'If only it *were* a bit more chewy.'
- 'Feathers. … That *would be* chewy!'

The Loaded Dog

- The party *were* fond of fish.
- It *was* big enough to blow the bottom out of the river.
- Andy *was* slow and heavy.
- It *was* a young sapling.
- Dave *was* desperate.

The Hand That Feeds Me

- I *was* wrong. But I *was* right.
- He *was* obviously friendly.
- This guy *seemed* genuine enough.
- The old guy's body *was* pretty warm.
- That *could not be* right.
- I *am* not a coward.

In the classroom

When exploring how authors build up a description of the characters or setting, get the class to identify examples of relating clauses, such as those above. Create a three-column table on the board (such as the one above) and into the columns insert the thing being described, the relating verb, and the description. (These can be colour-coded as red–green–red.)

Focus the students' attention on how well the author has exploited the description part of the clause. As they are revising their own stories, get them to conference with a peer about their use of this resource for description.

While the descriptive pattern above is the most common in narratives, there are a few other patterns created by relating verbs, such as identifying or naming something:

- 'The best thing for a gooey stew *is* mud.'

and using 'having' verbs to indicate possession:

- They *had* a big black young retriever dog.
- I am not a coward but they *did have* sticks.
- He's *got* a live cartridge in his mouth.

See Chapter 6 for more on relating verbs.

Existing verbs

Sometimes we just want to say that something exists. In this case, we generally use a 'being' verb preceded by 'there', as in the following sentences containing **existing verbs**:

Wombat Stew

- '*There are* no flies in this stew.'

The Loaded Dog

- *There was* plenty of fish in the creek.
- *There was* a small hotel or shanty on the creek.
- *There were* several casual Bushmen on the verandah.
- *There was* a vicious yellow mongrel cattle dog.

The Hand That Feeds Me

- *There was* blood on his face. *There was* blood on his clothes.
- *There was* also a fire.

existing verb: a verb or verb group expressing a process of simply existing, usually preceded by 'there' (e.g. *there is* a hole in the bucket).

Tense

In stories we generally use the **past simple tense**, as in most of the examples above. This typically consists of a single word ('Lizard *snapped* one hundred flies from the air and *flipped* them into the gooey, chewy stew.'). It is common, however, to find other tenses in stories, often consisting of more than one word, for example:

- 'I'*m brewing up* a gooey, chewy stew with that fat wombat.'
- 'I'*ve been listening* to all this advice.'
- 'You *haven't tasted* it!'
- Dave Regan, Jim Bently, and Andy Page *were sinking* a shaft.
- Andy *had slit and nicked* the firing end of the fuse well.
- In the fire they *had been burning* something belonging to the old man.
- … looking as if he *had been kicked* into a fire by a horse.

Some stories use the *historical present tense* to make the action more vivid ('He *tries to catch* him but he *escapes*.')

past simple tense: used to talk about actions and states that we see as completed in the past.

Think about it

If you are not familiar with the main tenses in English, you might want to consult a grammar reference book to find out about their uses and structure. This is not something that we would necessarily spend a lot of time on with most students, particularly with young children. But it is useful to be aware of the different shades of meaning we can achieve by employing a greater range of tenses. It is also often an issue for EALD students, particularly in the case of irregular verbs.

The verb group

These days we tend to use the term **verb group** as there is often more than one word representing what's going on:

- He *tried to make friends* with everybody.
- Dave *made a dive*.
- He *didn't notice* me.
- Nothing *could happen*.
- They are waiting till dinner *should be* ready.
- I *began to find* beer cans they had handled.
- They *picked up* stones.
- One of the louts *happened to turn around*.

    Even when there is only a single word, the term 'group' is still used.

WHO OR WHAT IS INVOLVED?

The Participants in the story

An important part of storytelling is to build up the characters and setting. This generally involves developing the Participants—human and non-human. We can find the Participants by asking the questions 'Who?' or 'What?'. The answer will not usually be a single word but a chunk of meaning.

Wombat Stew

- a very clever dingo *[ironic, of course, as he was in fact easily fooled]*
- big blops of billabong mud
- his bright blue tongue
- all sorts of creepy crawlies
- sleepy-eyed koala
- Gooey, brewy, yummy, chewy wombat stew!

The Loaded Dog

- a big black young retriever dog
- an overgrown pup
- a big foolish, four-footed mate called Tommy, who was always slobbering round them and lashing their legs with his heavy tail that swung round like a stock-whip
- his broadest and silliest grin
- the great, idiotic mongrel retriever
- his broadest, longest, and reddest smile of amiability
- a vicious yellow mongrel cattle dog sulking and nursing his nastiness
- the nasty yellow dog

- a sneaking, fighting, thieving canine whom neighbours had tried for years to shoot or poison
- spidery, thievish, cold-blooded kangaroo-dogs
- yapping, yelping small fry
- vicious black and yellow dogs that slip after you in the dark, nip your heels, and vanish without explaining.

Have a go!

Looking at the various canine Participants in *The Loaded Dog*, draw the dogs. Did the richness of the language help you to visualise the dogs?

The noun group

When we work with grammar from a functional perspective, we start first by looking at the meaning or function. Above, for example, we have started simply by asking the question 'Who?' or 'What?', and then introducing the functional term 'Participant'. At a certain point we might need to be able to recognise the grammatical choices that can be used to express the Participant. The main grammatical resource for describing the Participants is the **noun group**. At the core of the noun group is the head noun, which can be accompanied by some descriptive words coming before and after the head noun.

noun group: a word or group of words consisting of a head noun plus modifying words that can come before or after the head noun.

PARTICIPANT ('who?' or 'what?')		
the sickly smothering the astonished the	atmosphere stare doorway	of the summer sunrise of the publican leading from the passage
	head noun	
	NOUN GROUP	

Have a go!

In the examples below from *The Hand That Feeds Me*, circle the head noun of the noun group and underline any modifiers before and after the head noun.

- the quantity of food that human beings throw away
- the long, narrow park by the river

- the only real problem about getting a decent meal
- the scents of three different men
- the jacket of one of the men who had attacked him.

If we want to explore the descriptive resources offered by the noun group, we can go into further detail, again looking first at the function of each part of the noun group and then its grammatical form if necessary. We might want to ask questions such as:

- What is the thing we are talking about?
- How many (one, a dozen, many, 3000)?
- Which one/s in particular (this, that, these, those, my, our, your, his, her, their, Jim's, a, the)?
- What's it like? What qualities does it have (round, blue, big, old, sleazy)?
- What type is it (a *brick* house, a *vertebrate* animal, a *dining* chair)?

We could discuss these resources first by asking the relevant question, then by referring to their function and later, if of interest, by identifying their grammatical form:

	PARTICIPANT (taking the form of a noun group)				
	How many?	Which one/s?	What like?	What type?	What are we talking about?
	one of	those	long, sultry	summer	evenings
Function	*Quantifier*	*Pointer*	*Describer*	*Classifier*	*Thing*
Grammatical form	*number word*	*determiner*	*adjective*	*noun*	*noun*

Have a go!

In the following examples, identify the functions of each of the parts of the following noun groups, starting with the Thing (head noun) and working backwards:

- a spicy stew
- the bubbling billy
- one hundred flies
- her finest feathers
- that very clever dingo
- lots and lots of gumnuts
- munchy, crunchy wombat stew

- a vicious yellow mongrel cattle dog
- a murderer's finger marks
- the old guy's body
- these three men
- beer cans
- a dozen human beings.

As we have seen above, we can also add descriptive information *after* the head noun. The function of this part of the noun group is to qualify, so it is called a *Qualifier*.

PARTICIPANT (taking the form of a noun group)		
	TELL ME MORE	
one of those long, sultry summer	evenings	in July warm and humid that seem to go on forever
	Thing	*Qualifier*

Have a go!

In the noun groups (in italics) below, circle the head noun and underline the Qualifier.

- *Big blops of billabong mud.*
- He took a *great big slurp of stew.*
- They caught *more fish than they could eat.*
- They had *a cat that died in hot weather.*
- They were *young, boisterous men, rough with each other and loud.*
- He carted back *most of the camp rubbish that Andy threw away.*
- *The only real problem about getting a decent meal* is the competition.
- I picked up *the scents of three different men.*
- I began to find *beer cans they had handled.*
- *The long, narrow park by the river* is popular on a summer's night.
- They had been burning *something belonging to the old man. The old man who gave me meat. The old man they had beaten to death.*

- The scene looked as if the old man had grabbed *the jacket of one of the men who had attacked him.*
- There were *vicious black and yellow dogs that slip after you in the dark, nip your heels and vanish without explaining.*

embedded clause: a clause that is embedded inside a noun group (e.g. 'the old man *who gave me the meat*').

Qualifiers can take a variety of grammatical forms:

- In 'the long narrow park *by the river*' the Qualifier is a *prepositional phrase* (a phrase beginning with a preposition such as 'by', 'with', 'in', 'of', 'under')
- In 'the old man *who gave me meat*' the Qualifier is a *clause* (as it contains a verb: *gave*).

Clauses that form part of a noun group are referred to as **embedded clauses** because they are embedded inside the noun group.

Have a go!

Now go back to the noun groups in the previous Have a go! activity and see if you can decide whether the Qualifier takes the grammatical form of:

- a prepositional phrase (check to see whether it begins with a preposition)
- an embedded clause (check to see whether it contains a verb. It might also begin with words such as that, which, or who—though this isn't necessarily the case).

WHEN? WHERE? HOW? WHY?

When we tell stories, we need to provide details of the circumstances surrounding the activities such as time, place, manner, and reason. There are actually more types of Circumstances, but these are the most common ones in narratives.

Circumstances can take the grammatical form of an *adverbial*. There are various kinds of adverbials:

- prepositional phrases (a preposition + a noun group, e.g. 'on + a summer's night')
- adverbs (usually a single word, e.g. 'slowly', but can form up into a group, e.g. 'very *slowly*', 'so *slowly* that he fell asleep')
- noun groups (e.g. 'He woke up *the next morning*.'—though this is fairly rare)

When? (For how long? How often? At what point in time?)

Wombat Stew

- *One day* on the banks of a billabong a very clever dingo caught a wombat.
- *Just then* the sleepy-eyed Koala climbed down the scribbly gumtree.

The Loaded Dog

- Andy was cook *today.*
- He sniffed at the cartridge *twice.*
- Dave decided to apologise *later on.*
- *For years afterwards,* lanky, easy going Bushmen would cry: 'El-lo, Da-a-ve! How's the fishin' getting on, Da-a-ve?'

The Hand That Feeds Me

- *At first* he didn't notice me.
- I stayed with the old guy *for a while.*
- *A couple of hours later* it was semi-dark.
- *After another block* I began to find beer cans they had handled.
- The long, narrow park by the river is popular *on a summer's night.*
- Already drunk and unsteady, *most of the time* they missed.
- I left the old man *three more times. After each trip* I returned with a beer can.

Have a go!

As we have seen above, Circumstances of time can take various grammatical forms:

- adverbs or adverb groups (yesterday, soon after)
- prepositional phrases (phrases with the structure of preposition + noun group: *on* Monday, *for* ten days)
- noun groups (two days later).

From the examples of Circumstances above, can you identify these different grammatical forms?

Where?

Wombat Stew

- One day *on the banks of a billabong* a very clever dingo caught a wombat.
- Platypus came ambling *up the bank.*
- *Around the bubbling billy,* Dingo danced and sang.
- Waltzing *out from the shade of the ironbarks* came Emu.
- She arched her graceful neck *over the brew.*
- Old Blue Tongue the Lizard came sliding *off his sun-soaked stone.*
- *Up through the red dust* popped Echidna.
- Just then the sleepy-eyed Koala climbed *down the scribbly gumtree.*

- And *into the gooey, chewy, crunchy, munchy stew* Koala shook lots and lots of gumnuts.

  The Loaded Dog
- 'Run ! ! ! Look *behind you*, you fool!'
- Andy turned slowly and looked, and *there, close behind him*, was the retriever with the cartridge *in his mouth* wedged *into his broadest and silliest grin*.
- The dog had come *round the fire / to Andy*, and the loose end of the fuse had trailed and waggled *over the burning sticks / into the blaze*.
- snatched the cartridge *out of his mouth* and flung it *as far as he could*.
- The dog laid the cartridge *at the foot of the sapling*.
- There was a small hotel or shanty *on the creek, on the main road, not far from the claim*.
- There were several casual Bushmen *on the verandah* and *in the bar*; Dave rushed *into the bar*, banging the door to *behind him*.
- The retriever went in *under the kitchen, amongst the piles*.
- *Halfway across the yard* the yellow dog caught him and nipped him.
- The remains of the nasty yellow dog were lying *against the paling fence of the yard* looking as if he had been kicked *into a fire* by a horse and afterwards rolled *in the dust under a barrow*, and finally thrown *against the fence from a distance*.

  The Hand That Feeds Me
- And we'd move *elsewhere*.
- There was blood *on his face*. There was blood *on his clothes*.
- They were all fresh, hanging *in the tepid air*.
- They had headed *away / from downtown*.
- They were *down by the riverside*, whooping and hollering and throwing things *into the water*.
- I went *straight back / to the body of the old man*. I laid the jacket *down / by one of his hands* and pushed a sleeve as best I could *into its forceless grip*.
- I raised my eyes *to the moon*, and I cried for the dead man … Until I heard them come out *into the still summer night*. Until I heard them make their way *to the alley* to see what the fuss was about.

Have a go!

Focusing on the Circumstances of place in *The Loaded Dog*, draw a map and track the action during the chase scene.

Most of the Circumstances of place in *The Hand That Feeds Me* are prepositional phrases. Can you find any that aren't? What form do these take?

Think about it

We have seen previously that the grammatical form of a prepositional phrase can express the function of a Qualifier in the noun group. Here, we have seen that a prepositional phrase can also have a different function—to express a Circumstance. To tell which function it is performing, first of all ask whether it is telling you more about the Thing in a noun group (i.e. the function of Qualifier) or whether it is telling you about the Process (i.e. the function of a Circumstance). As a rule of thumb, you can tell a Circumstance if it can be moved around in the clause (whereas a Qualifier is attached to the Thing inside the noun group and cannot move):

- prepositional phrase functioning as Circumstance (telling you more about where the action was taking place—sometimes called an adverbial phrase):
  - *Around the bubbling billy,* Dingo danced and sang.
  - Dingo danced and sang *around the bubbling billy.*
- prepositional phrase functioning as Qualifier in <u>the noun group</u> (telling you more about the flies—which ones? Sometimes called an adjectival phrase.):
  - <u>The flies *around the bubbling billy*</u> were added to the stew.

Can you see why we need to work on two levels (function and grammatical form)? There is not a one-to-one relationship between function and form. A grammatical form can have many functions (as above) and a function can be expressed by different grammatical forms. From a functional perspective, it is preferable (and more engaging for the students) to focus on function or meaning and then (if relevant) to attend to how the meaning is expressed by a particular grammatical form rather than focusing on grammatical form alone.

How? (In what manner? By what means? Like what?)

Wombat Stew
- So Lizard snapped one hundred flies from the air *with his long tongue.*
- 'I'm brewing up a gooey, chewy stew *with that fat wombat,'* replied Dingo *with a toothy grin.*
- 'Blops of mud?' Dingo laughed *heartily.* 'What a good idea.'
  The Loaded Dog
- 'Why not blow the fish up in the big water-hole *with a cartridge?'*
- … lashing their legs *with his heavy tail that swung round like a stock-whip.*
- He seemed to take life, the world, his two-legged mates, and his own instinct *as a huge joke.*
- Dave and Jim stood *with their backs to the fire*
- Andy's legs started *with a jolt*
- Dave caught him *by the tail*
- The dog laid the cartridge, *as carefully as if it was a kitten,* at the foot of the sapling

- Andy chained the dog up *securely*
- Lanky, easy going Bushmen would cry, *in a lazy drawl* and *with just a hint of the nasal twang*: 'El-lo, Da-a-ve! How's the fishin' getting on, Da-a-ve?'

  The Hand That Feeds Me
- I checked the meat out *carefully*
- Topped me up *nicely*.
- I approached *cautiously*
- I followed the trail *with increasing confidence.*
- I saw them *clearly enough.*
- Other men might be able to track them *from the smell*, but each of the cans bore a murderer's finger marks.

Think about it

Circumstances of manner can have different meanings: in what manner? by what means? and like what? See if you can identify the meaning of the different Circumstances of manner above. What can you say about the grammatical forms that these Circumstances take?

Why?

Wombat Stew

- '... *for a munchy stew* you need slugs and bugs and creepy crawlies.'

  The Loaded Dog
- Dave Regan, Jim Bently, and Andy Page were sinking a shaft at Stony Creek *in search of a rich gold quartz reef*
- … to see about frying some chops *for dinner*
- 'My dog!' he gasped, *in reply to the astonished stare of the publican*
- They loved him *for his good-heartedness and his foolishness*

  The Hand That Feeds Me
- I cried *for the dead man.*
- I was pleased *with my justice.*

Have a go!

Have a look at the Circumstances above in italics. What grammatical form do they take (prepositional phrase or adverb/adverb group)?

FIELD AND NARRATIVES: STRATEGIES FOR TEACHING AND ASSESSING

- Regularly share narratives with students in a variety of media and formats. Guide them to notice how they are structured and the stages they go through.

- In raising their awareness of the language, start by asking the three questions, using an image from the story: 'What's happening?', 'Who or what is involved?', and 'What are the surrounding circumstances?' When students are comfortable with asking each other such questions, gradually introduce the terms that refer to the kinds of meanings being developed: various types of Processes, human and non-human Participants, and Circumstances that answer questions such as 'Where?', 'When?', 'How?', 'Why?'

- Innovating on a familiar text provides students with a scaffold until they feel confident to write their own stories. Choose a relatively simple (but well-written) story and ask your students in groups to write an episode of a parallel story, following the same outline as that of the original, but varying the main character, or the resolution, or some other aspect of the story (e.g. 'Parrot Pizza'— who caught the parrot? Which birds came to its rescue? What ingredients did they add to the pizza? How was the problem resolved?)

- Once the students have developed a very rough draft of their episode, model for them some of the language features of the original story that might provide inspiration for revising their draft (vivid action verbs, interesting saying verbs, the inclusion of sensing verbs, rich noun groups, and a variety of Circumstances represented by adverbials). Use some of these resources in collaboratively writing the Orientation or the Resolution. Then ask students to review and proofread their episodes, ready for collation into the final, published story.

- One Year 2 class, for example, noticed that the kookaburra in the illustrations of *Wombat Stew* played no part in the actual story, so they created a role for him, writing an episode where he featured and using images of the kookaburra and dingo from the other episodes. Notice how they used the language similar to the other episodes as a model for their choices, such as the action verb ('flapped in') and the saying verb ('cackled'):

> At that moment, Kookaburra flapped in. 'Crikey, Dingo!' he cackled. 'What are you cooking up?'
>
> 'Squishy wishy Wombat Stew!' replied Dingo.
>
> 'Stew isn't stew without worms,' laughed Kookaburra. 'Koo koo kaa kaa! Koo koo kaa kaa!'
>
> Dingo's ears pricked up. 'Now you tell me! Righto, in they go!'
>
> Kookaburra swooped down, plucked some worms from the loose soil and added them to the squishy, wishy stew.

Dingo danced and sang.

'Wombat stew, Wombat stew, Gooey, brewy, Squishy, wishy, Wombat stew!'

www.youtube.com/watch?v=QGjTrK9yvBM

- When assessing students' narratives and providing feedback, consider the quality of the Complication stage and the originality of the Resolution. How well has language been used in expressing the students' ideas and in developing the setting and characters? In carrying the action forward? In providing spaces for reflection?

CHAPTER SUMMARY

In this chapter we have looked at a variety of narratives and how they are structured to achieve their purpose of entertaining. We have seen how the language functions to build a story world, to develop a relationship with the reader and between the characters, and to create a cohesive text. In particular we have focused on how language functions to represent what is going on in the story—the Processes, the Participants in those Processes, and the Circumstances surrounding the Processes. We have considered some strategies for teaching narratives and have looked at how we can draw on our knowledge of functional grammar in modelling certain language features of narratives and supporting students' writing.

FOR FURTHER DISCUSSION

1   How are you coping with the various language features in this chapter? It's quite a bit to take in, so we would recommend that you do all the activities accompanying the chapter and keep looking at the sample texts to identify the various features mentioned. Don't try to analyse every word—just those features that we have focused on here. As with everything else that's somewhat new, it takes time and practice. We will revisit many of these features in the following chapters, but you might like to follow up the various points in greater detail by referring to a functional grammar reference book (see Further Reading at the end of the book).

2   Discuss whether a focus on meaning and function (e.g. Processes, Participants, and Circumstances) is a helpful way to introduce the grammar of the clause.

3   Do you feel that such knowledge about how language works will be useful in helping to support your students in appreciating how authors use language in creating narratives and how students themselves can focus on particular resources to improve their own writing?

REFERENCES

Lawson, H. (1970). *The Loaded Dog*. Sydney: Angus & Robertson.

Lewin, M.Z. (1998). The Hand that Feeds Me. In *Rover's Tales*. New York: St Martin's Press.

Rose, D. (2006). Reading genre: A new wave of analysis. *Linguistics and the Human Sciences, 2*(2).

Vaughan, M., & Lofts, P. (1984). *Wombat Stew*. Australia: Ashton Scholastic.

Zusak, D. (2005). *The Book Thief*. New York: Random House.

WEBSITES

Michael Z. Lewin's homepage
www.michaelzlewin.com/

Goodreads
www.goodreads.com

> Look here for reviews of thousands of stories.

BBC Teaching resources
www.teachingenglish.org.uk/britlit/hand-feeds-me

> This BBC site has some activities for teaching *The Hand That Feeds Me*, including an audio podcast of the story read by the author.

Sydney Story Factory
www.sydneystoryfactory.org.au

> 'We run free creative writing and storytelling workshops for young people aged 7 to 17, particularly those from marginalised backgrounds. Under the guidance of our expert storytelling team, young people work with volunteer tutors to write stories of all kinds, which we publish in as many ways as we can. Young people leave with the skills and confidence essential for future success.'

Units of work exploring literary texts
www.petaa.edu.au/imis_prod/w/Teaching_Resources/Literature_Singles/w/Teaching_Resources/lit_singles.aspx

> A number of units on children's literary texts developed by the Primary English Teaching Association of Australia (PETAA) for members. (See whether your educational institution is a member.)

Authors in Schools
www.petaa.edu.au/imis_prod/w/Teaching_Resources/Authors_in_Schools_Units_/w/Teaching_Resources/AIS/Copyright_Agency_Connect.aspx?hkey=657a426c-3c55-4868-bcfe-4eb06b61683e

> Units of works highlighting various Australian authors and activities dealing with such notions as plot development, characterisation, and the human spirit.

5

LANGUAGE FOR RECOUNTING WHAT HAPPENED

In this chapter we investigate the recount genres that students will encounter in their journey through school and consider some teaching implications. We look at how recount genres develop from the early years through to later secondary in a range of curriculum areas. Throughout the chapter, we will revisit some of the grammatical features introduced in Chapter 4. Towards the end of the chapter, our language focus will be the differences between spoken and written modes.

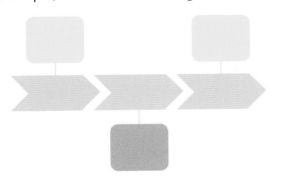

Learning objectives

In this chapter, you will:

- become familiar with the different genres used for recounting and how they are structured to achieve their purposes
- consider how students learn to read and write recount texts across the years of schooling
- identify the major language resources for recounting
- discover some useful classroom strategies for teaching the language of recounts.

Key terms and concepts

recount (personal, autobiographical, empathetic, memoir, biographical, historical, literary)

macrogenre

mode continuum

cohesion

reference (pronouns, possessives, demonstratives, comparatives)

extended reference

substitution

ellipsis

nominalisation

coordinating conjunctions

INTRODUCTION

What did you do on the weekend? What happened at the party last night? How was the skiing trip? How did you hurt your foot? We're always keen to share with others the details of what happens in our daily lives. This is usually done in oral interaction—in person, on the mobile, or using Skype—often embellished with interpersonal details relating to the emotions experienced, evaluations of what we did or saw, and judgments of people's behaviour.

When children begin school, they are usually encouraged to tell others what happened on their holidays or on an outing, often as part of morning news. At first the details pour out in a random jumble complete with irrelevant facts and comments. They make assumptions that you know what they are talking about and don't realise they have to fill in the details for those who weren't present. Over time, however, they learn to organise the events in an orderly sequence and to sort out the important elements from the not so important. This is a significant step into becoming literate—structuring a text coherently and becoming aware of the needs of the distant reader.

As the students move through school, their recounts of personal experience give way to recounts that involve more academic subject matter, generally in the written mode. They learn to explain how they managed to solve a maths problem by recounting their reasoning, or to report on what happened in a science experiment, or to represent an historical event.

Recounting, then, is an important part of our social lives—sharing experiences and creating solidarity—as well as our academic lives, where we reflect on what happened in the past in order to come to a better understanding of the present and the future.

Think about it

Have you recently recounted an event? Was it in the oral or written mode? Was it accompanied by visual images (e.g. photos, video, illustrations)? Was it in a social or academic context?

> **recount:** a text with the purpose of telling what happened.

All **recount** texts have in common the fact that they tell of a series of events in the past that are chronologically sequenced. They differ, however, in terms of their register: the subject matter (field), the intended audience (tenor), and whether they are more spoken or written (mode). Table 5.1 provides an overview of the recount genres we will be looking at in this chapter.

Table 5.1   An overview of recount genres in this chapter

Genre	Social purpose	Sample curriculum contexts
Personal recount	To give details of an incident involving personal experience	Our excursion to the zoo My holiday in Fiji
Factual recount	To report on events or incidents not experienced personally by the reporter	A class newspaper article on a recent incident The school sports carnival
Autobiographical recount	To recount episodes in someone's life as told by that person	Understanding someone's life experiences from their own perspective
Biographical recount	To recount episodes from another person's life	The life of significant individuals
Historical recounts and accounts	To record, explain, and interpret important or interesting events in a society's past	Australia's immigration history A history of games for children
Literary recount	To retell a sequence of factual or imaginary events, often with aesthetic features	Poems recounting a sequence of events Recounts of imaginary events

Think about it

Can you think of any other curriculum contexts in which recount genres might be focused on?

While both narratives and recounts relate a series of events, the difference is that narratives involve a major Complication, which creates suspense until it is resolved.

RECOUNTS OF PERSONAL EXPERIENCE

We saw in Chapter 2 that a major breakthrough in language development is when the toddler learns to go beyond using language that refers to the here and now and starts reconstructing an event from the past without the support of the immediate context. As their language continues to develop, their recounts become more elaborated. In recalling the event, they are often supported by an older conversation partner. Here, for example, 4-year-old Jodie is telling her aunt about her birthday party.

Aunt: It sounds as if you had a great birthday party yesterday. Tell me what you did.

Jodie: I liked the piñata when it fell down.

Aunt: How did the piñata fall down?

Jodie: I hit it with a stick and it fell down.

Aunt: And then what happened?

Jodie: All the sweets came out and we all grabbed them and I got the most 'cause it's my birthday and I like Minties best and …

Aunt: And then what did you do?

Jodie: I couldn't blow out the candles and my dad came over and he helped me and then he cut the cake with the knife and I gave the cake to all my friends.

Notice how Jodie's aunt is helping her to sequence the events in chronological order, prompting Jodie for relevant details and guiding her to stay on track—in the same way that teachers support young children when they are giving their morning news.

As children start to become literate, they are often asked to write recounts of holidays, excursions, school camps, the sports carnival, and the like. These are important in preparing students for the more demanding recounts that they will need to write in later years. A typical written personal recount would begin with an Orientation stage, letting the reader know something about the event: who was involved, when it took place, where they went, why they went. This is followed by the Record of Events, recounting what happened and often interspersed with comments. The recount might be rounded off with an optional Comment stage evaluating the event.

- Orientation
  - Providing background information (e.g. who? when? where? why?)
- Record of events
  - Chronological steps
- Comment
  - Evaluation of event or emotional response.

The following is a recount of Year 5's outing to the rainforest south of Sydney. Here, they are not simply telling what happened but they are also reporting on what they learnt from the excursion—an important point when so often students' recounts of excursions include details of the bus trip, lunch, and the fun bits, but very little on what they actually gained from the outing.

Table 5.2   Personal recount of excursion

Stages and phases	Our Excursion to Minnamurra Rainforest
Orientation	Yesterday all Year 5 students went on an excursion to the rainforest at Minnamurra for our project on ecosystems.
Record of events Event 1	When we arrived, we could smell the damp air and we could hear the sound of the lyrebirds.
Event 2	First we watched a video about the different plants and animals in the rainforest and how they live together. Then our guide took us into the rainforest and showed us the trees that formed the canopy. There were huge fig trees with massive buttress roots. Some were hundreds of years old and were as wide as the room of a house.
Event 3	After that we went to a spot with beautiful tree ferns that grew underneath the canopy, protected from the sun. Underneath them, we observed the smaller ferns, epiphytes, fungi, and lichen that grew on the trees and on the rainforest floor.
Event 4	We tried looking for animals but all we could see were some wombat burrows. But we heard the calls of many different birds, such as bellbirds and cockatoos.
Comment	We really enjoyed our visit to the rainforest and we learnt a lot about how an ecosystem works.

Have a go!

1   Identify parts of the recount in Table 5.2 that refer to the students' developing knowledge of the field from the excursion.

2   When we recount an experience, we use language that locates the event in a particular time and language that functions to sequence the activities.

   a   Identify language features that refer to time.

   b   Which ones locate the action in time and which ones sequence the activities?

3   Basic recounts usually use the *past simple tense* (e.g. *watched*)—most usually a single word ending in -ed that represents a completed event in the past.

   a   Identify the verbs in the text above and notice whether they are in the past simple tense.

   b   Can you notice any in the past simple tense that are irregular (i.e. that don't end in -ed)?

   c   Are there any implications for EALD students?

In the classroom

When introducing students to personal recounts, it is much easier when the class has a shared experience to refer to, such as an outing, the sports carnival, or an experiment.

Matt took his class to Canberra to see how parliament operates. Before leaving, they decided that they would write up a recount of their findings as a blog. At Parliament House, they took photos, conducted interviews with tourists, took notes during Question Time, and made videos of the surroundings.

Back at school, Matt helped them plan their recount, dividing the class into groups, each of which developed an episode of the recount by drawing on their fieldnotes, research, photos, interviews, and videos.

They assembled their episodes into a chronological sequence and uploaded them to their blog, together with the other multimodal items.

Matt projected their recount onto the interactive whiteboard and together they worked on revising it, focusing on such features as Circumstances of time and place, the choice of Process types (e.g. doing, saying, thinking, feeling, relating) and the use of rich noun groups to describe the Participants.

Because they had all participated in the trip, they had a common point of reference and were all able to contribute to the recount.

As we have seen, personal recounts are based on an event that the speaker or writer has experienced in their life. The following text is an example of a personal recount written by a soldier in the Second World War, who provides a first-hand account of his involvement in D-Day.

Table 5.3   Personal recount of wartime experience

Stages	*The Invasion of Normandy*
Orientation	The great day arrived, 6 June 1944, D-Day. I was in charge of the coal orders from Ashford and had to help with supplies for the troops who were about to invade Normandy.
Record of events	We were marched down to New Romney, and all along the route the locals were cheering and waving. It was impressive, but I somehow found it all a bit sad, as I knew it was the last thing some blokes would ever see, and that some of us would never see our loved ones again. During the night a storm had blown up as we crossed the channel, and God it was rough. Our supper had been sausages, lovely great big ones, but we were paying the price for them now—me and three others who were manning a Bren gun up on a raised platform—and as the boat wallowed, we felt every sway and dip, and was I ever sick! Once off duty I went to the toilets, and I was sitting on one toilet, and throwing up into another and sitting next to me, in the same predicament, was my mate, one Lt Hutchinson (Hutch).

Stages	*The Invasion of Normandy*
	Eventually the crossing was over, and we disembarked, cold, tired, wet, and ill but after a little while ashore we all felt a little better. We had just survived the worst storm in the English Channel in living memory.
	Next day, Major Stewart told us to get bathed in the River Don, so about 90 men stripped naked and leapt in, generally larking about, and so far enjoying the war. It was nice to get clean of the smells of the crossing.
	At this point a small punt came around the corner of the river and straight through the middle of us, with two women and a man in it.
Comment (optional)	I would imagine that it is a sight that none of them ever forgot.

Source: Richard Henry William Brew, 2 August 1915—13 August 1997

Have a go!

1 a   As with the text in Table 5.2, identify language features in Table 5.3 that refer to time.

   b   Which ones locate the action in time and which ones sequence the activities?

2   In the recount of the school excursion in Table 5.2, most of the verbs are in the past simple tense. In the recount in Table 5.3 there is a much greater variety.

   a   Identify the verb groups in Table 5.3.

   b   Which ones are in the past simple tense?

   c   Can you notice any in the past simple tense that are irregular (i.e. that don't end in -ed)?

   d   Note the more extended verb groups in the text. What could you say about the different kinds of meanings they express (e.g. *had to help*; *were about to invade*; *were cheering and waving*; *would never see*; *had survived*)?

   e   If you were teaching older students, what might you point out to them about the verb groups in the recounts they read and write?

3   In a recount of personal experience, there is usually an interpersonal tenor introduced. In the recount above, identify instances of interpersonal meaning.

   a   Which ones refer to feelings?

   b   Which ones refer to evaluating the qualities or significance of things?

   c   Are they positive or negative?

   d   Are they directly stated or implied?

   e   In which cases has the writer boosted the attitude to make it stronger?

macrogenre: a text that combines more than one elemental genre (e.g. an explanation that includes a recount).

Sometimes, recounts (such as the one above) are part of a larger text that includes various other genres such as information reports (e.g. facts about the Second World War) and arguments (e.g. moral issues surrounding war). When a text includes more than one genre it is sometimes called a **macrogenre**.

FACTUAL RECOUNTS

Factual recounts can be similar to personal recounts, except that the person recounting the incident or event was not personally involved. (See Recounts of personal experience for a typical organisation of stages.)

The following is a factual recount from the children's news website DOGO News: Fodder for young minds.

Table 5.4   Factual recount of an incident at the zoo

Stages and *phases*	*Orangutan's Hilarious Reaction to Simple Magic Trick*
Orientation *When? Where? Who? How?*	During a recent trip to the Barcelona Zoo in Spain, Dan Zaleski decided to entertain the resident orangutan with a magic trick.
Record of events	
Event 1	In the video, the orangutan is seen closely observing the Connecticut resident as he places a chestnut inside a Styrofoam cup, seals it with a lid and then shakes it vigorously.
Event 2	Zaleski then magically makes the chestnut 'disappear' by taking the cup out of the mammal's sight for a brief second and dumping its contents on the ground.
Event 3	The smart orangutan ponders over the empty cup for a brief second before rolling over the floor in laughter!
Comment	The mammal's joyous reaction to the 'magic' trick is guaranteed to put a smile on anyone's face.

Source: www.dogonews.com/2015/12/14/video-of-the-week-orangutans-hilarious-reaction-to-simple-magic-trick

Have a go!

1   We usually expect a recount to use the past simple tense. What do you notice in this recount? What is the effect of this?

2   Find the video by searching 'DOGO' and 'orangutan'.

AUTOBIOGRAPHIES

An *autobiography* relates significant events from a person's own life. Although similar to a personal recount, the writer needs to deal with longer stretches of time than when recounting a recent incident. It means sorting out the relevant details from the irrelevant and thinking about what would be of interest to the reader. And beyond simply telling what happened, there is often a broader purpose, such as providing a model for others, or justifying one's actions, or helping others to learn from the writer's mistakes.

In the following autobiography, a young refugee to Australia tells his story as part of a project to let Australians know about the immigration experience. Notice now that the stages are somewhat different from a personal recount in achieving the text's purpose. It begins by identifying the person writing the autobiography, followed by a series of episodes, which are longer periods rather than single events. Abdul has presented episodes in his life not only in writing but also in a sequence of images.

Table 5.5   Autobiography

Stages	*My Life Story*	
Identification of subject	My name is Abdul. I am 11 years old and I have two sisters. I grew up in a small village and went to school with my friends. After school I helped my mother to carry water and made food for the family. We didn't have much money but we were happy.	
Episodes	Then last year the earthquake happened. It was very frightening. It destroyed everything in my village. My parents, one sister and my grandparents died. We tried to find them for a long time but we didn't have tools to move all the stones and bricks.	

(continued)

Table 5.5　Autobiography *(continued)*

Stages	My Life Story
	We were taken to a shelter and lived there for a few weeks with the other survivors. It was very hard because it was very cold and we didn't have warm clothes or electricity.
Comment (optional)	Afterwards we went to live with our aunt in Australia. It is good in Australia but we miss our family very much.

Have a go!

When writing an autobiography, the author uses first person pronouns (I, me, my, mine, we, us, our, ours). This creates an interpersonal tone in the text. See how many first person pronouns you can find in the text in Table 5.5.

Empathetic autobiographies

Students are often asked to write autobiographies in which they need to imagine that they are a character in a novel, or a person from a different period in history, or from a different cultural or physical setting. These are sometimes called *empathetic autobiographies*. Many students find these difficult to write as they need to do quite a bit of research to familiarise themselves with the historical or cultural context in which their autobiographical subject is located. Such recounts can, however, enable the student to come to an understanding of a situation from a different point of view. The student needs to inhabit the character or subject, demonstrating an awareness of how the person would have felt and behaved. They need to project a certain voice that captures the status and life experience of the subject. Such tasks are not simply an invitation to fantasise about the life of a person from a different context but require a great deal of knowledge, interpretation, and evaluation.

Memoirs

Memoirs are a particular kind of autobiography. Rather than chronologically documenting the author's life span, memoirs selectively focus on certain periods or incidents that the author sees as memorable. The author might reflect on events from a personal perspective, bringing a distinctive interpretation to an issue. Historically, memoirs were written by people in public life such as politicians, military leaders, or business people, sometimes justifying actions taken or decisions made. These days, however, memoirs abound, from the light-hearted reminiscences of celebrities or comedians through to the profound consideration of such matters as addiction, mental illness, cult membership, genocide, sexuality, ageing, and death. Memoirs are typically published as books, but can also take the form of blogs, diaries, movies, and documentaries.

There are many memoirs of interest to students, such as *Dreams from My Father* (Barack Obama), *Running with Scissors* (Augusten Burroughs), *The Happiest Refugee* (Anh Do), *My Place* (Sally Morgan), *I Am Malala: The Girl Who Stood Up for Education and Was Shot by the Taliban* (Malala Yousafzai), *The Diary of a Young Girl* (Anne Frank), *Wild Swans* (Jung Chang), *Schindler's List* (Thomas Keneally), and *The Peasant Prince* (Li Cunxin and Anne Spudvilas). Such memoirs can intrigue and inspire students by providing insights into the human condition by people who have actually lived the experience.

Have a go!

1   Compose an autobiographical recount using a timeline as a graphic organiser to sequence the events chronologically.

2   Now take something significant you have experienced and write a memoir of a paragraph or two.

3   Discuss the different language choices made in the two texts.

In the classroom

Find a copy of the wordless picturebook *Mirror* by Jeannie Baker, which depicts a day in the life of two boys and their families—one from inner-city Sydney, Australia and the other from a small, remote village in Morocco, North Africa. Ask half the class to write an empathetic autobiography or memoir of the inner-city boy and the other to write an empathetic autobiography or memoir of the Moroccan boy. Ask them to consider similarities, differences, empathy, and point of view, and then to share the text with others.

BIOGRAPHIES

Students often engage with *biographies* of celebrities and sports people as well as of inspirational figures such as Ghandi, Martin Luther King, and Caroline Chisholm. Reading and writing biographies provides insights into why the person is regarded as having a significant place in society. Though biographies usually celebrate the lives of people who have made a contribution, they can also deal with those who are notorious for various reasons. In any case, biographies usually reflect the values of a culture as embodied in the biography: What do we revere? Who are our role models? What behaviour do we fear or condemn? Biographies also help us to appreciate the complexity of life and to understand how others have dealt with its trials and its gratifications.

INTRODUCTION TO PERSON
(e.g. name, role, era, qualities, prominence)

KEY EPISODES   CONTRIBUTIONS

SIGNIFICANCE

Biographies typically go through similar stages to autobiographies, beginning by identifying the subject followed by episodes from the person's life, often including reference to the significance of the person.

Table 5.6   Biography

Stages	Sally Morgan
Identification of person	Sally Morgan is one of Australia's best known Aboriginal artists and writers. She came from a very poor family and often went hungry. Her mother worked as a cleaner and her father was often sick. Sally didn't like school but loved English and drawing.
Episodes	Sally was born in Perth in 1951 and was the eldest of five children. As a child, Sally didn't know she was Aboriginal. She had been told by her mother that she was Indian, which made her very confused. It wasn't until she was 15 that she found out her true heritage. Her mother had had a very difficult life as both her grandmother and mother had been part of the Stolen Generations. So her mother felt that it was safer to pretend that they weren't Aboriginal. In 1983, Sally travelled to the Pilbara area of Western Australia to find out more about her family. There she discovered a large, warm family who welcomed her and gave her a sense of belonging. In 1987, she wrote a story of her family's experiences—children taken from their family, slavery, poverty, abuse, and fear because their skin was a different colour. Accompanied by her own illustrations, the book—*My Place*—became a bestseller.
Significance	Today, Sally is still writing and painting. Her stories continue to be enjoyed by children of all ages. She has received many awards, including from the Human Rights and Equal Opportunity Commission.

Biographies can take many forms using a variety of media: books, magazine articles, films and videos, family history websites, digital stories, and oral histories.

Recounts are often visually represented by a timeline or flowchart. We could show the sequence of events in Sally Morgan's life with a simple timeline diagram:

Sally Morgan: Significant events

1951	1966	1974	1983	1987	Today
Born in Perth	Discovers her Aboriginal heritage	Completes BA degree	Visits her family's homeland	Publishes *My Place*	Professor at the University of WA

Think about it

Biographical recounts usually include interpersonal elements from the Appraisal system that express attitudes. In the biography in Table 5.6, see if you can find references to Sally Morgan's life in relation to:

- feelings (Affect)
- evaluation of things and experiences (Appreciation)
- assessment of behaviour (Judgment): Is she esteemed? Special? What is valued in her achievements? Is there evidence of judging the behaviour of others?

   In each case, consider whether the appraisal is positive or negative, directly stated, or indirectly implied.

For further discussion of Appraisal, see Chapters 2 and 9.

HISTORICAL RECOUNTS

We have been looking so far at recounts that tell about individuals' and groups' experiences on a relatively small scale—from brief, recent incidents to longer life episodes. With historical recounts we are often concerned with much longer stretches of time:

- cosmological epochs (e.g. the Quark epoch)
- archaeological periods (e.g. palaeolithic, neolithic, bronze age)
- empires (e.g. the Roman empire, the British empire, the Ottoman empire)
- kingdoms and dynasties (e.g. the Tudors, the Ming dynasty)
- eras of civilisation (e.g. medieval, Renaissance, industrial)
- reigns (e.g. Edwardian, Victorian, Napoleonic)
- wars (e.g. the Opium Wars, the French Revolution).

   Many historical recounts deal with wars, as in the following recount of Operation Overlord during the Second World War.

Table 5.7   Historical recount

Operation Overlord

On 6th June 1944 (known as D-Day), in a daring operation, British, Canadian and American forces launched a massive attack by sea and air on the Normandy coast of France, which had been occupied by the German army. The coast was divided into five sections code-named Sword, Juno, Gold, Omaha, and Utah.

The landings were completed in two phases. Just after midnight, 24 000 airborne troops were parachuted behind the beaches in order to prepare the way for the seaborne forces—the largest invasion by sea in history. At 6.30 am, more than 7000 vessels landed on the Normandy coast. By the day's end, 160 000 soldiers had penetrated 6 kilometres inland, and their foothold in Normandy was secure.

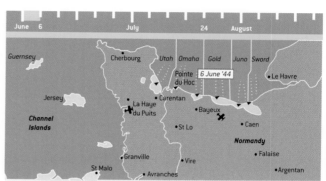

During the next few weeks, an enormous number of Allied troops built up along the coast, assembling for a major push. Gradually, over the rest of June, the Allied troops advanced into the areas neighbouring the coast. The German resistance was fierce, but by 24th July, the Allies had established a firm hold on the Normandy coast.

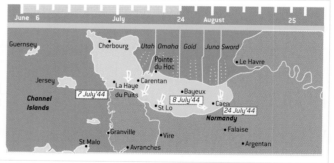

The battle for Normandy continued for the next several weeks, with the Allied troops advancing further into enemy territory to the south. On 27th July, the US Army launched Operation Cobra, wiping out most of the German forces west of St Lo.

From 28th July, the advance sped up, meeting little resistance from the Germans, until, on 31st July, the Americans arrived at Avranches to the south, creating a major breakthrough.

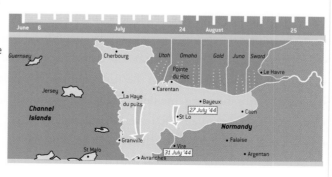

Operation Overlord

From here the American troops were able to drive deep into France towards the ports of Brest and Lorient, while the British and Canadian forces conducted local attacks to keep the Germans occupied.

On 6th August, the Germans rallied for a counter-attack, but the Americans retaliated with massive air strikes. After four days of fighting, the German fighting diminished.

On 8th August, the American 3rd Army made it to Le Mans and swung north while the British and Canadian forces pushed south to form an enormous pincer, surrounding the Germans on all sides.

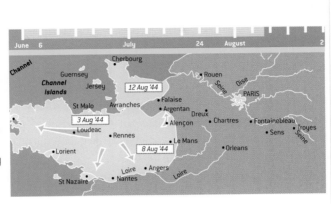

Towards the end of August, the Allied forces had established control over a major area of France and the German army was weakened and withdrawing.

On 25th August, the French army arrived at Paris and was given the honour of liberating the city. Operation Overlord was successfully completed ahead of schedule.

Over a period of twelve weeks, there had been some 600 000 casualties, but the stage had been set for the defeat of Nazi Germany.

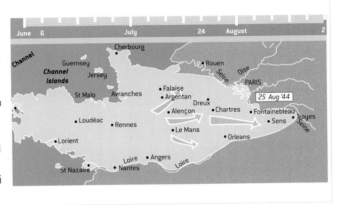

Source: www.bbc.co.uk/history/worldwars/wwtwo/launch_ani_overlord_campaign.shtml

We have seen previously that recounts can be represented visually by a sequence of photos, or pictures, or by a timeline. Here, however, the visual representation is much more complex. It still depicts a sequence of events in chronological order, but now the timeframe is overlaid on a series of maps so that the reader can see where the action took place, on which dates, and how the territory captured by the Allies expanded over the period of Operation Overlord.

Have a go!

Multimodal texts such as the one above can prove very difficult for students to read. Often such texts are simply skimmed without an attempt to interpret the complex information. And yet they are usually critical to a sound understanding of a topic. Students can be supported to read such texts through close reading activities, where they are guided to read the text carefully and to interact with the text by posing questions, summarising, noting bits that were hard to understand, and physically annotating the text. Here you will be given the opportunity to experience a close reading task—even if it means marking the textbook! It will take time, but it is worth the effort to better understand the challenges of reading complex texts and how students can be supported by revisiting the text in various ways, each time tackling a different aspect of the topic.

1   Cover up the maps and skim the text for the main gist. How well did you understand the text?

2   Now cover up the text and just try to work out the sequence of events from the maps alone. Try to interpret the maps out loud, perhaps with a partner. How much do you now understand of what happened?

3   Now read the text and the maps together. At what points did you need to consult the map? At what points did the text help to interpret the map?

4   Underline the Circumstances of time in the text and draw an arrow to a related time reference on the map. How does the map represent time differently from the written text?

From the underlined Circumstances of time, summarise the progress of Operation Overlord by creating a timeline, spacing the various dates/times along the timeline.

Note how the Circumstances of time represent timeframes differently, from the vague 'for the next several weeks' through to the very precise 'at 6.30 am'.

Do you think other cultures carve up time in the same way as Western cultures?

5   Now go back to the text and highlight the Circumstances of place. As you find each one, draw an arrow to its geographical position on the map.

On your timeline, insert the location where each event took place.

6   For each event/place on your timeline, locate and circle the Participants in the event (e.g. the Allied troops) and include them in the timeline. You might need to also include the accompanying Process (e.g. the Americans *retaliated*).

How do the Participants in this recount differ from those in the previous recounts?

How have Quantifiers been used to boost the impact of the recount?

7   Now go to the website by searching 'BBC Operation Overlord animated map'.

Here you will find an animated version of the invasion. Did the animation help to make the progress of the battle clearer?

You have now revisited the text from several different perspectives. Did this help to consolidate your understanding of Operation Overlord?

See Chapter 4 for further detail on Participants, Processes, and Circumstances (as well as features such as Quantifiers).

Quantifiers can be used to increase (or decrease) the strength of an utterance (see Chapter 2: Graduation).

Can you see the potential for doing close reading activities with other types of texts in order to reach a deep understanding of important content? (Of course, you would need to adjust the focus of the analysis depending on the topic and genre.)

HISTORICAL ACCOUNTS

Like historical recounts, *historical accounts* are ordered in a chronological sequence. However, they don't simply recount the events; they also provide an explanation of what happened along the way. The account of Operation Overlord in Table 5.8, for example, differs from the recount above in that it gives reasons for the success of the operation as we follow along with the events.

Table 5.8   Historical account

Stages	*Operation Overlord*
Orientation	The success of Operation Overlord during the Second World War was largely due to the high level of clever planning by the Allied generals. Previous efforts to defeat the Germans had failed because of a lack of equipment and manpower. But now they gathered together a massive force of 5000 planes and 6000 ships. Rather than choose the easier, more obvious French port for landing, they selected the less likely Normandy coast, thus confusing the enemy.
Episodes	For months before D-Day, the Allies seized bridges and key routes near Normandy to protect the troops from attack once they had landed. Prior to the landings, they also bombed road and rail communications so that movement of the German troops would be impeded. On D-Day, the Allied bombers dropped hundreds of life-size dummies by parachute all over Normandy in order to baffle the Germans and divert them from the actual landing place. Once the Normandy coast was secured, huge numbers of troops were landed by ship. Because the ports could not support such a large influx, the Allies built ingenious floating harbours called Mulberries, which they transported from England to provide for the safe landing of thousands of tons of supplies and equipment each day during the period of build-up.
Comment	Operation Overlord ultimately resulted in the destruction of German forces and the defeat of Germany.

Have a go!

1. Circle all the expressions that refer to the time when events took place.
2. Now underline all the instances in the text that indicate an element of causality (e.g. result, reason, or purpose).
3. Does this help you to observe how historical accounts are a combination of events in time and the causal relationships between them?

Think about it

Read the final sentence.

> Operation Overlord ultimately resulted in the destruction of German forces and the defeat of Germany.

Notice how it has summarised a whole stretch of activity by compacting it into a couple of noun groups (*the destruction of German forces*, *the defeat of Germany*). In spoken language, we would probably have said something like:

> 'Because of Operation Overlord, *the German forces were destroyed* and *Germany was defeated*.'

Now we have two clauses (in italics). It is typical of written language to compact events (represented by clauses) into things (represented by noun groups). This is called **nominalisation** and is a major challenge for students entering secondary school.

See if you can unpack the first sentence from the text back into the spoken mode by inserting verbs (noun groups are in italics):

> *The success of Operation Overlord during the Second World War* was largely due to *the high level of clever planning by the Allied generals*.

Nominalisation is a common strategy when trying to relate causes and effects in an historical account.

---

nominalisation: a process in which an idea or event (represented by a clause or clauses) is downgraded to a 'thing' (represented by a noun group). It is a language resource for creating more compact text, and is often a feature of academic and bureaucratic texts. See Chapter 10.

LITERARY RECOUNTS

So far, we have been looking at recounts that tell of past experience in the real world. Some recounts, though, tell of happenings in the world of the imagination. When these recounts use language in ways that we recognise as aesthetically pleasing, original, or carefully crafted, we can refer to them as *literary recounts*. They might take the form of prose, poems, or multimodal texts.

The literary recount in Table 5.9 is an award-winning text written by a 12-year-old girl from Otago, New Zealand. It begins with an Orientation stage that introduces us to the setting and the cheetah. There follows a series of events in which the cheetah, about to begin his hunt, himself becomes the hunted and is captured and taken away to live in an enclosure. Eventually, he is released—though in true literary form, gaps are left for our imagination. (Why was he captured? By whom? Why was he brought back?) Finally, we find the cheetah resuming his hunt in what we could call a Reorientation stage, taking us back to where we started. Notice that we have identified not only stages but also phases within the stages. Stages are the relatively broad stretches of text that are characteristic of most texts belonging to a particular genre. The phases are much more flexible and vary from text to text, depending on the particular topic or audience.

Table 5.9   Literary recount

Stages and *phases*	*The Cheetah's Hunt*
Orientation *setting* *main character*	A hot breeze fanned the top of the savannah grass. The grass swayed *slightly,* testing the sun-baked ground in which its roots were embedded. Crouched *low among the ground,* paws barely touching the hard ground, lay a cheetah. His fierce amber eyes were riveted on a herd of wildebeest.
Sequence of events *Development of character*	He stalked forward, making barely a rustle. Then*, with a sudden graceful bound,* he took off. He was flying, racing the wind. His claws slid *out from his paw-pads.* He was the hunter, he was **invincible**.
Problem *Reaction*	BANG! The shot echoed *through the savannah,* as though the mountain was collapsing. *Instinctively,* the animal swerved, then crouched. His head whipped around to focus on where the shot had sounded. It didn't seem **threatening**, so he ignored it, and turned back for the wildebeest. They were gone. The cheetah snarled *angrily.* He needed prey. Throwing caution to the wind, he stalked to where the shot had sounded. A new scent filled his nostrils. **Metallic**.
Further problem *Reaction* *Comment*	BANG! BANG! BANG! Three shots were fired *in rapid succession.* A new emotion filled his mind. Fear. The cheetah turned and bolted. Not running to kill, but running to hide. The tables had turned. He was the hunted.
Change of setting *in time* *Problem*	Night fell over the savannah *like a dark blanket.* The cheetah laid his heavy head on his paws and slept. His dreams were filled *with weird lights and crazy colours.* Shots echoed, *as though in a cave.* A sharp pain ripped through his body, and then everything stopped.
Change of setting *in place* *Reaction*	The cheetah *groggily* opened his eyes. A sharp, metallic smell reached his nose. He got up and walked around, revelling in the feel of life returning to his numbed limbs. *Ahead of him,* he could see lots of tree trunks bound together. *Behind him,* a metal wall. *To either side of him,* glass. A box. He was **trapped**.
Description of setting *Comment*	Something was thrown beside him, and he ate *gratefully.* He lapped up some water from a pond he'd found during his ramblings. Not that there had been far to ramble. He tried to run, to stretch his legs. Before he could get any speed, he saw a wall looming up ahead. He swerved, puffs of dust rising *from where his paws had been,* and stalked *over to one of the glass walls* and glared out of it. The harsh laughter of the humans hurt his ears. He padded *towards his den,* ears, tail and head drooping. The wild hunter was **tamed**. His spirit had been broken.
Change in character	The next few months meant nothing. Days came, days went. There was nothing left in the cheetah. His paws carried him without him knowing. His mouth ate, but he never felt **satisfied**. Neither did he feel **hungry**. He ate, drank, slept. He survived, but he didn't live. Then people started entering his cage. They poked him and examined him. They took him *to a room that was lit by bright lights.* Another pinprick. More darkness.

(continued)

Table 5.9 Literary recount *(continued)*

Stages and *phases*	The Cheetah's Hunt
Change in setting *Change in character*	A familiar rustle filled the cheetah's ears. He didn't allow himself to think that it might be grass. But the thunder sounded *like hooves*. He dared to open one eye. *Immediately*, he was on his paws. It was! He was home! He pounced around, trying to catch his tail. He felt **reborn**. He noticed things *in sharper detail*, noticed things he never had before. It was **perfect**.
Climax	Then, he ran. The cheetah ran. He was **truly magnificent**. His paws thrummed the earth, and a sense of overwhelming power filled his mind. But what was that? He slowed *to a trot*, *then a walk*. That smell … wildebeest.
Reorientation	Again he crouched, and stalked forward. It was time to finish the hunt.

Source: Romy Wales (aged 12), Roxburgh Area School, Central Otago

Have a go!

- Read the text aloud for enjoyment.
- Now read it again, and as you do, consciously visualise the setting, the characters, and the events. Visualisation is an important skill to support students' comprehension.
- What literary qualities are evident in the text in Table 5.9? In what ways is it different from a factual recount of what happened to the cheetah? If you were demonstrating to other students how they might also write a literary recount, what would you model for them? After you have considered how the whole text is structured and how meaning builds up in the text through the stages and choice of phases, tackle the following.

1 Circle some of the vivid verb groups. Are they well chosen? What types of Processes do they express: actions? thinking? feeling? perceiving through the senses? Are the perceiving Processes (seeing, smelling, hearing, touching, tasting) directly stated as verbs or do you have to infer them from the surrounding text?

2 Look at the noun groups (such as those underlined) representing the Participants. Discuss the effect they create. Does a noun group have to be long to be effective?

3 Look at the groups or phrases representing the Circumstances (such as those in italics). Discuss what they contribute to the meaning of the text, for example in terms of manner (How?), or setting in time (When?) or place (Where?).

4 How is language used to create a sense of place? Find evidence of how the setting changes throughout the recount.

5 Look at some of the choices of adjectives or adjective groups (in bold italics) that the author has used. What do they contribute to the recount?

6   What might you observe about the way the author has structured the following sentences? How has the author played with the typical structure of sentences?

- Crouched low among the grass, paws barely touching the hard ground, lay a cheetah.
- Behind him, a metal wall. To either side of him, glass. A box. He was trapped.
- He padded towards his den, ears, tail and head drooping.
- The next few months meant nothing. Days came, days went. There was nothing left in the cheetah. His paws carried him without him knowing. His mouth ate, but he never felt satisfied. Neither did he feel hungry. He ate, drank, slept. He survived, but he didn't live.
- Another pinprick. More darkness.

7   Which other sentences do you think are particularly evocative or well structured or literary? Can you explain why (e.g. the way they have been crafted, metaphorical language, similes)?

8   Even though the recount is not narrated in the first person ('I'), what gives the impression that the recount is being told from the point of view of the cheetah? Find some specific examples.

In the classroom

Literary texts should not be used simply as a vehicle for teaching grammar. When we engage with literary texts in the classroom, we enjoy them first, generally, by reading them aloud with the students. The *Australian Curriculum: English*, however, requires 'an informed appreciation of literary texts'. In order to do this, we need to explicitly support students in coming to an awareness of how the author has used language to create a mood, a setting, or a character, or to create suspense or to delight us by making unexpected choices. In turn, students are able to draw on examples from literary texts in writing their own. This is much easier when the class has a shared language for talking about language (a metalanguage).

When helping students to appreciate the language of literary texts:

- Carefully select a text that demonstrates effective and creative use of language.
- Use your knowledge about language to identify key features that you will later draw students' attention to.
- Share it aloud with the class (or a group) to savour the overall meaning of the text.
- Discuss with students those language features you have identified or any other particularly striking uses of language that the students notice. Get them to find evidence from the text.
- Ask the class to think about the effect of these language features and how they are functioning (e.g. to locate the setting in a particular time or place, to evoke a particular mood, to intrigue). In the recount above, for example, how has grass been used in the orientation and later in the text to suggest the location from the cheetah's point of view? What does metal represent? How do we come to know the cheetah through what it looks like (e.g. fierce amber eyes), what it does

(crouches low, paws barely touching the ground, stalked) and how it moves (with a sudden graceful bound, groggily).

- Gradually build up a shared metalanguage for talking about these features. Get students to identify, for example, the action verbs at the beginning of the story (crouched, stalked) and show how these have been used again at the end to show how the action is picking up where it left off. Include not only the terminology you are being introduced to here, but also terms for figurative language such as metaphor (his spirit had been broken), and simile (like hooves).

- With the class, develop word walls—collections of effective words and phrases from texts they are reading. These are organised in particular ways (e.g. various types of Processes, examples of different kinds of Circumstances) on sheets of cardboard attached to the wall. Encourage them to add to the lists over time and to refer to them when writing their own texts.

- Eventually, you can also get students to critique poorly written texts in terms of, for example, their use of clichés, lack of originality, or clumsy constructions.

DEVELOPING CONTROL OVER RECOUNTS

Recounts are often seen as one of the basic genres that children encounter in early primary school, and then move on. As we have seen from the texts above, recount genres continue to be used in spoken, written, and multimodal forms throughout the years of schooling. In early childhood, children start to use language to recount experiences. Adults provide scaffolding, guiding them to sequence events in chronological order. Gradually, they learn to reconstruct their past experiences in the written mode, often accompanied by drawings or photos. With the support of peers and their teacher, they might move from recounting recent individual experiences with a brief timeframe and only a couple of events to recounting group experiences such as excursions over a longer timeframe, where they have to select relevant information to include and organise the text into stages and phases. The teacher could, for example, guide the students to retell what they did as a class by displaying a series of photos of the events, or stopping a video of the activity at strategic points, or jointly constructing an illustrated storyboard that could act as a template for the students to write their own recount.

By mid-primary they are using procedural recounts in both spoken and written modes to explain how they solved a maths problem or how they carried out an experiment. And by late primary they are writing a range of recounts, many of which are not of personal experience, but concern much longer spans of time, such as biographies of other people's lives.

Moving into secondary school, they need to be able to deal with historical recounts, where time is carved up into epochs, ages, periods, and so on. Such recounts often involve the technicality of the historical discourse, referring to key historical figures and groups, movements, and settings. They might also be asked to write empathetic recounts, where they take on the persona of a character from another era or cultural context. Some students will engage in creating literary recounts, taking time to carefully craft the language and the flow of events.

By mid- to late secondary, they will be writing accounts that not only tell what happened but also include an element of explanation. Throughout the years of schooling, students still need support in reading and interpreting more complex recounts and accompanying images. And they need models of these recounts when they are attempting to write them, along with demonstrations from the teacher of how to research the topic, collect information from primary and secondary sources, organise notes, summarise key points, and construct a coherent text.

Think about it

1   Does the developmental sequence described above reflect what you have observed during, for example, field experience?

2   Would you be able to identify the increasing linguistic demands being made on students as they engage with recounts across the years of schooling?

3   What does such a progression suggest to you about the need to develop students' resources for recounting in primary school in order to meet the demands of secondary school?

WHAT ARE THE MAJOR LANGUAGE RESOURCES FOR RECOUNTING?

As students progress through schooling, the language resources needed for recounting become increasingly complex. The following summarises the language features that are important in recounting. You have already encountered most of these, either in this chapter or in previous chapters. For more detailed investigation of some of these language features, we would recommend that you consult relevant reference books (e.g. as listed in Further Reading at the end of the book).

Expressing and elaborating ideas: Developing control of field-related meanings

- Recounts reconstruct the field of events in the past through choices from the *Ideational* function of language.
- In personal recounts, biographies, autobiographies:
  - specific, familiar Participants (e.g. my family, Class 2Z, our school)
  - Processes representing actions, thoughts, and feelings, primarily in the past simple tense (e.g. went, was, were, had, watched)—noting potential difficulties for EALD students with irregular verbs (e.g. go → went) and negative verb groups (went → didn't go)
  - Circumstances of time to locate actions in the past and to sequence events (e.g. yesterday, for two weeks, at first).

- In historical recounts and accounts:
  - generalised, unfamiliar Participants, often representing key historical figures or groupings (e.g. King Henry, the Light Brigade), or events (the Eureka Stockade), or nominalised events (*the revolution* led to *a collapse of order*), or phases in time (the Dark Ages), or geographical locations (the Middle East), or technical terms (primary sources, battalion), or abstractions (peace, friendship). Participants are often expressed in lengthy noun groups (e.g. The Allies built *ingenious floating harbours called Mulberries that they transported from England.*).
  - Processes representing a wide range of activities, happenings, feelings, and thoughts, as well as building up description through relating verbs (Hitler *was* a wily, ruthless leader), using a variety of tenses and verb group constructions to express more nuanced meanings
  - Circumstances representing many different ways of packaging time, of indicating place, of expressing manner, of referring to causality, and so on
  - much more complex combinations of clauses to express higher-level thinking.
- In literary recounts:
  - carefully chosen Participants (*a sharp pain*), Processes (*riveted, whipped around*), and Circumstances (*in rapid succession*) to represent original ideas in vivid, engaging ways
  - the use of figurative language (e.g. *like a dark blanket*)
  - playfulness with the structure of the recount, the paragraphs, and the sentences (e.g. verb-less sentences: *Metallic*; short, punchy sentences: *He was the hunted*; *He was trapped*).

Interacting with others: Developing control of tenor-related meanings

See Chapters 2 and 9 for further information on the Appraisal system.

- Recounts (especially personal, autobiographical, and biographical ones) often involve the expression of interpersonal meanings. We can use insights from the Appraisal system to identify how an interpersonal tenor is being created in recounts:
- expressing attitudes
  - sharing feelings (*We miss our family very much; Sally didn't like school*)
  - evaluating the qualities of something (*clever planning; a successful operation; ingenious floating harbours*)
  - judging people's behaviour (*a large, warm family that welcomed her; slavery, abuse, poverty; she received many awards*)
- increasing and decreasing the force (*an enormous number of troops; deep into France; meeting little resistance*)
- establishing an I–you relationship
  - the use of first person pronouns where appropriate.

Creating cohesive texts: Developing control of mode-related meanings

- Recounts can be told in the oral mode, in the written mode, or in multimodal forms. The choice of mode and medium will have an impact on the choices made from the Textual function of the language system.
- Oral recounts:
  - fairly loose organisation of the text; not necessarily a coherent chronological sequence
  - language with a spoken quality—sentence fragments and/or long, rambling sentences
  - supported by oral features such as intonation, pauses, emphasis, volume.
- Written recounts:
  - more highly structured organisation
  - the use of text connectives to sequence the events of the recount (*at first, then, finally*)
  - tightly controlled internal cohesion.

See Chapters 8 and 9 for information on text openers, paragraph openers, sentences openers, and text connectives.

FOCUS ON MODE: FROM SPOKEN TO WRITTEN

The language focus for this chapter is on the Textual function and how it relates to the mode being used in a particular situation—in particular how the language changes in the shift from the spoken to the written mode. While we are focusing here on the modes used in recounting, of course the choice of mode will impact on the features of other genres as well.

Figure 5.1   Focus on mode

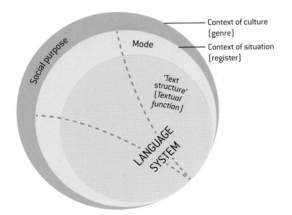

When children enter school, one of the biggest challenges is to move from the familiar spoken way of using language into the written mode. Here, we will look at some of the features of spoken and written language.

The mode continuum

mode continuum:
a way of thinking about texts in terms of whether they have more 'spoken' language features or more 'written' ones.

We can think of the shift from spoken to written language as moving along the **mode continuum**, with the 'most spoken' features at one end and the 'most written' at the other.

Spoken (language accompanying action)	Written (language in reflection)	
Dialogue (interactive, jointly constructed; shared knowledge and assumptions)	Monologue (sole responsibility; distanced in time and space from the reader)	
Spontaneous, fleeting, first draft	Planned, frozen, edited	
Flowing and intricate	Compact and dense	
Embedded in physical setting	Independent of physical setting	

During spoken interaction, the child receives lots of support from conversation partners, who prompt, question, complete sentences, supply unknown vocabulary, and so on. The meanings are jointly constructed and the child can make assumptions about shared experiences and understandings. In the written mode, the child must take sole responsibility for developing a sustained text that needs to be able to be understood by an unknown or distant reader.

Spoken language is spontaneous and first draft. There is no opportunity to think about what to say and to edit what has been said. In the written mode, the language is more highly structured as the writer has time to think, edit, revise, and organise their ideas.

coordinating conjunctions:
words such as *and, but, so, yet, or,* and *for* that link two or more independent clauses.

Language at the spoken end of the continuum is often free-flowing, consisting of intricate strings of clauses joined together by **coordinating conjunctions** such as *and*, *but*, and *so*, as in this oral recount about a lost dog:

But I couldn't find him anywhere

so I looked under the bed

and he wasn't there

and then I went outside

and called him

but he didn't come

and I was really worried

so then I thought

that he must have gone for a walk with Dad.

Looking back at the personal recount in Table 5.3, we can see that, even though it's written down, the language is closer to the spoken end of the mode continuum:

Our supper had been sausages, lovely great big ones,

but we were paying the price for them now—

me and three others who were manning a Bren gun up on a raised platform—

and as the boat wallowed,

we felt every sway and dip,

and was I ever sick!

Once off duty I went to the toilets,

and I was sitting on one toilet,

and throwing up into another

and sitting next to me, in the same predicament, was my mate, one Lt Hutchinson (Hutch).

Compare this with how similar meanings might have been expressed down the written end of the mode continuum where language is more compact and dense:

Following a magnificent sausage supper, *the wallowing, sway and dip of the boat* **resulted in** *mass bowel and gastric evacuation.*

The information in the 10 clauses of the spoken version has been reduced to a very dense single clause. Much of the meaning has been compacted into the two noun groups (in italics) brought together in a cause–effect relationship through the verb ('resulted in'). This is the kind of efficient use of language that students will encounter as they move into secondary school.

Both ends of the mode continuum play an important role in learning. At the spoken end, students engage in an exploratory, free-flowing exchange of information and ideas with heavy support from conversation partners and the physical setting. As they move towards the written end of the continuum, they have to take greater responsibility for constructing the text on their own, with time to look up references, to make notes, to draft and revise, to edit out irrelevancies, to think about relationships between ideas, and to structure the text into coherent stages.

Think about it

1   When planning units of work, why would it be important to include activities at the spoken end of the mode continuum and then move students towards the written end?

2   Can you think of instances you have observed where students do lots of oral activities but aren't then pushed along to the written end where they can consolidate the learning?

3   Can you think of instances where students have been thrown in the deep written end of the mode continuum without the opportunity to build up their understanding of the field through the oral mode?

COHESION

In the oral mode, there is support from the immediate setting—objects that can be seen, pointed to, and touched, so there is no need to be explicit, as in the following exchange:

Come and have a look at this.

I love this one. It's my favourite.

What about this one?

Ah yes, that's very special.

What's this on the back?

Let me have a look. I think I know what it is.

Can I keep it?

Think about it

Read the text above out loud.

1   Are you having trouble trying to imagine what is being talked about? What do you think it could be?
2   Can you see how most of the reference points outwards into the physical setting? Because the participants can see what is being referred to, they don't need to name them.

In the written mode, the reader is distanced in time and place, and the writer has to make the text independent of any shared physical context. In the excerpt below from a recount, the writer has now filled in the details of the conversation above.

Aunt Matilda came downstairs with a box of trinkets. As she sorted through the box, she called Jimmy over and shared with him the history of each piece. Picking up an old pearl necklace, she told him how she had worn it at the Queen's coronation. 'I love how the pearls glow against my skin. My father gave them to me for my 21st birthday, just before he passed away,' she murmured. Jimmy picked up an old cameo brooch. 'What about this one?' he enquired. 'Ah, that belonged to your mother.' Carefully, he replaced the brooch in the box, and as he did so, he noticed that it had an inscription on the back. He tried to read it, but he couldn't. 'Maybe I can,' offered his aunt. 'It looks like a love message from your father. They often gave each other presents.' Jimmy looked wistful. 'Can I keep it?' he whispered. 'Of course you may. It's yours.' It was all too painful for Jimmy, and tears began to roll down his cheeks…

The reference is no longer pointing outside the text, but is pointing internally to things that have been introduced previously: the text is cohesive within itself.

Have a go!

Identify each item in the exchange on page 150 that refers back to someone or something already mentioned in the text above.

Draw an arrow back to the thing being referred to. (The first one has been done for you. See Chapter 2 for an example.) Clue: To see whether there is a cohesive link in play, take a clause out of context and see whether it can be understood on its own, for example:

he noticed that it had an inscription on the back

Obviously, you have to read back to retrieve the meanings, so there is cohesion involved.

There are a number of different types of **cohesive devices**. Here, we will look at **reference** items (pronouns, possessives, demonstratives, articles, and comparatives), substitution, and ellipsis.

> **cohesive devices:** language features that create cohesion in a text.

Reference

Certain cohesive devices refer to something mentioned elsewhere in the text. These include pronouns, possessives, demonstratives, and articles.

> **reference:** the use of language resources to make a text cohesive by referring back (or forward) to something or someone mentioned elsewhere in the text.

Pronouns

Pronouns can be organised according to whether they are **subject or object pronouns** and whether they are singular or plural.

		Subject	*Object*
Singular		I	me
		you	you
		he, she, it	him, her, it
Plural		we	us
		you	you
		they	them

Have a go!

Identify examples of various types of pronouns that form cohesive links in the Aunt Matilda text above.

Possessives

Words indicating ownership (*possessive adjectives and pronouns*) can also form cohesive ties.

Singular	*my, mine*
	your, yours
	his, her, hers, its
Plural	*our, ours*
	your, yours
	their, theirs

Have a go!

Identify examples of various types of possessives that form cohesive links in the Aunt Matilda text.

Demonstratives (pointing words)

Demonstratives point to 'which one in particular': the farther one? the closer one?

Singular	this, that
Plural	these, those

Have a go!

Identify examples of various types of demonstratives that form cohesive links in the Aunt Matilda text.

Articles

Sometimes we introduce something by using the *indefinite article* (a/an). Once it has been introduced, we can use the *definite article* (the), making a link between new information and old information. For example, 'a dog' later is referred to as 'the dog'.

Have a go!

Identify examples of definite articles (*the*) that refer back to something introduced with an indefinite article (*a/an*) in the Aunt Matilda text.

Comparison

Another way of making a cohesive link is to make a comparison between two items, for example:

1 She had the fillet steak and he did *likewise*.
2 She ordered a strawberry ice-cream and he wanted *the same*.

Extended reference

Sometimes words such as 'it' and 'this' will refer back to a whole stretch of text, as in this excerpt from *The Loaded Dog*.

> extended reference: when a word such as *this* or *that* or *it* refers back to a whole stretch of text.

Jim swung to a sapling and went up it like a native bear; it was a young sapling, and Jim couldn't safely get more than ten or twelve feet from the ground. The dog laid the cartridge, as carefully as if it was a kitten, at the foot of the sapling, and capered and leaped and whooped joyously round under Jim. The big pup reckoned that this was part of the lark.

Source: Lawson 1970

Think about it

Can you imagine any cases where extended reference might cause difficulty in following the build-up of meaning through the text (e.g. an argument or an explanation)?

Substitution

substitution: cohesion can be created by substituting an all-purpose, general word such as *do*, *one*, *some* or *so* for a word met previously.

In English, we often use a **substitute word** instead of repeating a word, thereby making a cohesive link. The substitute words are usually general, all-purpose words:

- The verb 'do' (does, did) substitutes for verbs or verb groups (He wasn't supposed to *go out* but he *did*.)
- Words such as 'one' are substituted for noun groups (*The cakes* looked delicious so he tasted each *one*.)
- Words such as 'so' are substituted for a whole clause or clauses (*He felt quite sick*. 'I told you *so*,' said his mother.)

Have a go!

Can you find any examples of substitution in the Aunt Matilda text above?

Ellipsis

ellipsis: cohesion can be created by leaving words out, forcing the reader to retrieve the meaning from the surrounding text.

Another way of making a cohesive link in English is to use **ellipsis**, leaving words out, thereby forcing the reader to go back into the text to find the word/s being referred to, for example:

- He didn't object to her manners, though he wanted to (i.e. he wanted to *object to her manners*).
- The red wine looked good so they ordered some (i.e. they ordered some *red wine*).

Have a go!

1 Identify as many examples as you can of ellipses in the Aunt Matilda text above.
2 Go back to the stories in Chapter 4 and see how many examples of ellipsis and substitution you can find.

Think about it

Do you think cohesion can have implications for students' reading? Would this continue throughout schooling as students encounter increasingly complex texts? How might you support students in tracking meaning through the text?

See Chapters 2 and 8 for other ways of making texts cohesive.

FOCUS ON MODE: STRATEGIES FOR TEACHING AND ASSESSING

The mode continuum offers a planning tool for teachers. It emphasises the importance of hands-on, face-to-face engagement in the oral mode, and then works slowly along the continuum, providing high levels of support as students gradually distance themselves from the here and now towards the more reflective end of the continuum. This is sometimes referred to as 'shunting along the mode continuum', where carefully planned learning activities move along the continuum in a back-and-forth manner, as suggested in Figure 5.2.

Figure 5.2   Shunting along the mode continuum

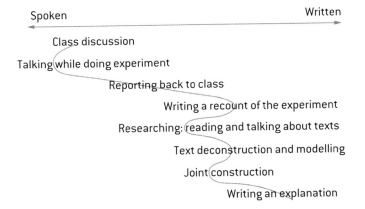

Source: Adapted from South Australian Department of Education and Children's Services 2010, p. 2

Consider the following strategies.

- Provide opportunities for students to step back from the here and now of an activity and orally recount what they have observed. This is an important step along the mode continuum as a precursor to writing.

- Cut up a recount into its stages and phases, and then ask the students to reassemble it. Ask them to explain what helped them to decide how to organise it. They might point out text connectives such as 'then' or 'after that'. Or they might use hints from various types of cohesive devices. ('This', for example, usually assumes something that has been previously referred to.) This is also a good activity to do on the interactive whiteboard.
- Select part of a story being read by the class, project it onto the whiteboard, and then get students to create cohesive strings (as above) using different colours to track the different Participants.
- If students are writing rambling, spoken-like sentences, demonstrate how to combine them into more compact, written-like ones.
- Get older students to compare the oral language features of a transcription of an oral recount and a written version of the same recount. Get them to look at the mode continuum earlier in the chapter and see if they can identify those features listed at the oral end and those at the written end of the continuum.
- When reading texts with dense, nominalised sentences, demonstrate how to unpack these to more spoken-like language, for example:

More written	More spoken
The success of Operation Overlord during the Second World War *was* largely due to the high level of clever planning by the Allied generals. Previous efforts to defeat the Germans *had failed* because of a lack of equipment and manpower.	Operation Overlord during the Second World War *succeeded* because the Allied generals *were* very clever and *planned* very well. When they *had tried to defeat* the Germans beforehand, they *weren't* able to because they *didn't have* enough equipment and there *weren't* enough soldiers.

See Chapter 10 for further detail on nominalisation and density at the written end of the mode continuum.

Notice how we've used more verbs (in italics) in the more spoken version.

When assessing students' language we often develop a set of criteria (e.g. a rubric) that we will be looking for in our evaluation. It is important to use a rubric that reflects the features of the particular genre in question. Even though an oral recount of personal experience and a written historical recount are both recounts, the assessment criteria will need to differ depending on the mode being used, the field, and the tenor. Remember to share the rubric with the class beforehand so that the students know what they are aiming for and so they can assess their own work. Focus on assessing those features that you have actually dealt with in class.

CHAPTER SUMMARY

In this chapter we have examined how language is used to recount various kinds of personal experiences and historical events. We have seen how different recount genres are organised into significant stages. We have also investigated the characteristic language features of recounts, including various ways of talking about time, the past simple tense, and figurative language in literary recounts. We have focused on the mode continuum, moving from the exploratory spoken mode and working across to the more crafted, compact language of the written mode. We have also looked at how cohesion changes in the shift from oral to written language. Strategies for teaching and assessing these have been suggested.

FOR FURTHER DISCUSSION

1   What have you learnt from this chapter that you didn't know before? What provided useful insights? Which bits did you find challenging? What still needs clarification? How will you do this?

2   Design a series of lessons around recounts using the mode continuum as a guide.

3   How does the mode continuum map onto the teaching-learning cycle in Chapter 3?

REFERENCES

Lawson, H. (1970). *The Loaded Dog*. Sydney: Angus & Robertson.

South Australian Department of Education and Children's Services (2010). Engaging in and Exploring Writing. Literacy Secretariat Resource Paper, consultative draft, p. 2.

WEBSITES

The Learning Place
http://learningplace.com.au/deliver/content.asp?pid=36766

> This website has been developed by and for Queensland teachers. It has suggestions for teaching a variety of genres as well as notes on functional grammar.

TeachFind
www.teachfind.com/primary-literacy-framework

> This is a UK website that provides a very detailed lesson plan for teaching recounts.

100 Biographies & Memoirs to Read in a Lifetime: Readers' picks
www.goodreads.com/list/show/85102.100_Biographies_Memoirs_to_Read_in_a_Lifetime_Readers_Picks

> A collection of outstanding memoirs, including several suitable for older students.

6

LANGUAGE FOR OBSERVING AND DESCRIBING THE WORLD

This chapter examines the language used for observing and describing the world; for identifying, contrasting, comparing, and classifying entities in our natural and social environments.

Learning objectives

In this chapter, you will:

- discover the various genres for observing and describing the world and how they are organised to achieve their purpose
- learn how they combine with each other and other genres to form macrogenres
- understand how students develop control of these genres over the years of schooling
- become increasingly familiar with the major language resources for observing and describing
- consider how visual elements of text contribute to their purpose
- acquire some useful strategies for teaching the language of observation and description.

Key terms and concepts

macrogenres

reports (descriptive, classifying, compositional, comparative, historical)

action verbs

relating verbs

auxiliary verbs

lexical cohesion

infographics

visual metalanguage

vectors

viewing angle

INTRODUCTION

The genres used for informing and describing are generally known as information reports. Information reports organise our experiences of the world for us; they are used to record, organise, and store information relating to categories of things. Information reports are closely connected to educational settings and workplaces; in particular, they are a major vehicle for apprenticing individuals into the discourse communities connected with science and technology. They frequently occur with other genres and in longer texts such as posters and textbooks, and on websites. A website for a government environment department, for example, is likely to have information reports on endangered species. These larger texts are referred to as macrogenres (Martin & Rose 2008, p. 218).

So far in this book, we have focused on genres that are 'activity-oriented' and thus organised around events sequenced in time. In contrast, the focus of this chapter shifts to genres that are 'thing-oriented', that is, they are organised around an entity in relation to such features as its description, its classification, and its composition. An entity may be either physical (e.g. an animal species, a particular form of technology, a food, a country) or abstract (e.g. democracy, electromagnetic radiation, sustainability).

Young children encounter simple descriptions of people, places, and things in the early years of school. In these years, students learn to give a simple spoken description of objects through games such as 'What's in the Bag?' and 'I Spy' and other hands-on activities. These are forerunners to the more objective descriptions. A key distinction is that early descriptions tend to be about particular, individual participants such as 'My cat Indiana'. In contrast, curriculum areas such as science and technology require descriptions of general classes of entities such as 'cats'. Gradually, these descriptions include increasingly detailed information about the characteristics of the entity. Spoken descriptions give way to more carefully crafted texts that are often multimodal as information is distributed across print, visual, and graphic elements. In these texts, students represent the knowledge gained from class discussions and guided research across the school curriculum from mid-primary onwards. By the upper primary and junior secondary years, students are expected to manage information about entities according to their composition and their extended classifications, to compare and contrast phenomena as well as to analyse specific sites in terms of a range of natural and built features.

Have a go!

Compare the two texts below. Both are introductory paragraphs: the first is from a literary text, the second from a factual text. How do the language choices differ? Think about the purpose of each text. Who or what are the Participants? What do you notice about the noun groups in the different texts? What kind of Processes do we find in each?

The fabric clung perfectly to the body of the woman in her parents' backyard that Sunday afternoon. Its hem falling like water just below her knee, its sleeves settling around the folds of her elbows and shoulders. She had bought the dress a few weeks earlier from a small boutique in the western suburbs, her girlfriend telling her how much it suited her. The woman walked around the backyard with her family that afternoon, from her uncle standing over by the BBQ, to her great-aunt holding her nieces hostage under the stiff canvas umbrella …

Introduction to a short story, 'Journeys'—Year 11 student

Ultraviolet light (UV) is electromagnetic radiation that has a wavelength shorter than visible light but longer than x-rays, in the range of $7 \times 10^{-7} - 3 \times 10^{-9}$ m. It has a frequency range of $7.5 \times 1014 - 1017$ Hz. It is called ultraviolet because it occurs right after the end of the visible part of the light spectrum, just beyond 'violet'.

Introduction to a descriptive report on UV light—Year 9 modelled text

What do you think are the implications of such differences for teaching factual texts?

As we have seen above, information reports are concerned with general categories of things rather than events and happenings and with informing about technical and scientific topics. Because of this, they can seldom be interpreted and constructed without knowledge of the field and its associated language. Students require time and support to come to grips with the topic and to recognise, understand, and use an abstract and technical vocabulary in order to engage with these texts. Teachers need to plan carefully for students' encounters with information reports in curriculum contexts from the early years of schooling through the primary years and into junior secondary school.

TEXTS THAT OBSERVE AND DESCRIBE

There are different kinds of information reports. This chapter explores these different genres and identifies the major features through which these texts achieve their purposes. Table 6.1 summarises the genres used for informing and describing. Many of the texts described below are embedded in macrogenres such as textbooks, websites, and information books.

Table 6.1   Different types of information reports

Genre	Social purpose	Sample curriculum contexts
Descriptive report	To give information about a particular entity by describing its features, history, special characteristics (Specific description). To give information about a species or class of things by describing physical attributes, behaviours, uses, etc.	Sydney Harbour Bridge China The platypus Diamonds Bridges

Genre	Social purpose	Sample curriculum contexts
Classifying report	To organise and describe a field or topic into a class and subclass hierarchy	Types of whales What bird is that? Environment disasters
Compositional report	To organise and describe a field or topic according to its parts (a part or whole report)	Boundary Road Reserve: Site Report Layers of the rainforest
Comparative reports	To identify the similarities and differences between two or more classes of things	Stars and planets 3D shapes Natural and built environments
Historical reports	To give information about the way things were in relation to a particular historical period or site	The goldrush in Australia Roman cities The Renaissance

So far, we have referred to texts that are made up of different genres as **macrogenres**. Macrogenres may also comprise different instances of the same genre. A comparative report on stars and planets, for example, will frequently include descriptive reports about both stars and planets in order to be able to describe their similarities and differences. A descriptive report about koalas will feature a compositional report on the description of its appearance.

> **macrogenres:** texts comprising a number of elemental, shorter genres that are organised and related in particular ways. Macrogenres are commonly found in textbooks and on websites.

Have a go!

Because they are typically bundles of information about an entity, texts that inform and describe are said to have a box-like structure; it is possible to move some paragraphs around or to leave one out. In contrast, texts that are sequenced according to time cannot be reorganised and still make sense. What do you think are the implications of this for designing worksheets to support students' reading and writing of these different texts?

When students interpret and construct different kinds of information reports, they encounter language for:

- generalising
- defining
- classifying
- describing
- comparing and contrasting

- developing technicality
- analysing.

Figure 6.1   Information retrieval chart for a descriptive report

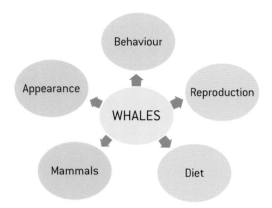

Descriptive reports

Descriptive reports are also known as 'all about reports'; they describe one kind of entity whose typical characteristics are bundled together, each elaborating on a particular aspect. Descriptive reports are most common in primary schools. They are often referred to as *information reports.* In this chapter, we use the term 'information reports' as a general (rather than technical) term to refer to all of the different kinds of texts described in Table 6.1. The structure of a descriptive report at its most simple is:

- Title
- General statement
  - identifies the entity
- Description
  - describes particular features, characteristics, activities, and behaviours.

Some General statements will also classify the entity into a particular category or taxonomy (such as mammals or reptiles), define the entity and locate it in a time or space, as well as preview the rest of the report.

The nature of the description stage of descriptive reports varies according to the type of entity under focus. In animal reports, the description is subdivided into sections to do with aspects such as physical attributes, habitat, diet, reproduction, and behaviour. They will also often have an optional stage describing environmental threats. A country report (e.g. China or Australia) will have bundles of information describing landforms, economy, and climate. A technology report (e.g. electric cars) will typically feature a description stage that is divided into car parts (that is, an embedded compositional report). Many descriptive reports will have a mini-explanation embedded in them. A report on frogs, for example, will have a sequential explanation of a frog's lifecycle. Similarly, a report on electric cars will usually include a general explanation of how they work.

Table 6.2 contains a descriptive report of a fish species known as the red-bellied piranha. The stages and phases are labelled.

Table 6.2   *Red-Bellied Piranha*: A descriptive report

Stages and *phases*	
Title	Red-Bellied Piranha
General statement *Entity classification*	The red-bellied piranha is a type of fish that lives in the Amazon River.
Description *Features*	It has an orange belly, grey back, and very sharp teeth set in strong jaws. It grows up to 33 centimetres in length.
Diet *Behaviour*	The red-bellied piranha hunts in shoals of 20–30 fish. They feed on a diet of fish, insects, snails, plants, and river animals. They hide in vegetation in order to ambush prey, and they also chase prey and scavenge for food. The younger, smaller fish hunt by day, and the older, bigger fish hunt at dawn and dusk.
Reproduction	The female lays a clutch of up to 1000 eggs.
Life expectancy	Piranhas can live for about 10 years.

Source: Chancellor 2010

The text in Figure 6.2, overleaf, comes from an early reader, *The Dinosaur Hunters* (Alcraft 2014). Other texts in this book (an example of a macrogenre) include biographies in the form of graphic novels. However, most pages include brief descriptive information reports like that of the brachiasaurus shown here together with graphics such as the timeline and comparison chart. Such early readers are useful resources for developing students' knowledge of a particular field as well as for engaging them in reading information texts.

Have a go!

Think about how the image and language in Figure 6.2 have been carefully laid out to engage the young reader. What do you notice about the language choices (technical or everyday) and the elements of print and image used? Which information is emphasised and how?

Figure 6.2   Descriptive reports in an early reader

Hunting Dinosaurs

Dinosaurs lived on Earth millions of years ago. Dinosaur hunters look for clues, such as fossils of bones, teeth and claws. These clues help us understand more about these amazing creatures.

How fossils are made

Fossils are the **impressions or remains** of bones and body parts that have been **preserved** over a very long time.

After an animal dies, its remains start to rot.

Its bones sink into the mud.

Time passes. Mud, sand and bones turn to stone.

Over time, the sea disappears and the land moves.

Millions of years later, fossils can be discovered.

brachiosaurus

human

Compare their size

This is a brachiosaurus (*say* brak-ee-oh-sore-us).

It was taller than a two-storey house, and as heavy as a truck. It ate about 200 kilograms (kg) of plants every day!

Classifying reports

Classifying reports describe the entity in terms of a taxonomy, that is, they subclassify members of a general class of things.

The typical structure of a classifying report is as follows:

- General statement
  - classifies and defines
  - names the classes.
- Description
  - describes subclasses and their characteristics.

Figure 6.3   Taxonomic diagram for a classifying report

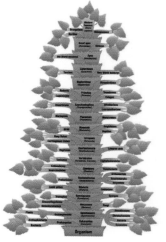

The following text represents a classifying report written for learner readers in the middle years of primary school.

Table 6.3   *Environmental Disasters*: A classifying report

Stages and *phases*	
Title	Environmental Disasters
General statement	A disaster is something that does a lot of damage.
Definition	Sometimes, disasters hurt living things and the place where they live. These disasters are called environmental disasters.
Identification of classes	Water pollution can be an environmental disaster. Water is polluted when people put things such as rubbish into it. Air pollution can also be an environmental disaster. Air can be polluted by things such as gas or smoke.
Description *Water pollution*	*Oil spills* Sometimes oil is spilled into water. Most oil spills are accidents. The most common accidents are when an oil tanker hits another oil tanker, or when an oil tanker hits the rocks …
Air pollution	*Toxic gas* Toxic means poisonous. Companies use toxic gas to make chemicals. Large amounts of toxic gas can be very dangerous. It can hurt or kill animals and humans.
	Nuclear power Nuclear power can be very useful, but it can also be very dangerous if something goes wrong. If there is an accident, it can cause dangerous radioactive fallout. This cannot be seen, but it quickly spreads over a large area …
	Smog Smog is a big cloud of polluted air. It is like very thick fog. It hangs just above the ground. In some big cities, a lot of coal and oil are used. These can make smog. In some cities there are lots of cars and trucks on the road. The fumes from the cars and trucks can make smog. The more pollution there is, the worse the smog gets …

Source: Thomas 2008

In the general statement stage of text in Table 6.3, the phenomenon 'environmental disasters' is grouped into those disasters that pollute water and those that pollute air. The subsequent chapters of this brief text then describe the effects of oil spills on water and give some examples. The text can be summarised in the taxonomy shown in Figure 6.4.

The criteria for classification vary according to the field (or subfield) and the age of the learner. The taxonomy presented in Figure 6.4 is organised around relatively commonsense categories of water pollution and air pollution, thus reflecting the ways in which such environmental issues are introduced in the early years of school. Similarly, animals can be classified initially according to covering, habitat, and movement, but later they will be organised into vertebrates and invertebrates, with further subcategories or deeper taxonomies that include mammals, reptiles, fish, etc. In secondary science, the phenomenon of electromagnetic radiation is categorised into different kinds of waves (infrared, gamma rays, x-rays, ultraviolet rays, etc.) according to their wavelength and the amount of energy they carry. In another example, rocks are classified into whether or not they are igneous, sedimentary, or metamorphic. Classification reports are the texts that enable writers to represent these important ways of organising and describing the world in the curriculum areas related to science and technology.

Figure 6.4   A simple taxonomy of environmental disasters

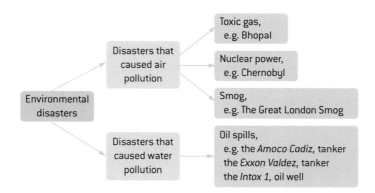

Think about it

The contents pages of many textbooks present taxonomies of the text contained in the book. Locate some information texts written for different audiences (e.g. a secondary science book, an education textbook, a factual text for a learner reader), and identify any taxonomies of the kind described above. Are these readily identifiable? How does a well-designed contents page assist the reader? What does this tell you about selecting texts for your students?

Compositional reports

Figure 6.5   Labelled diagram for a compositional report

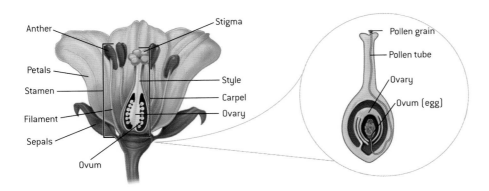

Compositional reports describe an entity in terms of the parts of the whole. They are typically structured as follows:

- General statement
  - identifies entity
- Description
  - of parts or components
  - functions of components.

In the early years, compositional reports are often introduced to students in the form of labelled diagrams of entities that students can see and study. Drawing is an important way to encourage learners to observe parts of entities and their functions. Kindergarten children may, for example, observe ants in a classroom ant colony as part of a Minibeasts unit of work in science. Other readily observable entities that lend themselves to labelled diagrams include firefighters' protective clothing (community helpers), plants (living things), bicycles, cars, and motorbikes (transport), and household tools (simple machines). From such labelled diagrams, teachers and students will often jointly construct compositional reports. Students in upper primary and lower secondary years encounter compositional texts such as that in Table 6.4. Such texts are frequently accompanied by photographs or drawings, which are often labelled with key terminology from the written text.

Table 6.4   *The Acoustic Guitar*: A compositional report

Stages and *phases*	
Title	*The Acoustic Guitar*
General statement *Entity identification*	The acoustic guitar as we know it is a six- or 12-stringed instrument that is played with the fingers or a plectrum. There have been many forms of the guitar but the current form was developed in Spain and dates back to the Renaissance.
Description *of parts and their functions, including mini-explanation*	The acoustic guitar consists of multiple parts that work together to create sound. It has a hollow body that amplifies the tone created by the vibration of the strings when strummed or plucked. The important parts are the body, the fretboard, the sound hole, the capstan, the tuning pegs, the strings, and the bridge. The body of the acoustic guitar is considered to be very important as it provides the resonance that shapes the tone of the guitar as well as the volume. The fretboard is commonly made from rosewood and has a number of metal frets embedded in it (20–24). Strings are pressed down behind a fret to change the note that the open string will produce. Most fretboards have marker inlays on the third, fifth, seventh, ninth, and twelfth frets; they function as a quick recognition indicator. The sound hole is where the soundwaves made by the strings via the bridge saddle (see diagram) exit the body leading to what is ultimately heard. The headstock, which is attached to the end of the guitar's neck, houses the tuning pegs. It can also be where the guitar identification or brand can be found. The tuning pegs are attached to the capstan, which allows the strings to be lowered or raised in pitch. The capstan has the string tied though it. The bridge is found between the hole and the bottom of the body. Its function is to allow the strings to pass over it and sit at a certain height, which is called the action.

Have a go!

We have pointed out that the genres used for observing and describing are focused on entities rather than activities. How does this difference influence language choices? Think about the patterns of choices for verbs and for noun groups in the texts above. How do these differ from those in the recounts in Chapter 5?

Comparative reports

Comparative reports are those texts that compare or contrast particular characteristics of an entity with those of a similar entity. These may draw upon classification systems to do so.

Comparative reports are typically structured as follows:

- General statement
  - introduces entities to be compared.

- Description
  - systematic analysis of similarities and differences.

Figure 6.6   Information retrieval chart for a comparative report

CHARACTERISTICS	ITEMS BEING CONTRASTED		
	SOLOMON ISLANDS	NEW ZEALAND	AUSTRALIA
MAJOR NATURAL FEATURES	1000 islands, Volcanoes, Tropical beaches	2 main islands, Snowfields, Thermal springs	1 main island, Desert, Rainforest
NATURAL DISASTERS	Earthquakes Volcanoes Tsunamis	Earthquakes Volcanoes	Drought Floods Cyclones
LANGUAGES	67 different languages	Mainly English and Māori	English, Migrant and Aboriginal languages

Table 6.5   *Stars and Planets*: A comparative report

Stages and *phases*	
Title	*Stars and Planets*
General statement *Entities*	Our solar system comprises the sun (a huge star) and all the planets orbiting it as well as other material. Have you ever wondered what the difference is between a star and a planet?
Description *Similarities and differences in terms of light production* *Movement*	The basic distinction is that a star gives off light while a planet only reflects light. A star is a ball of gas. Pressure at the centre of the star causes a nuclear fusion reaction to start. This fission burns and creates light for millions of years. A planet is a spherical ball of rock or gas that is usually found orbiting a star. Over time a star will eventually change properties and become a planet but a planet will remain relatively unchanged.
Appearance	When observing planets and stars through a telescope, several differences can be seen. Stars appear to twinkle whereas brighter planets don't. The closer, larger planets appear as disk-shaped; in contrast, the stars tend to be points of light.

Have a go!

Locate the words in the text in Table 6.5 that the writer uses to compare and contrast the entities. Make a list of these and others that express this kind of relationship.

Figure 6.7   Sorting information for a comparative report

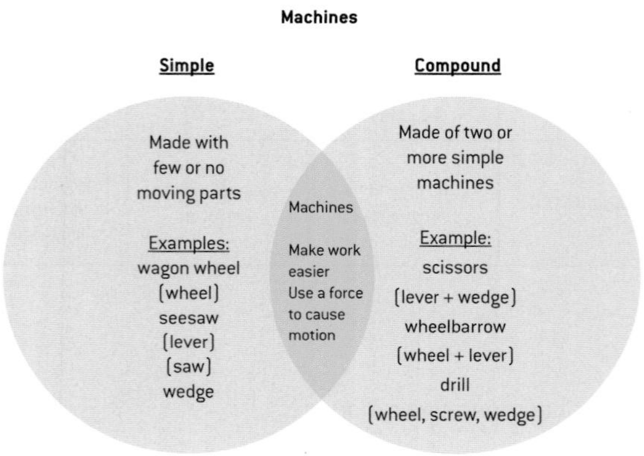

Machines

Simple   **Compound**

Made with
few or no
moving parts

Made of two or
more simple
machines

Machines

Examples: Make work
wagon wheel   easier
(wheel)   Use a force
seesaw   to cause
(lever)   motion
(saw)
wedge

Example:
scissors
(lever + wedge)
wheelbarrow
(wheel + lever)
drill
(wheel, screw, wedge)

Historical reports

Figure 6.8   Image accompanying an historical report

Historical reports, which provide information about the way things were in a particular historical period, have a structure that is similar to that of other reports and comprise:

- Title
- General statement
  - identifies historical period or site
  - defines and locates it in time and place.
- Description
  - features or characteristics
  - activities
  - behaviours
  - artefacts
  - historical significance.

Historical reports are important precursors to period studies in secondary history. Year 6 students typically study the Australian goldrushes, reading and jointly constructing texts such as that in Table 6.6.

Table 6.6   *The Australian Goldrushes*: A historical report

Stages and *phases*	
Title	*The Australian Goldrushes*
General statement *Identification* *Time* *Place*	The Australian goldrushes are significant in Australian nineteenth-century history. The first verified discovery of gold was around Bathurst, New South Wales, in 1851. Goldfields were then established in areas around the nation. People came from all over the world with the intention of striking it rich. Between 1845 and 1896 Australia's population more than doubled, going from 400 000 to 1 000 000 people.
Description *Environment* *Accommodation* *Transport*	At first, goldfields were established in rough environments alongside rivers. As the claims of success and wealth grew, the sites became busy. The surrounding ridges became huge campsites housing prospectors and their families as well as tradespeople attracted by other work prospects. People lived in tents at first; later, huts made from wood, canvas, and bark were common. Over time the goldfields became towns and cities. At the start of a goldrush site, there were very few roads, meaning that everything had to be carried in from the surrounding townships. As the site developed, people travelled on horseback or wheeled their possessions in barrows.

(*continued*)

Table 6.6   *The Australian Goldrushes*: A historical report (*continued*)

Stages and *phases*	
Employment opportunities	While it was the opportunity of striking it rich that attracted many, other people stayed for the other job opportunities. Mostly, the people who flourished at the goldfields were the tradespeople selling food and equipment and the landowners selling land to people for homes. The diggings also provided employment in services such as laundry, inns, and boarding houses, and even hospitals.
Nutrition and health	Health and hygiene became an issue on the diggings. People lived on a basic diet of damper, tea, and mutton, which didn't provide the necessary nutrition and variety. Sewage was not correctly disposed of and, as a result, clean drinking and washing water became contaminated. In addition to this, diseases and epidemics were brought to the diggings by the people arriving from overseas by ship. While there were doctors and nurses, they could not deal with the numbers so many people died from illnesses such as dysentery and typhoid.
Historical significance of the goldrushes	The goldrushes played an important role in building the Australian nation. They were responsible for diversifying an economy formerly based on wheat and sheep. The influx of immigrants contributed to a multicultural society. The heritage of the goldrush era is still apparent in many of the public buildings in cities such as Bathurst and Ballarat.

Think about it

Consider an upper primary class you know. Would all the students be able to read the text in Table 6.6? What language features could be challenging for students? Think about passive voice (see also Chapter 7), ellipsis (Chapter 5), noun groups (Chapters 4 and 5), metaphors (Chapter 4), and idiomatic phrases.

Have a go!

We described skimming and scanning in Chapter 3.

Pre-reading: How would you introduce the text in Table 6.6 to the students? What pre-teaching of vocabulary, technical and abstract terms would you do? What kind of visual aids (timelines, etc.) would support students' understanding? How would you encourage talk around the text?

Reading the text: At what points might you stop to check understanding? How would you introduce skills such as predicting, skimming, scanning, and guessing from the text? What questions would you ask?

After reading: What might you do to consolidate students' understanding of the text? How would you ensure that they revisit the text to retrieve specific information? Think about strategies such as transforming it into another mode or medium, retelling the overall gist, rewriting from detailed notes, and using it to research related topics such as housing on the goldfields.

DEVELOPING CONTROL OVER INFORMATION REPORTS

This chapter has begun to describe the ways in which learners are apprenticed into the genres for observing and describing. It has been pointed out that these texts do not, in the main, deal with everyday observable events and that students need time to acquire background knowledge of the topics they are researching. Overall there is a movement from the specific to the general in terms of the entities that are represented in the group of texts we have called information texts. Students also require explicit teaching of the kinds of texts through which entities are described, classified, contrasted, analysed, and generalised.

The primary years are critical for developing students' capacity to interpret and construct genres for observing and describing. Initially, students will encounter brief descriptions and descriptive reports about concrete, familiar entities such as animals, places, and buildings as their teacher points them out in texts read in the classroom. Together, the teacher and students write and read back brief factual descriptions and simple descriptive reports. Gradually, teachers introduce more detailed texts, pointing out classification and description stages to students and some language features. From the very beginning, students interact with multimodal information reports. Their own descriptions are often captured as labelled diagrams (as we have seen above); photographs, drawings, maps, and call-out boxes will accompany those they read. They will also be presenting their texts in spoken performances, orchestrating voice, text, and image using various technologies.

From mid-primary onwards, students engage with unfamiliar topics and undertake guided research using expert individuals and digital and print resources to locate and record information for joint and independent construction. They will encounter compositional, classifying, and comparative reports as they study more complex physical entities such as rainforests, natural disasters, and the solar system. Students also engage with abstract entities such as social movements and historical phenomena. From late primary, they interpret and construct historical reports, thus laying the groundwork for period studies and site interpretations later in secondary school History. Language becomes increasingly technical and abstract, reflecting the more sophisticated ideas and concepts in the secondary curriculum areas. Students also learn to use a range of multimodal resources to construct texts, including video documentaries in addition to pamphlets and posters and social media forms. The audiences for students' texts widen beyond the classroom to include those more unfamiliar as students participate in a wider range of activities, often adopting an expert stance in the later years of schooling.

WHAT ARE THE MAJOR LANGUAGE RESOURCES FOR OBSERVING AND DESCRIBING?

As students gain control over the genres for observing and describing, we have noted how they acquire the capacity to deal with increasingly abstract and technical language. The shift from texts that are activity-focused to those that are entity-focused is also reflected in the language choices.

The following list summarises the language features that are associated with observing and describing.

Expressing and elaborating ideas: Developing control of field

- Generalised Participants are initially represented in simple noun groups ('stars and planets', 'the acoustic guitar', 'the red-bellied piranha') but become increasingly complex with technical information ('White box [*Eucalyptus albens*]'; 'electromagnetic radiation that has a wavelength shorter than visible light but longer than x-rays, in the range of 7×10^{-7} to 3×10^{-9} m').

- The noun group is also important for developing description by using factual Describers (the end of the *visible* part of the light spectrum, a *spherical* ball of rock or gas, a *basic* diet of damper, tea, and mutton) and Classifiers (a *red-bellied* piranha, *greenhouse* gases). Describers answer the question 'What is it like?' or 'What are its qualities?' and can be intensified (the *most* visible part, a *very* basic diet). Classifiers answer the question 'What type?' (a *polar* bear, an *extinct* species) and cannot be intensified with the addition of words such as 'very'—they are either that type or not. Describers and Classifiers can occur together in the same noun group ('a *large female* piranha').

- Technicality is a feature of defining and classifying ('The Australian sea-lion is a *pinniped—a fin-footed mammal*', '*Cardiomyopathy* is the deterioration of the function of the *myocardium* [or heart muscle] for any reason').

- *Relating verbs* link an entity with its attributes ('Leaf cutter ants *have* powerful jaws', 'This species of parrot *was* once very common in the Amazon').

- Timeless present tense (with the exception of an historical report) ('Our solar system *comprises …*', 'The tuning pegs *are attached …*').

- **Action verbs** will be used where the behaviours of entities are described (e.g. 'They *chase* prey and *scavenge* for food', 'when the strings *are pressed*', 'this fission *burns*').

Acquiring an expert voice: Gaining control of interpersonal meanings

- Attitudinal vocabulary is unusual in genres for observing and describing, as the emphasis is on facts rather than opinions. However, descriptive reports on endangered and threatened species may include evaluative terms ('*Sadly*, there are only about 5000 giant anteaters left in the wild', 'The green turtle is *threatened* by *loss* of nesting beaches to coastal development', 'accidental *capture* by *longline fishing*, *predation* of eggs by *feral animals*, *illegal killing* and *entanglement* or *ingestion* of marine *debris*').

- Images to accompany these persuasive textual elements are often deliberately chosen to reinforce the verbal text, evoking powerful reactions from readers. Other information reports

action verb: a verb or verb group expressing a material Process of doing or happening.

set out to enthuse as well as inform and include explicit evaluative language; a television documentary about wildlife in the Amazon, for example, may include terms such as 'extraordinary' and 'magnificent'. Information texts for young readers frequently include evaluative language under subheadings such as 'amazing facts' and call-outs ('*Wow! 43 species of ants found on one tree! That's more than there are in the whole of the UK!*'). An important point with respect to attitudinal language is that what is modelled by the teacher in the context of jointly constructing text for different audiences and purposes will send strong messages to students about what is appropriate to include in their independently constructed texts.

- Modality is used to temper claims where there is room for options and speculation or evidence is inconclusive ('Guitars *can* be made from wood or polycarbonate materials', '*Mostly* the people who flourished at the goldfields were the tradespeople').

- Because information reports are based on research, it is not uncommon to find the different sources of information acknowledged through the use of vague references ('Some scientists …'), specific citations ('Smith [2011] found …'), and reference lists containing books, expert interviews, websites, and other digital sources.

Creating coherent and logical texts: Developing control of textual meanings

- Paragraph and sentence openers (see Chapters 8 and 9) usually refer to the entity being described, either by naming and renaming it or a subclass ('*The Australian sea-lion* is a pinniped—a fin-footed, marine mammal. *Australian sea-lion males* are typically … *The females* are …'), or by using a pronoun ('*They* are found …').

- Cohesive patterns tend to be predictable in information reports. **Lexical cohesion** is commonly achieved through whole–part and class–subclass relations (acoustic guitar: body, neck, fretboard, sound hole, etc.; vertebrates: fish, amphibians, reptiles, birds, mammals). Pronoun reference and repetition are other important resources for creating texts that hang together.

- Texts for observing and describing usually draw on a range of meaning-making resources, including language, image, sound, and music integrated into multimodal texts.

FOCUS ON FIELD: LINKING INFORMATION

In this chapter we look at relating verbs, the language used to link information in order to identify, describe, classify, and exemplify.

Relating verbs are used to link two pieces of information in information reports. Relating verbs often take the form of the verbs *to be* and *to have*, for example 'Insects *are* the only invertebrates with wings', 'A star *is* a ball of gas', and 'The Australian goldrushes *were* significant'.

lexical cohesion: cohesion between content words through word associations such as repetition, synonyms, antonyms, collocation and word patterns (class–subclass, whole–part).

relating verb: a verb or verb group expressing a process of creating a relationship between two pieces of information (e.g. between a thing being described and its description).

Being verbs include *am* (*is*, *are*), *was* (*were*), *mean*, *become*, *turn into*, *seem*, *appear*, *represent*, *is called*, *symbolise*. Having verbs include *have* (*has*, *had*), *possess*, *own*.

Generally speaking, relating verbs either *identify* an entity or they *describe* it in terms of its attributes. The examples in Table 6.7 indicate some of the relating verbs that are used to link an entity and how it is being identified or described.

Figure 6.9   Choices from the language system in building up the field

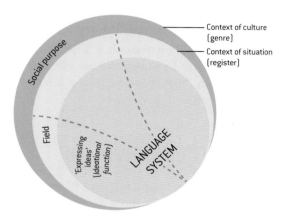

Table 6.7   Relating verbs that identify

Entity being identified	Relating verb	Identification
The classical acoustic guitar	is	a six-stringed instrument.
A neuron's capacity to respond to a stimulus	is known as	excitability.
An outlier	is defined as	an observation that is numerically distant from other data.
The dove	symbolises	peace.
Yellow	represents	the sun.
Toxic	means	poisonous.
The shell of the turtle	is called	a carapace.

In contrast, the list in Table 6.8 illustrates some of the verbs that are used to link the entity being described and its description.

Table 6.8   Relating verbs that describe

Entity being described	Relating verb	Description
The malleefowl	has	a conspicuous vertical black streak on its throat.
The Bathurst copper butterfly	became	an endangered species as a result of habitat destruction.
The red-bellied piranha	possesses	teeth sharp enough to strip a tapir to a skeleton in minutes!
The 1990s	was	a warm decade.
The diamond	seemed	insignificant until it was cut and polished.
The band	comprises	a lead guitarist, a bass player, and a drummer.

Have a go!

Look again at the text about ultraviolet light earlier in this chapter (p. 160). Identify the relating verbs in that text. Think about the function of each and determine if it is identifying or describing the example. Begin a list of relating verbs together with examples of their use in whole sentences. You will find this useful for your own academic writing as well as for teaching the language of technicality.

Many relating verbs that identify are definitions. Good definitions can be reversed. *The Amazon is the world's largest river* can be reversed—*The world's largest river is the Amazon*—so it is a good definition. In a good definition, the definition has to exclude all other possibilities. For example, *a bird is an animal* isn't a good definition. Neither is *a bird is an animal that has wings* (because flies also have wings). And neither is *a bird is an animal that has wings and lays eggs* (because turtles also lay eggs). The defining factor, feathers, needs to be included to distinguish birds from all other animals.

Have a go!

Which of the following are good definitions?

	Yes	No
Vertebrates are animals with backbones and spinal columns.		
The platypus is a monotreme.		
Yeast is a single-celled fungus.		
Asbestosis is the lung disease that occurs as a result of breathing in asbestos.		
A chicken is a bird that lays eggs.		
A robot is a machine that can move and do the work of humans automatically.		

Can you write good definitions for the following entities: an epidemic, a vegetable, global warming, a tablet computer? What resources did you have to use to do this? Where are good definitions likely to be found? What is the difference between commonsense understandings of these entities and more technical scientific ones? What does this mean for the classroom?

A caution about auxiliary verbs

auxiliary verbs:
parts of the verb group that modify the main verb in a range of ways such as tense (e.g. she *was* eating) and modality (she *might* leave).

Many students confuse relating verbs and **auxiliary verbs**. Not all uses of the verbs *be* and *have* are relating verbs. They often function as auxiliary or helping verbs that locate an action or an event in time.

Be can be used to convey an ongoing action (the progressive aspect), for example 'The spider *is spinning* her web' and 'The web *was being built* at night'. *Have* is often used to refer to action already done (the perfect aspect), for example 'The spider *has built* a perfect web'. Further examples are given in Table 6.9.

Table 6.9   Sorting out auxiliary and relating verbs

Auxiliary verbs (in bold)	Relating verbs
Oil **is** *spilling* into the ocean.	Toxic gas *is* an environmental threat.
One-fifth of the Amazon rainforest **has** *disappeared* in 50 years.	The rainforest *has* an amazing diversity of species living there.

A note on the passive voice: *be* can also be used to help form the passive, for example 'Animal habitat *has been destroyed* by land clearing', 'The bridge *is found* at the bottom of the body of the guitar'. The passive voice is another feature of texts that inform and describe. It enables the writer to maintain the focus of information in the sentence opener (*Animal habitat* and *The bridge*). The passive is also one way in which informational reports achieve an objective tone because it is possible to leave out the Participant, for example 'The sex of the turtle *is determined* by the temperature at which the eggs are incubated' (by whom?), and 'Thousands of hectares of animal habitat *have been destroyed*' (by whom?).

The passive voice is explained in Chapter 7.

FOCUS ON FIELD: STRATEGIES FOR TEACHING AND ASSESSING

- Have younger students collect familiar items such as leaves. Together, make a list of all of the shared characteristics. Compare and contrast the leaves on the basis of certain features. Classify them into groups according to shared characteristics. Students might describe the plant that a leaf comes from in terms of a part–whole taxonomy. They might also learn how to define what a leaf is. In this way they are building up skills to understand and write information texts that classify, describe, and compare. Older students will need more technical classifications, often based on a key characteristic that isn't visible, such as the different types of chemical elements.

- Assist students to recognise taxonomies in text by providing information retrieval charts/ graphic organisers. These may be drawn up and collaboratively completed during shared reading sessions. They may also be provided to students who complete them during or after reading the text. Figures 6.3, 6.4, 6.5 and 6.6 give some good examples of worksheet outlines.

- Locate examples of relating verbs in the texts that students read. Begin a list for the classroom wall (be sure to include examples). See whether your students can decide whether they are describing or defining.

Figure 6.10   Snakes: Class–subclass

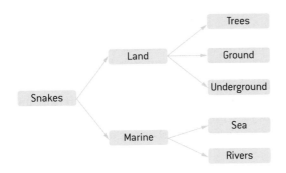

Figure 6.11   Snakes: Part–whole

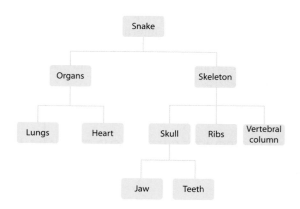

- Ask students to identify definitions from a list provided. Have them check to see which are good definitions.

- Provide students with an information report cut up into sentences. Ask them to put the sentences into bundles or paragraphs containing the same kind of information (e.g. habitat or appearance). Students may add a subheading or they may be provided.

- Give students an information text cut up into paragraphs without topic sentences and ask them to construct topic sentences. Alternatively, they can match topic sentences with the relevant paragraphs.

- Use cloze tasks that focus on sentence openers (or Theme; see Chapter 2). Jointly constructed texts are useful for this. For younger students or those who are new to English, a list of the answers can be provided.

- Provide students with proformas for researching an entity before constructing texts. These should guide the students to organise information in preparation for writing. A proforma for a descriptive report about an animal, for example, will have headings such as Appearance, Habitat. A proforma for a comparative report will probably have columns representing the entities to be compared. A matrix is a useful way to collect and organise information collected by the class for later retrieval, either during joint construction or as students work independently.

- Distinguish between factual and opinion Describers in noun groups when jointly constructing informing and describing texts. Colour-code for younger students. Encourage students to locate examples in the texts they read.

- Ask students to identify any Classifiers in the noun group from an information report and to consider whether they are important in defining or classifying the entity, e.g. 'a hammerhead shark' as opposed to 'a great white shark' as opposed to 'a mako shark'.

FOCUS ON MULTIMODAL MEANINGS: IMAGE AND LANGUAGE

While we recognise the central role of language in learning, in this book we have also noted the multimodal nature of texts. We have described how, in negotiating genres, language users draw on a range of meaning-making resources such as image and gesture as well as language. Learning about image is an important aspect of curriculum. In this section we explore some useful ways for talking about how an image contributes to a text's meaning using some terminology that will be familiar to you by now. Images include drawings, paintings, photographs, diagrams, and tables. We also look at the relationship between image and text (or verbiage).

Because students are comprehending and composing multimodal information reports, teachers must be explicit about how image works alongside language. A shared metalanguage for talking about image is as important as it is for talking about language with students. Indeed, there is a good deal of overlap in the ways of talking about language and image. In the following section we discuss how images make meaning as well as how they interact with language.

VISUAL REPRESENTATION

Just as language can be described with respect to the situation in which it is used, so too can image. An image can be discussed in terms of its field (What is it about? What ideas does it convey?), its tenor (How does it engage with the viewer?), and the mode (How is it organised?).

Consider, for example, the image in Figure 6.12 (Nichols 2004). We can ask the following questions to discuss what is happening in the image.

With respect to field, we can ask: What is happening? Who or what is in the image? What extra information is evident, for example: Where was the image taken? How was it taken? We might identify the activity as sorting and weighing diamonds (the caption assists us) but the diamonds are most prominent in the image. Processes of action are represented by action lines or **vectors**. In this image, there is a very clear vector between the man's hands and his eyes. The Participants in the image are the diamond grader and the diamonds. If we look for extra information or Circumstances, the means by which the grading is done—the scales and weights—are evident.

vector: connects one element in an image with another element through the use of a line or arrow, pointed finger, or extended arm.

Other images depict relationships rather than action; these are *classifying* and compositional images. Classifying images organise entities into particular categories. The diagram in Figure 6.13, for example, classifies diamonds in terms of their colour and worth.

Figure 6.3 introduced earlier is another example of a classificatory image. Both of these are abstract images, although not all classificatory images are abstract. *Compositional* images depict part–whole relationships; the diagram accompanying Table 6.4 for example, depicts the parts of a guitar.

Figure 6.12   Reading an 'action' image

Figure 6.13   Images that classify

Source: Nichols 2004

With respect to tenor and Figure 6.12, we can ask: Why was the image taken? How do the people and things in the image relate? How does the viewer engage with the image? What emotions and sensations does the image evoke? The diamond-sorting image is juxtapositioned with a factual text about weighing diamonds and the carat as a unit of measurement. As might be expected of a text that informs and describes, the viewer is a detached observer of the action in this photograph. The viewer looks down on the action and the viewing distance is a social rather than personal distance, that is, the viewer doesn't see the diamond grader's facial expression but is close enough to recognise the nature of his task. There are no overtly subjective elements in the image. The painstaking nature of this work and the valuable nature of the commodity being weighed is evident in the close relationship between the two major Participants (the diamond grader and the diamonds). In Figure 6.13, the bold, contrasting typeface and cartoonish repeated icons representing sparkling diamonds can be seen as choices made by the writer and text designer in order to account for the needs of the learner reader.

Modality in images refers to the degree to which the image is realistic. The use of a photograph (as opposed to, say, a drawing or cartoon) suggests a naturalistic orientation, a common feature of primary school science texts. In late primary and secondary school science, images are more likely to be more abstract and technical than naturalistic.

With respect to Mode and Figure 6.12, we can ask such questions as: How are the elements of the image organised? Which elements have prominence? The image is presented within a frame, suggesting that what is inside the frame is connected in some way. At the same time, the text on the opposite page is presented in a frame of similar shape and size, thus indicating that the two are connected in some way. Within the frame, the image is organised with the diamonds and the hand of the diamond grader as the central elements. Thus their salience is reinforced. The tools for weighing and the other individuals can be said to be of peripheral importance by their arrangement on the very outside edge of the image. In Figure 6.13, the relevant information—both verbal and visual—is clearly framed for the reader and the grading of diamonds in terms of hardness indicated by the upward-pointing arrow. The layout of the text is evidently motivated by the writer's awareness of the needs of the learner reader.

Have a go!

Figure 6.14   Training like an athlete

Source: Kramer 2008

Consider Figure 6.14. Analyse the image using the register variables, that is, field, tenor, and mode. Some additional questions have been provided for you.

Field

- What is happening? Who or what is in the image? What extra information is evident, for example where was the image taken?
- What kind of Process is taking place? Is it action or relational?
- Are there any vectors to indicate movement in a certain direction? How many? Are they clear?
- Who or what is represented? Are Participants reacting to someone or something in the image?
- Are they directing or pointing to someone or something? Are they symbolic? Are they concrete or abstract?

Tenor

- Why was the image taken? How do the people and things in the image relate? How does the viewer engage with the image?
- What feelings does the image evoke? Do the participants interact with the viewer by gazing directly at us (a demand)? Or do they not (an offer)?
- From what **angle** is the viewer looking at the image? A high angle in which the viewer looks down on the image positions the viewer more powerfully than a lower angle. An eye-level angle suggests a

viewing angle: the angle from which the viewer perceives an image can convey different relationships. A high angle means that the viewer is looking down on characters or subjects, suggesting a sense of power or dominance; low-angle shots make characters and objects seem more powerful than the viewer; eye-level angles are relatively neutral and suggest an equivalent relationship between the viewer and the characters or subjects in the image.

more equal relationship. A low angle in which the viewer looks up to the image is said to suggest less power to the viewer.

- Close-up shots suggest an intimacy between viewer and what is viewed, medium shots reflect more social rather than personal relationships, and long shots suggest an impersonal, public relationship. What kind of relationship is suggested in this shot?

- Realism can be described in terms of colour and detail. Full, saturated colours represent higher modality than black and white. Naturalistic photographs have higher modality than diagrams and drawings. The further the image moves from a photograph towards a sketch or a diagram, the more the reader becomes engaged in interpreting the meaning.

Mode

- How are the elements of the image organised? Which elements have prominence?
- Is there an obvious *centre-margin layout* with one element in the centre and other elements around it?
- Are the elements of the image disconnected via borders, lines, etc.? Are they connected in some way through vectors from within images, overlapping or superimposition of elements?
- Does one or more elements of the image have greater salience because of its size, colour, sharpness, or location on the page? Is it part of a reading pathway?

Diagrams in information texts

Thus far, our discussion has focused on the use of photographs in information texts. Other kinds of images such as graphs, tables, figures, videos, and interactive images are frequently found in information texts because they can convey complex and multiple forms of information efficiently.

Have a go!

Consider the following images. In what kind of information reports are they likely to be found? What fields are represented? Try explaining the information presented in each using spoken language. Which mode is most efficient? Why?

Figure 6.15   Abstract images

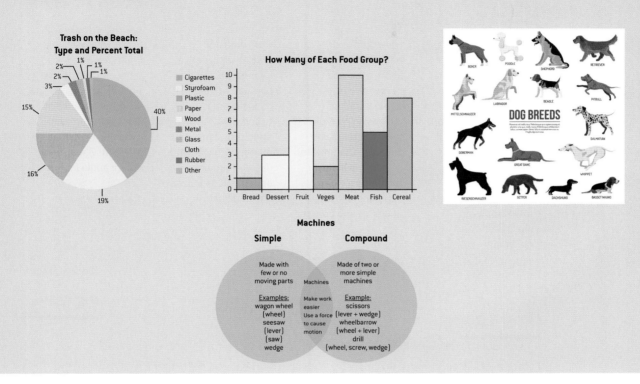

Learning to interpret and use these more abstract types of images (and visual language more generally) is an important skill in the English curriculum, one which develops over time as students encounter increasingly challenging curriculum fields (see Table 6.10).

Table 6.10 Developing skills and understandings about images

Year 1	Year 4	Year 6	Year 9
Learning to read visual language			
Compare different kinds of images in narrative and informative texts and discuss how they contribute to meaning	Explore the effect of choices when framing an image, placement of elements in the image, and salience on composition of still and moving images in a range of types of texts	Identify and explain how analytical images like figures, tables, diagrams, maps, and graphs contribute to our understanding of verbal information in factual and persuasive texts	Evaluate the impact on audiences of different choices in the representation of still and moving images

(*continued*)

Table 6.10 Developing skills and understandings about images (*continued*)

Year 1	Year 4	Year 6	Year 9
Learning to use visual language			
Create short imaginative and informative texts that show emerging use of appropriate text structure, sentence-level grammar, word choice, spelling, punctuation and appropriate multimodal elements, for example illustrations and diagrams	Plan, draft and publish imaginative, informative and persuasive texts demonstrating increasing control over text structures and language features and selecting print and multimodal elements appropriate to the audience and purpose	Plan, draft and publish imaginative, informative and persuasive texts, choosing and experimenting with text structures, language features, images and digital resources appropriate to purpose and audience	Create imaginative, informative and persuasive texts that present a point of view and advance or illustrate arguments, including texts that integrate visual, print and/or audio features

Source: ACARA 2015

Have a go!

Locate a double page from a textbook. Try to identify something of the relationships between the language and the image. Ask such questions as: Are they separate or do they overlap? Are there labels and captions? Are there thought or speech bubbles? How are they integrated? Do they convey similar meanings? Or do they provide different information?

Image and language working together

infographics: hybrid texts that combine image and language to convey information (usually factual) quickly and succinctly. Examples of infographics include transport maps, site plans, and graphs that summarise data.

As the curriculum content indicates, another important aspect of learning to work with images is their relationship with language or verbiage in texts that inform and describe. Students begin to construct and understand this relationship by explicitly linking image and language in labelled diagrams. Images and texts can be separated in a text or they can overlap. It is important that students understand that images do not simply mirror language, rather, that the two work together in a range of ways. Images and language can expand on each other by *adding* (or *extending*), *elaborating* (*restating, specifying, summarising*), and *enhancing* (*explaining*) information. In Figure 6.12, for example, the image of the diamond grader elaborates the linguistic text by exemplifying the work of weighing and sorting diamonds. In informing and describing texts that are written for young readers, images are frequently used to also project words through thought or word bubbles. Some texts, called **infographics**, comprise an almost equal amount of image and language and thus can stand alone. However, many other informative texts rely on both image and language to achieve their purpose. Because of this, figures, graphs, and other abstract diagrams require some interpretation in the written text. Integrating images and language in multimodal texts can be challenging for students. While a summary of the information may be sufficient, the writer may wish to draw readers' attention to some detail of the image; for example, the problem of cigarette butts in beach rubbish or perhaps the fact that the elephant is one of the largest mammals.

Have a go!

Collect a range of images from information texts. Label each type of image as a figure, a graph, or a map, etc. Can you place the images on a continuum from concrete or 'most real' to abstract? How does the information represented differ across the images? Are some easier to read than others? Are some more effective than others? Think about the purpose of the image and the intended audience. What implications does this have for teaching young writers about working with image? How will you support your students to select or construct and integrate abstract images in their informative texts? What kind of metalanguage will you use with students to talk about the images, about how they are composed and about their contribution to the whole text?

MULTIMODAL MEANINGS: STRATEGIES FOR TEACHING AND ASSESSING

Working with multimodal texts is an important aspect of becoming literate, as we have seen. The following suggestions are just some of the ways in which teachers incorporate image into their classroom language programs:

- Explicitly teach **visual metalanguage** to students. Label large-format images with questions to ask in order to analyse the image.

- Locate a variety of images to construct an image bank for students working on a particular theme. This saves valuable class time and can circumvent problems with copyrighted images.

- Have students make brief video recordings of class excursions and other events, such as expert visitors (with permission), so that moving images can be incorporated into digital information texts.

- Mine the tools of presentation software such as animation trails and teach students to use them so that they can produce simple, effective moving graphics to indicate pathways and sequences.

- Examine a variety of texts comprising image and language with students. Discuss the types of images (photographs, diagrams, maps) and point out the relationship between each and the accompanying language.

visual metalanguage: an explicit, shared language for talking about the meanings of image, for example placement, salience, viewing angle, and composition.

- Have the students draw arrows from the image to those points in the surrounding text that describe or explain the image.
- Incorporate the reading or viewing of image into guided reading sessions with students. Encourage oral interpretations of images by themselves but remind students to consider the relations between the image and language as they are reading.
- Younger students can experiment with changing elements of an image, for example by taking the Participants out of one image and adding them to a different image. Discuss the effect of placing Participants in different settings (Circumstances of place, time, and accompaniment).
- Publish different versions of texts by incorporating different images; compare the impact on how the text can be understood and read.
- Have students experiment with digital images by varying distance, angle, and colour saturation in relation to the same subject.
- Encourage students to plan the use of images in their own writing, to consider the selection of different kinds of image, and to justify the selection in terms of the contribution to meaning.

Think about it

How important do you think images are to informing and describing? How will you teach students about reading images? How will you teach them how to write about the use of images in their own writing? At what points in the teaching-learning cycle would you be exploring images?

In the classroom

Peter teaches a Year 4 class in a rural city. As part of the human society and its environs curriculum, he and the class were examining national parks. They investigated the activities that go on in national parks as well as their environmental, educational, and social purposes. The children were familiar with a range of genres, such as recounts, descriptive reports, literary descriptions, procedures, and narratives. They had also learnt a good deal about the grammatical features associated with these different purposes for using language. Peter decided that the literacy focus for the unit would be a macrogenre in the form of the mixed multimodal text types found in pamphlets and posters. The students were to construct a pamphlet or site guide for a newly established nature reserve in close proximity to the school. Since their kindergarten year, the students had planted a good many trees at the reserve and several school parents were involved in the ongoing development and maintenance of its facilities. The pamphlet was to be aimed at children visiting the reserve with their parents.

Literacy lesson 1: Examining national parks pamphlets

Prior to this lesson, the students had discussed their experiences of national parks and located the parks they had visited on a class map. A National Parks and Wildlife Service staff member had visited the class to talk about her work. She had also provided a number of pamphlets and posters.

The lesson began with students working in groups to examine a selection of pamphlets and posters from national parks and other public recreation areas. In order to complete the worksheet shown in Table 6.11, the students had to consider the image–language relationship, to recognise mini-genres and their language features and examples of technical vocabulary.

Table 6.11 Collaborative text analysis worksheet

Which of the following can you find in your pamphlets and posters? Put a tick beside each feature as you find it.		
title	information about wildlife	opening hours
photographs	information about plants	subheadings
drawings	information about the site history	scientific language
maps	advertisements	action verbs
diagrams	amenities (café, toilets, etc.)	relating verbs
logos	cautions	descriptive noun groups
legends	rules/dos and don'ts	statements
icons	walking times	commands
dot points or numbers	directions	questions
What is *always* in these texts? What is *usually* in these texts? What is *sometimes* in these texts?		

The class shared their findings, locating examples of each feature, discussing their functions, and deciding whether they were essential.

Peter then led the joint construction of a design brief for their pamphlet. The brief noted the purpose of the pamphlet (to guide a visitor around the newly constructed path), the audience (children accompanied by adults), the essential information (history, some details of flora and fauna, a map with legend), rules (protocol), and cautions.

Literacy lesson 2: Site visit

The class visited the site accompanied by some of the parents with special knowledge of the site. As they walked around the path, the students stopped several times and engaged in activities designed to help them notice aspects of the reserve. For example, plastic hoops were used as transects for observing a small section of the ground in detail. Here, the students noticed different native grasses, and photographed and drew them. At other points, they drew flowering plants, stopped for silent reflection and observation, observed wildlife through binoculars and magnifying lenses, and took digital photographs from a range of angles and distances. Under close supervision of the adults, they also collected specimens of grasses, flowers, and bark.

Upon their return to the classroom, the students pooled the information and sorted it under the headings of flora, fauna, and amenities. Parents assisted by labelling the specimens collected, taking care to use noun groups that were both accurate and descriptive without being overly technical. Then, one of the parents spoke to the students about the history of the reserve and provided copies of a simple map of the reserve that showed the path so that the students could plot their walk on it. This was also an opportunity for the students and adults to identify some of the rules and cautions that might be included in the pamphlet.

The students then spent some time working in pairs to lay out mock versions of the pamphlet, using the map and the headings of flora, fauna, dos and don'ts, activities and Introduction.

Literacy lesson 3: Constructing the pamphlet

In preparation for the lesson, Peter used the students' mock pamphlets to devise two potential layouts for the pamphlet in large format. He also collected several photographs, some showing the reserve in distance shots, others in close-up.

The lesson commenced with the class identifying their preferred pamphlet layout after considerable animated discussion about reading pathways and the order of information. They also discussed the different photographs, comparing them in terms of the information represented and their contribution to the pamphlet. Suggestions as to suitable uses for the different types of images on the pamphlet were also elicited. Peter referred to several of the published brochures and other material during this phase.

The students were then organised into groups, each of which was given a section of the pamphlet to draft, for example flora and fauna, history or introduction, map and activities, dos and don'ts, and cautions. This task was supported by a good deal of information in the form of dot point notes collated from the earlier research and supplemented where necessary by Peter. Each group also had original notes, photos, and drawings as well as specimens of grass, leaves, bark, etc. Computers and cameras were available to the students. Peter recognised that the job of drafting the flora and fauna sections was the most challenging, so he worked with them to jointly construct the opening paragraphs of these sections. A support teacher and parent helper worked with other groups.

Each group's section was drafted in large format and placed around the room so that students could read and make suggestions about various parts of the pamphlet. Peter encouraged the students to revisit the design brief in order to assess the draft pamphlet. The issue of whether it was suitable for a young reader arose. A significant addition at this point was the inclusion of questions that directly addressed young readers and encouraged them to do things at particular times and points during their visit (e.g. Can you see some different types of gum trees? Draw a leaf from each type.). In the context of this activity, students were able to identify statements, questions, and commands and to discuss their functions at different parts of the text. The other change that was made here was the substitution of some written information for a student-drawn image of a child wearing suitable bushwalking clothing.

Follow-up lesson: Editing and publishing the pamphlet

Peter produced a draft version of the pamphlet, which he and the students read together and checked, making minor changes. This version was polished by one of the parents and printed by the local university before being distributed to families and to the local visitors' information centre. The students went on to publish individual pamphlets on a site of their choice.

Figure 6.16   The finished pamphlet—a multimodal macrogenre

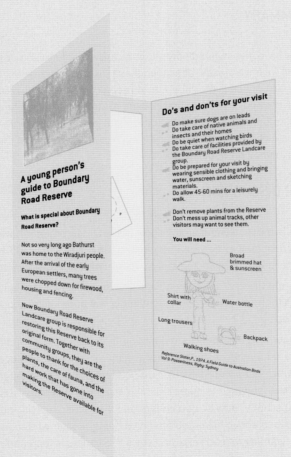

Think about it

Reread the descriptions of Peter's lessons.

1   Can you identify the stages of the curriculum cycle? At what points is he building the students' field knowledge? When is he modelling or deconstructing the genre? Where is he explicitly teaching about language or image? Why?

2   What activities foster oral language development? How are students supported into written language?

CHAPTER SUMMARY

In this chapter we have investigated how students learn to inform and describe entities over the years of schooling. While we have broadly described these texts as information reports, there are a number of different genres that function to describe, classify, and compare. We have identified their varying staging and language features and have described classroom strategies for teaching them across the curriculum areas. We have also considered the contribution of image to texts that inform and describe, arguing that students must be taught to comprehend and compose image as part of their literacy program in a world that is increasingly reliant on visual media.

FOR FURTHER DISCUSSION

1   At what points in the teaching-learning cycle will you draw students' attention to the place of images and/or to the relationship between image and language? How will you do so? Think about the functions of the stages. What resources can you collect now to anticipate this work?

2   What benefits are there in selecting a local site for building a curriculum context? What are some challenges? Peter (In the classroom) identified a real purpose for constructing text. What are some other ways of doing this?

3   Think about your own experiences of learning to control texts that inform and describe. Which of these can you remember reading and/or writing in primary and secondary school? Which ones were easy? Which ones were difficult? Do you remember being taught about their purpose, their structure, and the language features? Did this teaching take place systematically through primary and secondary school? How do you understand the terms 'explicit' and 'systematic' now? Which of the texts described above have you observed being read or written in classrooms recently? Look through some 'learning to read' texts and see if this variety is represented.

REFERENCES

Alcraft, R..Illust by Baldanzi, A. & Lowe, W. (2014). *The Dinosaur Hunters*. Melbourne: Oxford University Press.

Australian Curriculum, Assessment and Reporting Authority (ACARA) (2015). *The Australian Curriculum: English, version 8.1*. Sydney: ACARA.

Kramer, N. (2008). *Fireflies*. Oxford Reading Tree Series. London: Oxford University Press.

Martin, J.R. & Rose, D. (2008). *Genre Relations: Mapping culture*. London: Equinox.

Thomas, G. (2008). *Environmental Disasters*. Oxford Reading Tree Series. London: Oxford University Press.

WEBSITES

Australian Broadcasting Corporation: ABC Science

www.abc.net.au/science

> This website is an excellent source of reliable information on a range of science-related topics in a variety of formats. It also includes lesson plans on a range of scientific concepts and model texts for teaching information reports and explanations.

BBC News

www.bbc.co.uk/news

> The BBC website contains a host of digital resources to support the teaching of texts for informing and describing. The pages devoted to science and nature are particularly useful.

English for the Australian Curriculum

http://e4ac.edu.au

> This collection of units of work deals with informative texts from early primary through secondary. In the early primary and primary resources, you'll find examples of units on information reports of various kinds.

NSW Board of Studies Assessment Resource Centre

http://arc.boardofstudies.nsw.edu.au/go/stage-2/english/activities/information-report-on-an-animal

> This website contains graded and annotated descriptive information reports written by students aged between eight and 10 years old. As part of a larger resource comprising work samples across the curriculum areas, it is useful for understanding the expectations of students at particular points in schooling (K–10), as well as the range of achievements that are evident.

NSW Department of Education: Living things

http://lrrpublic.cli.det.nsw.edu.au/lrrSecure/Sites/LRRView/7397/applets/Living_Things_Database/livingthings/start.htm

> This link provides an excellent interactive and multimodal series of lessons on 'Living Things'—they include lessons on Plants and Animals, Classification, Scientific definitions, Photosynthesis and many more. A very useful resource for working with Information Reports.

Taronga Conservation Society: Taronga Zoo, Sydney

https://taronga.org.au/education

Zoos South Australia: Adelaide Zoo

www.zoossa.com.au/adelaide-zoo

> These websites offer online information for students researching a range of rare and endangered animals. There are rich multimodal resources suitable for building students' field knowledge in preparation for writing information reports, as well as for modelling aspects of the genre and language features. Many of the resources are downloadable to print.

LANGUAGE FOR EXPLAINING HOW AND WHY

This chapter will examine how language is used to explain how something works or why something happens. We will look at various kinds of explanations and how they are typically structured. We will also investigate the kind of language that is characteristic of explanations, along with some implications for the classroom. The language focus at the end of the chapter deals with how we combine clauses to connect our ideas, creating different types of sentences.

Learning objectives

In this chapter, you will:

- learn about the major genres for explaining and how they are structured to achieve their purposes
- consider how students learn to read and write explanation texts across the years of schooling
- become familiar with the major language resources for explaining
- explore how explanations can be represented visually
- discover some useful classroom strategies for teaching the language of explanation
- learn how clauses are combined in creating sentences.

Key terms and concepts

explanations (sequential, causal, cyclical, system, factorial, consequential)

timeless present tense

nominalisation

passive voice

types of clauses (independent, dependent, embedded, non-finite)

combining clauses (simple sentence, compound sentence, complex sentence)

conjunctions (coordinating and subordinating)

INTRODUCTION

From early childhood, children can be heard constantly asking 'Why?' and 'How?' in an effort to satisfy their curiosity about the world: Why does the moon come up at night? Where do babies come from? How does the toilet work? Why do I have freckles? Why do we yawn? Why do people die? How do fingernails grow? Why do cats purr? Older children continue to ask such questions, wondering about how the solar system operates, or how the internet works, or why they get pimples.

Questions about how and why are raised in all areas of the curriculum: How does our political system work? Why did Hamlet kill his father? How does an ecosystem function? Why do earthquakes happen? How do plants grow?

The answers to such questions require language that supports higher-order thinking as students attempt to understand and explain the phenomena of their world.

Think about it

What things were you curious about as a child? How satisfactory were the explanations that were given? Do you think children today have the same kinds of questions?

In school, we often expect students to be able to provide explanations. These might be explanations of natural phenomena (e.g. volcanoes), of social phenomena (e.g. the taxation system), and of built phenomena (e.g. escalators). We don't always give them enough support in learning the language needed to explain why things happen and how things work. Students need to be able to explain phenomena using both spoken and written modes and to comprehend and produce explanations when they are presented as written texts, diagrams, videos, or animations. Explanations involve the kind of reasoning that requires an understanding of cause and effect.

In the school curriculum, the genres of explanation involve a shift from simple sequential explanations through to more complex explanations of systems and phenomena with multiple causes and multiple effects.

In the following section we will look at the various genres employed in explaining and how they are structured, as well as their typical language features.

Table 7.1   An overview of explanation genres in this chapter

Genre	Social purpose	Sample curriculum contexts
Sequential explanation	To explain a phenomenon that involves a linear sequence	From farm to supermarket How does a garbage truck work?
Cyclical explanation	To explain a cyclical phenomenon	Life cycle of a butterfly How does an electrical circuit work?
Causal explanation	To explain a phenomenon that involves an element of causality	How do we hear?
System explanation	To explain how a system works	The desert as an ecosystem How does the internet work?
Factorial explanation	To explain the factors that lead to an outcome	What led to the Second World War? What causes obesity?
Consequential explanations	To explain the consequences of a particular input	What are the effects of global warming? What are the consequences of smoking?

SEQUENTIAL EXPLANATIONS

sequential explanation: typically uses a linear sequence to explain how something works.

Sequential explanations are relatively simple ways of explaining phenomena that involve a linear sequence without an attempt to introduce causal elements. While recounts and narratives also involve a sequence, they represent specific events located in the past. Sequential explanations represent generalised phenomena and use the **timeless present tense** or **present simple tense**. They usually explain 'how' rather than 'why' and can include both natural and human-made phenomena.

timeless present tense: a tense that is typically used to express general truths (*The flammability of materials varies*).

Sequential explanations sometimes look similar to procedures. A procedure tells someone how to do something, usually using commands (e.g. how to make an electrical circuit). A sequential explanation, on the other hand, explains how something operates (e.g. how an electrical circuit works).

Sequential, causal, and cyclical explanations typically move through the following simple sequence of stages:

- identification of phenomenon
- explanation sequence.

The teaching-learning cycle was the subject of Chapter 3.

A phenomenon is something that needs to be explained, so these explanation genres generally begin by identifying the phenomenon they are dealing with. This is followed by a linear explanation of the phenomenon.

Table 7.2 is a sequential explanation written by a 9-year-old student, explaining how honey is made. It begins by identifying the phenomenon to be explained—honey—followed by the explanation sequence. The final draft is the outcome of support provided during the teaching-learning cycle.

Table 7.2   Sequential explanation

Stages	*How is honey made?*
Phenomenon identification	Honey is a sweet, thick, sugary solution made by bees.
Explanation sequence	The first step in making honey begins when field bees fly from flower to flower collecting the sweet nectar from the flowers. With their tongues, the nectar is sucked out by the field bees and stored in sacs within their bodies. After filling their sacs with these sweet juices, the field bees fly back to their beehive and the stored nectar is regurgitated into the mouths of house bees. These house bees then add enzymes from their bodies to the nectar. Lastly, the nectar is stored in a cell of a honeycomb. Over time, the nectar ripens and becomes honey. When the honey is ready, it is collected by the beekeeper from the beehive and put into jars that are later delivered to the shops.

How honey is made

Getting nectar — Adding enzymes — Ready to eat! — Making honey — Collecting the honey

Have a go!

1   As this is a sequential explanation, it uses time expressions to sequence the events. See how many of these you can identify.

2   Sequential activities are organised not only in terms of time, but also in relation to the places where the events occur. Underline all the Circumstances of place in the text in Table 7.2 and think about how they also help to sequence the explanation.

3   When we explain something, we often want to focus on the thing being explained rather than who is doing the action. To do this, we use the passive voice. Looking at the examples below, how would you explain the use of the passive voice to students in your class?

Active voice	Passive voice
The field bees *suck out* the nectar and they *store it* in sacs within their bodies.	The nectar *is sucked out* by the field bees and *stored* in sacs within their bodies.
They *regurgitate* the stored nectar into the mouths of house bees.	The stored nectar *is regurgitated* into the mouths of house bees.
Lastly, they *store* the nectar in a cell of a honeycomb. The beekeeper *collects* it from the beehive and *puts* it into jars, which trucks *deliver* to the shops.	Lastly, the nectar *is stored* in a cell of a honeycomb. It *is collected* by the beekeeper from the beehive and *is put* into jars, which *are delivered* to the shops.

4   How would you help EALD students to understand the structure of the passive voice? If you are not sure about the passive voice, consult a grammar reference book or online resource.

Sequential explanations can be represented by a simple timeline as shown in Figure 7.1.

Figure 7.1   A timeline diagram to represent sequential explanations

Such diagrams are abstract and general and can be used to describe any sequential explanation, providing a visual representation of the relationship between events. The timeline of the honey-making process uses images that are specific to that particular explanation.

Think about it

When and why might you use the more general diagram or a diagram specific to the particular explanation?

Sometimes a sequential explanation diagram can have a degree of complexity. In the flowchart in Figure 7.2, for example, there are a number of decision points and alternative pathways to explain how iron ore is made into steel products.

Figure 7.2   Diagram representing a specific, complex sequential explanation

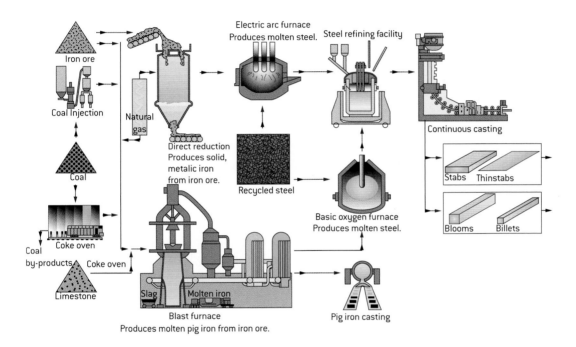

Think about it

What other phenomena can you think of that could be explained using a sequential explanation?

In the classroom

Images are an integral part of explanation genres. Throughout this chapter you will be asked to engage with images that both accompany and represent explanations. The tasks you will be doing are called information transfer activities, in which information presented in one mode (e.g. an image)

is transformed into a different mode (e.g. an oral explanation of the image). Such activities can involve the following processes:

Oral mode (e.g. an oral explanation)	to the written mode (e.g. a written version of the oral explanation)
Oral mode (e.g. an oral explanation)	to the visual mode (e.g. a visual representation of the oral explanation)
Visual mode (e.g. diagram of an explanation)	to the oral mode (e.g. oral explanation of the diagram)
Visual mode (e.g. diagram of an explanation)	to the written mode (e.g. written explanation based on the diagram)
Written mode (e.g. written explanation)	to the visual mode (e.g. a visual representation of the written explanation, or labelling of a diagram)
Written mode (e.g. written explanation)	to the oral mode (e.g. an oral retelling of the written explanation, possibly scaffolded by a diagram)

Information transfer activities involve a close, purposeful reading of the text, provide a scaffold for students' oral and written explanations, enable students to visualise the explanation (e.g. when graphic organisers are used), and help teachers to assess students' understanding of the explanation.

CAUSAL EXPLANATIONS

causal explanation: explains a phenomenon in terms of a time sequence that includes an element of cause and effect.

Causal explanations are very similar to sequential explanations, but are somewhat more demanding as they involve an element of causality.

Table 7.3 gives an explanation of how a tsunami happens. It begins by identifying the phenomenon, defining in general terms what is meant by the word 'tsunami'. This is followed by an explanation sequence that begins by announcing the three stages of a tsunami, followed by a description of how the three stages impact on each other.

Table 7.3 Causal explanation

Stages	How does a tsunami happen?
Phenomenon identification	The term 'tsunami' comes from the Japanese word for 'harbour wave', referring to the way that such waves can overwhelm an entire harbour. Tsunamis are a series of massive waves that are caused by a sudden and tremendous undersea movement such as a landslide, earthquake, or volcanic eruption.

Stages	How does a tsunami happen?
Explanation sequence	A tsunami typically happens in three stages. The first stage is when an initial burst of energy is created by an undersea movement. As a result of an undersea earthquake, for example, water is displaced, causing the water above the sea floor to rise up and produce a large ripple.
	The second stage is when the waves of energy pulse through the deep ocean at great speed. If the water is very deep, the speed of the tsunami will be faster. Tsunamis can travel as fast as 950 kilometres an hour in deep water.
	The third stage is inundation. As it approaches the coast, the leading wave of the tsunami is forced to slow down by the friction where the ocean floor meets the beach. When the following waves arrive, they pile up on top of the leading wave, creating a huge wave that has great power. Sometimes the water on the coast will drain away, leaving the beach exposed before the series of waves hits the shore five to 20 minutes later.
	The nature and height of the tsunami will depend on the shape of the sea floor and coastline. If the waves arrive in a bay or harbour, the water has nowhere to go, causing them to be funnelled inland. In such cases, significant devastation can result. Because it is very difficult to see a tsunami in the open ocean, it is hard to predict its arrival.

Have a go!

1   Identify all the verbs in Table 7.3 in the form of the timeless present tense.

2   See how many references to causality you can find. Are they in the form of a verb (e.g. *produces*), a noun (e.g. *effect*), or a clause beginning with a causal conjunction (e.g. *because, since, so*)?

3   Can you find any instances of the passive voice in the text above? For each instance, discuss why the passive might have been used rather than the active voice.

Causal explanations can be represented by a timeline or flowchart but now with an element of causality.

Figure 7.3   Diagram representing a causal explanation

Think about it

Referring to the diagram above, give an oral explanation of the three stages of a tsunami without looking at the written text. Discuss how a visual representation (e.g. a poster or a PowerPoint slide) can provide support for students when they give an oral presentation. This is another example of an information transfer activity.

CYCLICAL EXPLANATIONS

cyclical explanation: explains a phenomenon that involves a cycle of events.

Rather than explain a linear sequence, **cyclical explanations** explain a cycle of events. They sometimes involve an element of causality. The water cycle in Table 7.4, for example, explains a recurring sequence within which there is a degree of cause and effect. It begins by identifying the phenomenon to be explained, and then proceeds to explain the endless cycle of evaporation, condensation, precipitation, and collection.

Table 7.4   Cyclical explanation

Stages and *phases*	*The water cycle*	
Phenomenon identification	The water cycle is the journey water takes as it circulates from the land to the sky and back again. The water cycle goes through four main stages: evaporation, condensation, precipitation, and collection.	
Explanation sequence	When the sun heats water in oceans, lakes, rivers, and on the ground, it causes the water to change from a liquid to a gas and to rise up into the sky. This is called evaporation.	
Phase 1	As the evaporating water reaches colder temperatures, it cools, turning back into tiny water droplets, which in turn form clouds. We refer to this as condensation.	

Stages and *phases*	*The water cycle*
Phase 2	Eventually, clouds become too full of water droplets. As they become too full, the water droplets fall and we have rain or snow or some other type of precipitation.
Phase 3	At the collection stage, some of the water stays on the earth's surface in reservoirs, lakes, and oceans. Other water seeps down into the ground.
Phase 4	When the water reaches the ground it is again heated by the sun and the cycle begins again. It takes about nine days to complete the water cycle.

Have a go!

To help consolidate your familiarity with the language features of explanations, see if you can identify:

- time expressions (and the various forms they take)
- place expressions (Circumstances of place)
- any expressions of causality
- verbs in the timeless present tense.

  What do you notice about the form of 'it *is again heated* by the sun'?

Cyclical explanations can be represented by an abstract, generalised cycle diagram, as shown in Figure 7.4.

Figure 7.4   Diagram representing a cyclical explanation

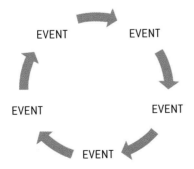

More specific cycle diagrams can involve the use of drawings or photographs of the components of the cycle. They can also be accompanied by a written explanation, either inserted in the diagram itself or as an accompanying text.

In the classroom

Different diagrams offer different ways of explaining a phenomenon, but not all diagrams are equally effective. The following activity supports students in becoming critical interpreters of cycle diagrams.

1   Get students to look carefully at a collection of diagrams that attempt to explain the same phenomenon, such as the water-cycle diagrams below.

2   In pairs, ask the students to use each of the diagrams to orally explain the phenomenon (e.g. the water cycle).

3   Get them to choose which diagram they preferred in terms of how well it represented the phenomenon.

4   Ask them to explain why they chose that particular diagram. What did it offer that others didn't?

Do the above activity yourself with the diagrams in Figure 7.5. If you were scaffolding the students' understanding of the diagram, at which point of the diagram would you start? Could you have started elsewhere?

Figure 7.5   Diagrams of the water cycle

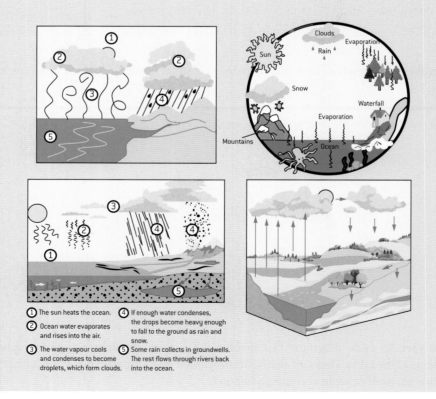

System explanations, *factorial explanations*, and *consequential explanations* differ from those above. They are not organised in a sequence. Rather, they are organised around relationships between parts of the system or between causes and effects. They still, however, typically use the timeless present tense as they deal with generalised phenomena that are not located in any particular time. The exceptions to this are explanations of historical phenomena.

SYSTEM EXPLANATIONS

Students often need to explain how a system works. They might, for example, want to understand how technological systems such as the internet or cloud technology work, or how social institutions such as the system of government or a hospital operate, or how a natural ecosystem functions. When we explain a system we usually begin by identifying the system and then describing its various parts (and perhaps their function). This part of the explanation is very much like an information report. The difference is that the **system explanation** then proceeds to explain the relationship between different parts of the system and how they interact. In the text below, for example, the phenomenon is identified (how an ecosystem or biome such as the rainforest works) and the author foreshadows how the text will unfold. The parts of the rainforest ecosystem are then described, and finally the interaction between the various components of the rainforest system is explained. Not all system explanations will follow this pattern exactly, but most will include these basic elements.

system explanation: explains how a system works in terms of the relationships between its parts.

See Chapter 6 for further detail on information reports.

Table 7.5   System explanation

Stages and *phases*	The rainforest
Phenomenon identification	A rainforest is an ecosystem—a system of living and non-living things that interact in a particular location. The plants and animals in the system depend on each other to survive. Each component of the rainforest—soil, rainfall, sunlight, ponds, plants, and animals—has a role to play in the life of the system.
System description *Foreshadowing Parts and their function*	The rainforest ecosystem can be separated into three main layers: the canopy, the understorey, and the forest floor. The canopy refers to the dense ceiling of leaves and tree branches that shades the forest floor. It provides a home for a great variety of birds along with tree-dwelling animals such as frogs, lizards, snakes, insects, and possums. The understorey offers a space for shade-loving shrubs, saplings, and large ferns to grow. The forest floor is dark and damp as it is heavily shaded by the levels above. It is home to many animals and insects along with plants such as vines, small ferns, mosses, fungi, and seedlings.

(continued)

Table 7.5   System explanation (*continued*)

Stages and *phases*	The rainforest
System explanation *Interaction between the levels*	At each level of the rainforest, the components interact to keep the system in balance. Let us imagine, for example, that a branch falls from a tree in the canopy. The branch decays and is decomposed through the activity of insects and micro-organisms, contributing to the soil. The branch might contain seeds that are nourished by the soil and grow into seedlings. Because there is now a hole in the canopy, the sunlight is able to reach the seedlings. The rain provides moisture for the seedlings to grow. The seedlings develop into trees that give shelter to numerous birds, animals, and insects and provide them with food such as leaves, nuts, and fruits.
Interaction between the components	The animals in the rainforest depend on each other as well as on the plants. Some, such as the ants that protect a certain type of caterpillar in return for the sweet juices that it produces, have mutually helpful relationships. Others form a food chain of predators and prey. A lizard, for example, might have a meal of insects. Then a bird might eat the lizard. When the bird dies and falls to the ground, its body will be consumed by insects and other small animals.
Generalisation	The organisms in an ecosystem are usually well balanced with each other and with their environment. Introduction of new environmental factors or the disappearance of a component can lead to the collapse of an ecosystem and the death of many of its native species.

Have a go!

Explanations often include technical terms. Which ones can you find in the text of Table 7.5?

Technical terms are usually accompanied by a definition. Can you find any definitions? Are all the technical terms defined? Why not?

System explanations can be represented by a diagram that identifies the system as a whole, the elements of the system (sometimes accompanied by their role or function in the system), and the various kinds of relationships between the parts (often indicated by arrows, sometimes indicating the process taking place and the flow through the system).

Figure 7.6   Complex system diagram

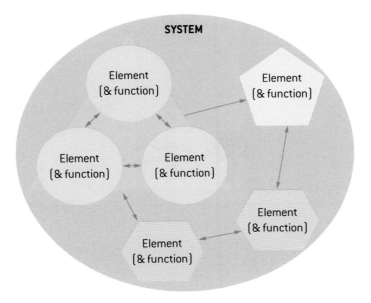

The rainforest ecosystem, for example, could be represented as in the following system diagram:

Figure 7.7   Diagram of rainforest ecosystem

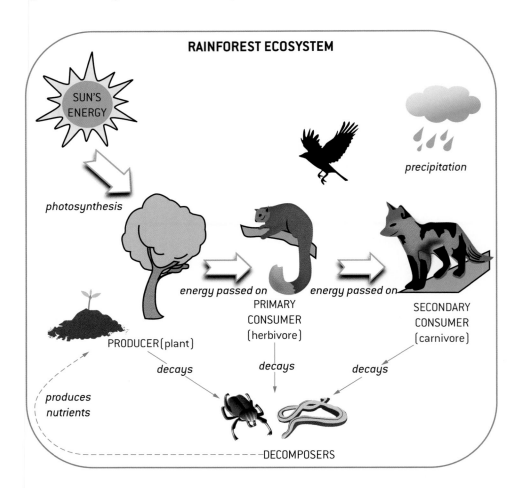

Have a go!

Read through the text in Table 7.5 and underline all the elements in the rainforest ecosystem.

Now read the text again, referring back and forth to Figure 7.7. See if you can map the elements and the interaction between the elements from the text onto the diagram. You might like to draw arrows on the diagram to show the kinds of interactions described in the text.

Notice how this information transfer activity forces you to read the text carefully and purposefully and provides a clear, visual understanding of the text.

Have a go!

Find an explanation of a system (e.g. an eggbeater, a cow's digestive system, the feudal system, the solar system, an electric circuit) and represent the system diagrammatically (as above), indicating the elements (components) of the system, the relationship between the elements, and any processes involved.

Does the diagram enable you to better understand the explanation?

FACTORIAL EXPLANATIONS

Factorial explanations identify the factors that contribute towards a particular outcome. Table 7.6 is not organised sequentially, but in terms of the various human factors contributing towards the spread of the desert. It begins by identifying the outcome (desertification), followed by a number of factors, and ends with a general statement about the phenomenon.

> **factorial explanation:** explains a phenomenon in terms of the factors that contribute towards a particular outcome.

Table 7.6   Factorial explanation

Stages and phases	What factors contribute to desertification?
Outcome *Definition* *Foreshadowing of factors*	Desertification is the process that turns productive land into non-productive desert *as a result of poor land management*. Desertification occurs mainly in semi-arid areas bordering on deserts. Although natural factors such as weather and drought *contribute* to desertification, *many of the causes* are related to human actions.
Factors *Factor 1*	Overgrazing is *the major cause of desertification* worldwide. Historically, dryland livelihoods have been based on a mixture of hunting, gathering, farming, and herding. This mixture varied with time, place, and culture, *since* the harsh conditions *forced* people to be flexible in their use of the land and to move around to where the plants have grown *in response to rain*. These days, however, the use of fences and bore water *has meant* that animals stay in the same place and overgrazing *has often resulted*.
Factor 2	*Another reason for desertification* is the cultivation of marginal lands, i.e. lands on which there is a high risk of crop failure and a very low economic return, for example some parts of South Africa where maize is grown.
Factor/s 3	Increasing human population and poverty also *contribute* to desertification as poor people *may be forced* to overuse their environment and may not be able to invest in land maintenance and rehabilitation. This *is made worse* by bad policy decisions, such as encouraging frontier expansion.

(continued)

Table 7.6   Factorial explanation (*continued*)

Stages and phases	What factors contribute to desertification?
Factor/s 4	Humans also *contribute* towards desertification in other ways. They destroy vegetation in arid regions, often for fuelwood and building material. They use inappropriate technologies and incorrect irrigation practices in arid areas, *causing* salinisation (the build-up of salts in the soil), which can prevent plant growth.
General statement e.g. *prediction*	Unless urgent measures are taken, desertification will continue to spread. While it is difficult to regulate natural *factors* that *contribute* to desertification, human *factors* are within our control.

Have a go!

Language features expressing causality have been placed in italics in the text in Table 7.6. Group them according to whether they are:

- Circumstances of reason (in the form of prepositional phrases)
- abstract Participants (in the form of noun groups)
- causal Processes (in the form of verb groups)
- causal conjunctions linking two clauses.

    Note that there are no expressions of time in this text as it is not organised around a time sequence.

Factorial explanations can be represented by a diagram such as Figure 7.8, which indicates the factors that contribute to a particular outcome.

Figure 7.8   Diagram of factorial explanation

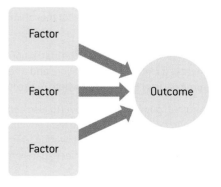

Think about it

Referring to the text in Table 7.6, develop a diagram like that above which represents the factors leading to desertification. Discuss how this activity guided you to read the text with a focus on its key purpose. How would such a diagram also provide a scaffold for students in writing an explanation?

Factorial diagrams can become quite complex as they attempt to depict the variety of factors involved. In Figure 7.9, for example, which shows the causes of repetitive strain injury (RSI), the initial outcomes lead into a feedback loop that intensifies the outcomes, which ultimately lead to more serious outcomes.

Figure 7.9   Diagram of a specific, complex factorial explanation

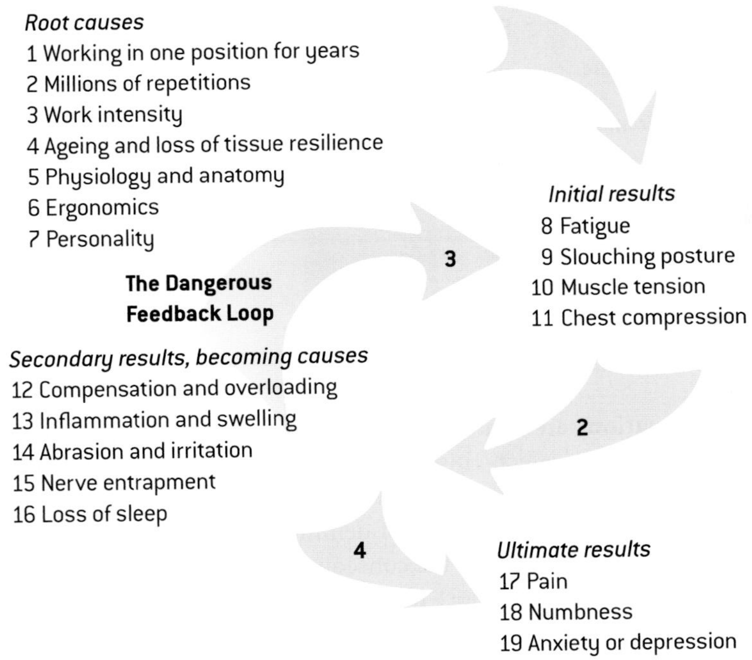

Root causes
1 Working in one position for years
2 Millions of repetitions
3 Work intensity
4 Ageing and loss of tissue resilience
5 Physiology and anatomy
6 Ergonomics
7 Personality

**The Dangerous
Feedback Loop**

Secondary results, becoming causes
12 Compensation and overloading
13 Inflammation and swelling
14 Abrasion and irritation
15 Nerve entrapment
16 Loss of sleep

Initial results
8 Fatigue
9 Slouching posture
10 Muscle tension
11 Chest compression

3

2

4

Ultimate results
17 Pain
18 Numbness
19 Anxiety or depression

Think about it

Referring to Figure 7.10 (an Ishikawa Fishbone diagram), explain orally the factors leading to incorrect delivery of parcels. As you do so, notice how the complexity of the factors is depicted in visual form.

Figure 7.10   Fishbone diagram of factorial explanation

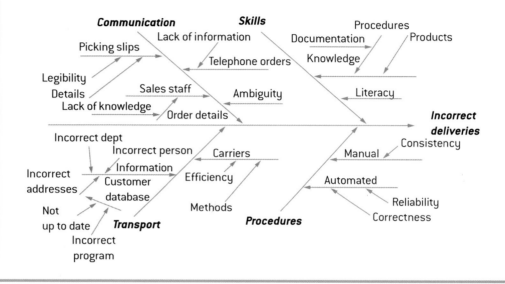

CONSEQUENTIAL EXPLANATIONS

consequential explanation: explains a phenomenon that involves an input and the consequences of that input.

Consequential explanations are similar to factorial explanations in that they are concerned with relationships of cause and effect. This time, however, the focus is not on the reasons but on the results. The text in Table 7.7 begins by identifying the input—in this case, binge drinking. In the opening stage it goes through phases of defining the input and providing background information. It then moves on to outline the consequences of binge drinking, organised in this instance into phases concerned with short-term and longer-term effects.

It is not always the case that a consequential explanation will follow exactly the stages above. Often they are part of a longer text, sometimes in combination with a factorial explanation (e.g. the causes and effects of erosion) or an exposition (e.g. the consequences of erosion and what we should do about it).

Table 7.7   Consequential explanation

Stages and phases	The effects of binge drinking
Input *Definition* *Background* *information*	The term 'binge drinking' generally refers to consuming large quantities of alcohol on a single occasion or over a number of days with the intention of becoming intoxicated. More than 16 per cent of 20–29-year-old females drink at levels that increase their risk of long-term alcohol-related harm. Alcohol is a major cause of injury and death among young people. When you're drunk, you're more likely to put yourself in risky situations, such as getting into a car with someone who has been drinking, or being the perpetrator or victim of violence.
Consequences *Short term* *Long term*	Binge drinking can have a number of adverse effects. Short-term consequences include hangovers, headaches, nausea, shakiness, vomiting, memory loss, falls, car accidents, exposure to risks and assaults, unplanned pregnancy, STIs, shame, severe abdominal pain, embarrassment, impact on self-esteem, loss of valuable items, loss of licence, over-spending, and alcohol poisoning sometimes leading to death. Longer-term consequences involve physical or psychological dependency on alcohol resulting in liver or brain damage, risk of cancer of the mouth or throat, sexual problems such as male impotency, depression, strokes, economic adversity, anxiety, high blood pressure, poor educational outcomes, and problems with work and relationships, heart disease, criminal convictions, and lower socio-economic status.

Consequential explanations can be represented by a diagram indicating the consequences flowing from a particular input, such as the simple consequential diagram provided in Figure 7.11.

Figure 7.11   Diagram of consequential explanation

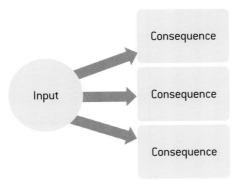

Think about it

When we list consequences, we often put them into groups.

1   a.   Read the text in Table 7.7 and identify the consequences of the input (binge drinking). Develop a diagram that represents the input and the consequences. Organise the consequences into short-term and longer-term (you will need to adjust the diagram in Figure 7.12). Then organise the consequences in each group into further categories, such as medical, social, and personal.

    b.   Did the diagrammatic representation help you to understand, summarise, and visualise the explanation? How would such an information transfer activity help students in their reading comprehension?

2   From the diagram in Figure 7.12, write a brief consequential explanation. Did the diagram make it easier to write the text than simply composing an explanation without such support? What implications might there be for supporting students in writing complex explanations such as these?

Figure 7.12   Diagram of complex consequential explanation

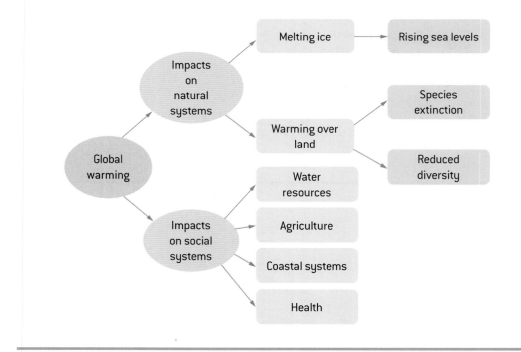

COMBINATION: CAUSES AND EFFECTS

It is often the case that different causality patterns are combined in the one text. In the following explanation written by a 12-year-old student explaining why Britain established a colony in Australia, for example, we find the reasons followed by the effects.

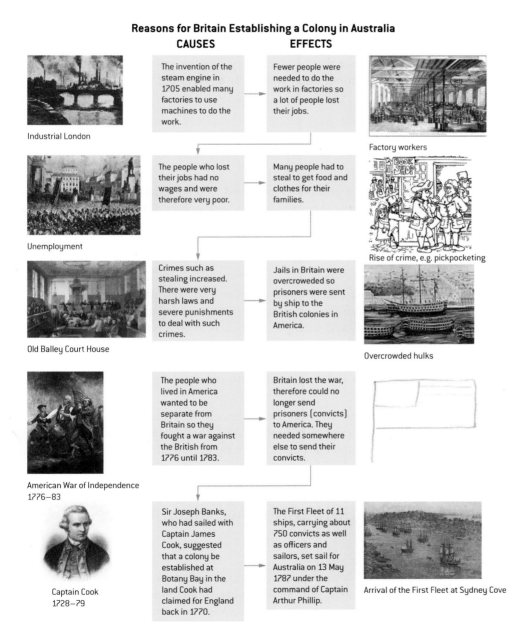

Reasons for Britain Establishing a Colony in Australia

CAUSES | **EFFECTS**

The invention of the steam engine in 1705 enabled many factories to use machines to do the work.

Fewer people were needed to do the work in factories so a lot of people lost their jobs.

Industrial London

Factory workers

The people who lost their jobs had no wages and were therefore very poor.

Many people had to steal to get food and clothes for their families.

Unemployment

Rise of crime, e.g. pickpocketing

Crimes such as stealing increased. There were very harsh laws and severe punishments to deal with such crimes.

Jails in Britain were overcroweded so prisoners were sent by ship to the British colonies in America.

Old Bailey Court House

Overcrowded hulks

The people who lived in America wanted to be separate from Britain so they fought a war against the British from 1776 until 1783.

Britain lost the war, therefore could no longer send prisoners (convicts) to America. They needed somewhere else to send their convicts.

American War of Independence 1776–83

Sir Joseph Banks, who had sailed with Captain James Cook, suggested that a colony be established at Botany Bay in the land Cook had claimed for England back in 1770.

The First Fleet of 11 ships, carrying about 750 convicts as well as officers and sailors, set sail for Australia on 13 May 1787 under the command of Captain Arthur Phillip.

Captain Cook 1728–79

Arrival of the First Fleet at Sydney Cove

In this case, there is a chaining sequence, in which each cause is followed by an effect that results in another cause followed by another effect. A more common pattern is to list a number of causes (or factors) followed by a number of consequences.

DEVELOPING CONTROL OF EXPLANATIONS

Students learn how to understand explanations first in the oral mode supported by visual images. In the early years, students will often engage with everyday explanations about phenomena close to their personal experience that involve a very simple sequence, as in this explanation about the causes and effects of tooth decay written by a 7-year-old following scaffolding from the teacher:

> If we don't clean our teeth we will end up with cavities. Unless we begin to use fluoride toothpaste, the cavities will become larger and need to be filled. If we don't visit a dentist when we have a cavity, the decay will spread. In fact, the tooth can become so decayed it will turn black and rot in your mouth.

In mid-primary, students are generally introduced to brief sequential explanations about relatively concrete phenomena that they can observe, such as how a bean plant grows or how a toy works. Sometimes these are cyclical explanations, such as the lifecycle of a frog. Gradually, they learn to explain phenomena that include causal relationships, such as why a volcano erupts. By the end of primary school they are dealing with basic systems, such as the school community or an ecosystem in a pond.

These explanations become much more complex and abstract as students move into secondary school, where they also encounter explanations involving multiple factors (the factors leading to endangered species) and multiple consequences (the outcomes of deforestation), often dealing with phenomena that can't necessarily be seen by the naked eye, as in explanations in physics, chemistry, and mathematics. In learning to comprehend and produce explanations, students are dealing with higher-order skills such as analysing, defining, and identifying causal relationships.

Most of these explanations will be accompanied by visual representations of the phenomenon—an integral aspect of most explanations. These diagrams become increasingly sophisticated, complex, and abstract. We can't take it for granted that students will know how to interpret such diagrams—they will often need help in learning how to read them.

WHAT ARE THE MAJOR LANGUAGE RESOURCES FOR EXPLAINING?

Here, we will focus just on field-related meanings as explanations require students to be able to deal with increasingly complex ideas. The following list summarises the language features that are important in explaining phenomena. We have already encountered many of these features in earlier chapters.

Expressing and elaborating ideas: Developing control of field-related meanings

- Generalised Participants ('These *house bees* then add *enzymes* from their bodies to the nectar.'; '*the animals in the rainforest*').
- Vocabulary often representing abstract concepts (e.g. system, effects, factor, result, cause, relationship).
- Technical vocabulary (e.g. evaporation, condensation, precipitation, predator, food chain).
- Various ways of creating definitions:
  - using a relating Process: 'The Water Cycle *is* the journey water takes as it circulates from the land to the sky and back again; This *is called* evaporation; This process *is referred to* as photosynthesis'.
  - using dashes and parentheses: 'A rainforest is an ecosystem—*a system of living and non-living things that interact in a particular location*'; 'Desertification (*the process that turns productive land into non-productive desert as a result of poor land-management*) is on the increase.'
  - using 'that is': marginal lands, that is, *lands on which there is a high risk of crop failure.*
  - using relative clauses: salinisation, *which is the build-up of salts in the soil.*
- **Nominalisation**, for example, where whole clauses are compacted into noun groups.

> **nominalisation**: a process in which an idea or event (represented by a clause or clauses) is downgraded to a 'thing' (represented by a noun group). It is a language resource for creating more compact text, and is often a feature of academic and bureaucratic texts.

Whole clauses	Nominalisations
If new environmental factors are introduced	*The introduction of new environmental factors*
or if a component disappears,	or *the disappearance of a component*
the ecosystem can collapse	can lead to *the collapse of an ecosystem*
and many of its native species can die.	and *the death of many of its native species.*
= four clauses	= a single, compact clause

- The use of mainly action and relating Processes in the timeless present tense (the branch *decays*; the forest floor *is* dark).
- The use of the **passive voice** to keep the emphasis on the main topic rather than who or what is doing the action (the nectar *is sucked* out; it *is stored* in sacs; the nectar *is regurgitated*; the nectar *is stored*; the honey *is collected*; it *is put* into jars; the jars *are delivered*).
- Various ways of expressing a time sequence in sequential, causal, and cyclical explanations (noun groups: *the first step*; verb groups: *begins*; prepositional phrases: *over time*; adverbs: *lastly*; clauses: *after filling their sacs*; *when the honey is ready*).

> **passive voice**: a structure in which the subject of the verb is the recipient of the action (e.g. *the thief was caught by the police*), as opposed to the active voice, in which the subject of the verb is the source of the action (e.g. *the police caught the thief*).

- Various ways of describing a system: the parts of the system, their function, and the relationship between the parts (noun groups: *each component* has a role to play; *mutually helpful relationships*; verb groups: the animals in the rainforest *depend* on each other; the components *interact*).
- Various ways of expressing cause-and-effect relationships.

Cause-and-effect relationships construct a connection between a cause and its effect. They can, however, emphasise meanings related more specifically to purpose, reason, or result, as in Table 7.8. These meanings can be expressed through a variety of language resources.

Table 7.8   Purpose, reason, and result

Meaning	Language resources
'Purpose' refers to intention and generally points forward towards a result.	For example, a clause beginning with a conjunction: *In order* to suck out the honey, the bee uses its tongue. Binge drinkers sometimes need to go into rehabilitation programs **so that** *they can recover.*
'Reason' refers backwards to the cause of an outcome.	For example, clause beginning with a conjunction: *As/because people used inappropriate technologies,* desertification increased. This mixture varied with time, place, and culture, *since the harsh conditions forced people to be flexible.* For example, Circumstance of reason expressed by a prepositional phrase: The plants have grown *in response to rain*; *Due to the cultivation of marginal lands* …; For example, causal Process expressed by a verb group: The disappearance of a component *can lead* to the collapse of an ecosystem. The sun's heat *causes* the water to change from a liquid to a gas.
'Result' refers to the outcome of an action.	For example, clause beginning with a conjunction: They use incorrect irrigation processes, *so salinisation occurs.* For example, causal Process expressed by a verb group: Poor policy decisions *result in* increasing desertification. For example, Circumstance of result expressed by a prepositional phrase: Desertification takes places *as a consequence of poor land management.* *As a result of an undersea earthquake* water is displaced. For example, text connective: The clouds become too full. *Therefore/consequently* the water droplets fall.

FOCUS ON FIELD: COMBINING IDEAS

We have previously seen how we use clauses to express our ideas. In this chapter, the language focus is on creating relationships between ideas by combining clauses in various ways. Here, we are dealing with choices from the *Ideational function* of language, as indicated in Figure 7.13.

Although we have been dealing with explanations in this chapter, the issue of how to combine ideas applies to all genres.

See Chapters 2, 4, and 5 for information on clauses.

Figure 7.13   Choices from the language system in building up the field

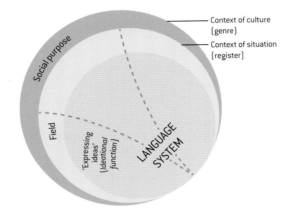

One of the major functions of language is to enable us to represent our experience: to express and develop ideas. We do this by using clauses. We could say that one way of thinking about a clause is that it expresses a single idea.

A sentence containing a single clause is often referred to as a simple sentence. A sentence containing two or more independent clauses joined by coordinating conjunctions such as *and*, *but*, *or*, and *so* is called a compound sentence. A sentence containing an independent clause and one or more dependent clauses is called a complex sentence. Clauses in a complex sentence are joined by subordinating conjunctions such as *after*, *although*, *as soon as*, *because*, *before*, *if*, *in order that*, *since*, *though*, *unless*, *until*, *when*, *while*.

See Chapter 2 for an outline of the Ideational function of language.

Expressing ideas using simple sentences

In representing a slice of experience, we use a clause. From this perspective, we can say that a clause represents a Process, the Participants in that Process, and any accompanying Circumstances.

These days,	many young people	drink	too much alcohol.
Circumstance	Participant	Process	Participant

simple sentence:
a sentence that consists of a single independent clause.

We can refer to a single, independent clause as a **simple sentence**. This doesn't necessarily mean that the content is simple. It means that the structure is relatively simple as there is only one clause.

Combining ideas using compound sentences

We can expand on an idea by linking it to another idea. In the following sentence, we have taken the original idea and developed it further by adding another clause and connecting the two with a conjunction.

The trees give shelter to animals	and	they provide them with food.
clause	conjunction	clause

compound sentence:
a sentence consisting of two or more independent clauses joined by a coordinating conjunction.

When we join clauses together in this way, they are called **compound sentences**. A compound sentence uses the following conjunctions:

1   *and, but, so, or*
2   as well as some less frequent ones such as *nor, for, yet, either … or.*

These are called **coordinating conjunctions** (or linkers). A compound sentence joins two or more **independent clauses** using coordinating conjunctions.

coordinating conjunction: a conjunction that joins two or more independent clauses to form a compound sentence (e.g. *and, but, so, or*).

Table 7.9   Compound sentences

Independent clause	Coordinating conjunction	Independent clause
The nectar ripens	*and*	*it becomes honey.*
Some animals live on the forest floor	*but*	*most animals live in the canopy.*
Binge drinkers might end up with brain damage	*or*	*they might even die.*
Animals are forced to stay in the same place	*so*	*overgrazing occurs.*

independent clause: a clause that is not dependent on another clause for its meaning. Sometimes called a main or principal clause.

Clause	Conjunction	Clause	Conjunction	Clause
Humans destroy vegetation	*and*	*they use inappropriate technologies*	*so*	*the desert continues to spread.*
Responsible drinking is relatively harmless	*but*	*binge drinking has negative consequences*	*and*	*it can ruin your life.*

Table 7.10   Coordinating conjunctions

Meaning	Coordinating conjunction	Example
Adding information	and	The branch decays *and* is decomposed through the activity of insects and micro-organisms.
Contrasting	but, yet	Desertification is a recognised problem *but* poor policy decisions increase the risk.
Indicating result	so	The cloud becomes heavy *so* the raindrops fall.
Indicating reason	for	Binge drinkers often have accidents, *for* their judgment is impaired.
Providing alternatives	or, either … or, neither … nor	*Either* they seek assistance, *or* their lives are significantly affected.

Have a go!

Here is a sorting activity to try out. Make up a number of compound sentences using a variety of coordinating conjunctions. Write them up on strips of cardboard using capital letters. Then cut up the sentences into the two clauses and the conjunctions, for example:

DROPLETS CAN FALL AS RAIN	OR	THEY CAN FALL AS SNOW.

Mix up all the clauses and put the conjunctions into a separate pile. See if you (or your students) can combine the clauses using an appropriate conjunction. (A similar activity can be done with complex sentences; see below.)

Contrary to popular belief, it is possible to use coordinating conjunctions to begin a sentence, as in this example from *The Hand That Feeds Me*:

The old guy was grazing too and at first he didn't notice me. *But* when he did, though I couldn't make out the words, he was obviously friendly. *And* then he threw me a piece of meat. (Lewin 1998)

Combining ideas using complex sentences

Complex sentences use a different set of conjunctions to combine ideas. These are called **subordinating conjunctions** (or binders), joining a **dependent clause** to an independent clause.

complex sentence: a sentence consisting of an independent clause and at least one dependent clause.

subordinating conjunction: joins a dependent clause to an independent clause (e.g. *when*, *because*, *unless*, *although*).

dependent clause: a clause that depends on another clause for its meaning. Sometimes called a subordinate clause.

Table 7.11   Subordinating conjunctions

Meaning	Subordinating conjunction	Example
Time (when?) point in time	after, before, when	*After* filling their sacs with these sweet juices, the field bees fly back to their beehive. Sometimes the water on the coast will drain away *before* the series of waves hits the shore. *When* it is ready, the honey is collected by the beekeeper.
at the same time	while, just as, as	*As* it approaches the coast, the leading wave of the tsunami is forced to slow down.
how long?	as long as, since, until	Binge drinkers often keep drinking *until* they are incapable of thinking clearly.
how often?	whenever	*Whenever* the field bees visit a flower, they suck out its nectar with their tongues.
Manner means (how?)	by, through, with	*By* decomposing dead leaves and branches, insects and micro-organisms help to enrich the soil.
comparison (like what?)	as if, as though, as, like	Binge drinkers behave *as though* they are invincible. This is made worse by bad policy decisions, *such as* encouraging frontier expansion. Binge drinkers put themselves in risky situations, *like* getting into a car with someone who has been drinking.
Cause reason	as, because, since, as a result of	*Because* it is very difficult to see a tsunami in the open ocean, it is hard to predict their arrival. The forest floor is dark and damp *as* it is heavily shaded by the levels above.
purpose	so that, in order to, so as to, in order that	Better policy decisions are needed *so that* desertification can be slowed.

Meaning	Subordinating conjunction	Example
Condition	if, as long as, in case, unless, on condition that	*Unless* urgent measures are taken, desertification will continue to spread. *If* the water is very deep, the speed of the tsunami will be faster.
Concession	although, even though, even if, while, whereas, despite, much as	*Although* natural factors such as weather and drought contribute to desertification, many of the causes are related to human actions. *While* it is difficult to regulate natural factors that contribute to desertification, human factors are within our control.
Adding	besides, as well as	The canopy offers shelter to a great variety of birds *as well as* providing them with food.
Replacing	except for, other than, instead of, rather than	*Rather than* moving around from place to place, animals stay in the same place.

Complex sentences typically (though not necessarily) involve higher-order thinking as students learn to express more subtle and intricate relationships between ideas. They are often used to convey the logical reasoning needed for explanation.

One way to test whether a sentence is compound or complex is to see whether the clauses can be reversed. In a compound sentence, the clauses cannot be reversed.

1   ✓ The nectar is sucked out by the field bees *and* it is stored in sacs within their bodies.

We couldn't reverse these two clauses and say:

2   ✗ *And* it is stored in sacs within their bodies, the nectar is sucked out by the field bees.

In a complex sentence, the clauses are usually able to be reversed.

3   ✓ *Because* there is now a hole in the canopy, the sunlight is able to reach the seedlings.

4   ✓ The sunlight is able to reach the seedlings *because* there is now a hole in the canopy.

Note that when the dependent clause is placed first, it is followed by a comma. When it is placed second, there is no comma.

Have a go!

See whether you can reverse the clauses in the sentences in the right-hand column of Table 7.11. What does this tell you? Does it always work?

Combining ideas using compound-complex sentences

When we combine an independent clause with two or more other clauses (independent and dependent), we have a compound-complex sentence, as in the following:

Dependent clause	Independent clause	Independent clause	
After filling their sacs with these sweet juices,	*the field bees fly back to their beehive*	*and the stored nectar is regurgitated into the mouths of house bees.*	

Have a go!

Identify whether the following sentences are compound, complex, or compound-complex. Explain how you made your decision. Discuss the kind of meaning/s created by combining the clauses (e.g. time, condition, reason). Hint: Look for the verb group to identify the clause, then look for the conjunction/s for the meaning.

	Compound	Complex	Compound-complex
When the honey is ready, it is collected by the beekeeper from the beehive and put into jars.			✓ meaning: time, addition
The nectar is sucked out by the field bees and is stored in sacs within their bodies.			
If the waves arrive in a bay or harbour, the water has nowhere to go.			
When you're drunk, you might put yourself in risky situations.			
As the evaporating water reaches colder temperatures, it cools and turns back into tiny water droplets.			
These days farmers are using fences and bores so the animals stay in the one place all the time.			
They destroy vegetation in arid regions, and they use inappropriate technologies and incorrect irrigation practices in arid areas.			

Non-finite clauses

You might have noticed that some of the dependent clauses have no subject and no indication of tense. These are called **non-finite clauses**. They are very common in complex and compound-complex sentences. They often aren't signalled by a conjunction.

Independent clause	Non-finite dependent clause
The waves pile up on top of the leading wave,	creating a huge wave with great power.

In the sentence above, 'creating a huge wave with great power' is a non-finite clause as there is no subject (e.g. they) or tense (e.g. past or present).

Non-finite clauses have an -*ing* form (as above), a *to*- form, and an -*ed* form, as below.

Independent clause	Non-finite dependent clause
The plants and animals in the system depend on each other	*to survive.*

Non-finite dependent clause	Independent clause
Stored in cells of the honeycomb,	*the nectar ripens over time.*

Here are some more examples.

Independent clause	Non-finite dependent clause
Sometimes the water on the coast will drain away,	*leaving the beach exposed.*

Dependent clause	Independent clause	Non-finite dependent clause
If the waves arrive in a bay or harbour,	*the water has nowhere to go,*	*causing them to be funnelled inland.*

Independent clause	Non-finite dependent clause
At each level of the rainforest, the components interact	*to keep the system in balance.*

> **non-finite clause:** a dependent clause that has no subject and is not marked for tense (e.g. *Crossing the road*, she was struck by a car).

Have a go!

Underline the non-finite clauses in the sentences below.

- Field bees fly from flower to flower collecting the sweet nectar from the flowers.
- After filling their sacs with these sweet juices, the field bees fly back to their beehive.
- The term 'tsunami' comes from the Japanese word for 'harbour wave', referring to the way that such waves can overwhelm an entire harbour.
- As a result of an undersea earthquake, for example, water is displaced, causing the water above the sea floor to rise up and producing a large ripple.
- They use inappropriate technologies and incorrect irrigation practices in arid areas causing salinisation.
- When you're drunk, you're more likely to put yourself in risky situations, like getting into a car with someone who has been drinking.
- At each level of the rainforest, the components interact to keep the system in balance.

Embedded clauses

embedded clause: a clause that is embedded inside a noun group (e.g. the first step *in making honey*; the bees *that guard the queen*).

In Chapter 4, we encountered embedded clauses as part of the noun group. These are a type of dependent clause, but they are embedded inside the noun group, so don't really have the status of 'ranking' clauses. They often begin with relative pronouns such as 'that', 'which' or 'who' (in which case, they are often called relative clauses), though these pronouns (and other words) are often omitted (e.g. I can't stand *the cat ~~that is~~ making all that noise*).

Here are some examples from the texts in this chapter. The embedded clause has been placed in double brackets. The noun group is italicised.

- More than 16 per cent of 20–29-year-old females drink at *levels [[that increase their risk of long-term alcohol-related harm]]*.
- Another reason for desertification is the cultivation of marginal lands, i.e. *lands [[on which there is a high risk of crop failure and a very low economic return]]*.
- *The first step [[in making honey]]* begins when field bees fly from flower to flower collecting the sweet nectar from the flowers.

Embedded clauses can do other jobs, but here we are just interested in their role within the noun group, telling us more about the head noun.

Have a go!

Put double square brackets around the embedded clauses in the noun groups in italics below:

- Honey is *a sweet, thick sugary solution made by bees*.
- Tsunamis are *a series of massive waves that are caused by a sudden and tremendous undersea movement*.
- The term 'tsunami' comes from the Japanese word for 'harbour wave', referring to *the way that such waves can overwhelm an entire harbour*.
- The canopy refers to *the dense ceiling of leaves and tree branches shading the forest floor*.
- Desertification is *the process that turns productive land into non-productive desert as a result of poor land management*.
- When you're drunk, you're more likely to put yourself in risky situations, such as getting into a car with *someone who has been drinking*.
- Desertification occurs mainly in *semi-arid areas bordering on deserts*.
- The term 'binge drinking' generally refers to consuming large quantities of alcohol with *the intention of becoming intoxicated*.

Sometimes a noun group can contain more than one embedded clause.

- The branch might contain *seeds [[that are nourished by the soil // and grow into seedlings]]*.

Verbless clauses

It is possible to have a clause with no verb—though usually you can infer the verb. These are sometimes called 'sentence fragments'. They are usually found in literary texts, as in this example from *The Hand That Feeds Me*:

- It never ceases to amaze me the quantity of food that human beings throw away. Especially in warm weather.

Have a go!

Go back to look at *The Hand That Feeds Me* in Chapter 4 (page 94) and see how many verbless clauses you can find.

FOCUS ON FIELD: STRATEGIES FOR TEACHING AND ASSESSING

We teach students about combining clauses not simply because compound and complex sentences are often items in assessment tasks. More importantly, we combine clauses in various ways to create different kinds of relationships between ideas. Students are able to combine clauses in the spoken mode before they enter school. The teacher's job is not to start from scratch but to extend students' capacity to make increasingly complex meanings.

Think carefully about why you might teach students about combining clauses. Are they developmentally ready? Do they know what a clause is? What benefit will they get from an explicit knowledge about different ways of connecting ideas through combined clauses? What will it enable them to do?

See Chapters 2 and 4 to revise how we use clauses to express ideas.

Share with students examples of poorly constructed sentences (e.g. choppy, rambling, consisting only of a dependent clause, incorrectly punctuated) and see if they can suggest improvements.

Introduce students to the notion of combining clauses by providing them with a number of independent clauses written on strips of cardboard along with a collection of coordinating conjunctions (*and*, *but*, *or*, *so*). Demonstrate how to choose two clauses and join them with a conjunction, then ask students to come up and do the same. This can be done with the whole class or in groups. (It is an ideal activity for the interactive whiteboard if you have access to one.)

Make it slightly more complex by seeing if they can combine three independent clauses using coordinating conjunctions. You might even get them to notice that combining too many clauses in this way makes a text sound spoken and a bit clumsy. You could show them how to compact a string of clauses into a single clause, e.g.:

I have a friend
and his name is Joey   ⟶   I have *a 10-year-old friend called Joey who likes*
and he is 10 years old   *skateboarding.*
and he likes skateboarding

Notice how we have used the information in the clauses to build up a long noun group (italics), which is more typical of written language.

For more advanced students, give them a collection of independent clauses and a collection of dependent clauses beginning with subordinating conjunctions. See if they can combine them to make complex sentences.

Get them to notice whether they can reverse the clauses and to think about what effect it has to put the dependent clause at the beginning or end of the sentence.

See if they can combine more than two clauses.

Now give them some non-finite clauses and see whether they can use these to create complex sentences, again seeing whether the dependent clause can come first or last.

As you read various types of texts with the class, get them to identify sentences that combine clauses in different ways and to think about the kinds of meanings being created (e.g. cause, time, concession, contrast). Ask them also to identify effective simple sentences.

In literary texts, see if students can notice how authors carefully craft their sentences and often play around with the expected structure. Older students might even be able to notice a particular author's style in constructing sentences (e.g. how compound-complex sentences are used by writers such as Jane Austen, Herman Melville, and Henry James).

Get students to notice how compound, complex, and compound-complex sentences are punctuated, including the use of commas, semicolons, colons, and dashes. (You might need to consult a punctuation guide to refresh your memory of punctuation conventions.) Demonstrate how poor punctuation can make reading difficult and how good punctuation can enhance comprehension.

Monitor students' reading by asking questions to probe whether they understand the relationship between ideas (particularly the more challenging meanings created by conjunctions such as *although, unless, since, if*).

Monitor students' writing to observe whether they are using appropriate and effective combinations of clauses and extending their potential to create higher-order meanings.

CHAPTER SUMMARY

In this chapter we have examined how language is used to explain how something works or why something happens. We have looked at the major genres for explaining in the school curriculum: sequential explanations, causal explanations, cyclical explanations, system explanations, factorial explanations, and consequential explanations. We have described their stages and phases, and the language features that are typical of explanation texts, focusing in particular on the language resources for sequencing in time and for expressing cause and effect. We looked in some detail at how to combine clauses to form compound, complex, and compound-complex sentences.

FOR FURTHER DISCUSSION

1   Explanations are required in all areas of the curriculum. Fill in the boxes below, giving as many examples as you can of explanations in the selected curriculum areas (though not each box needs to be filled). One has been done for you.

	Science	Geography	History	Technologies
Sequential				
Causal				
Cyclical				
System	the respiratory system			
Factorial				
Consequential				

2   Go on the internet and try to find some explanations relating to the topics you named above. Use these as the beginning of a database of texts that you will be able to use later on. Will you need to modify the texts to suit a particular age group or to provide a clear model of the particular type of explanation?

3   How will your knowledge about the language features of explanations help you in selecting texts, modifying them, modelling how they are organised and their characteristic language patterns, and assessing students' writing? At what point/s in the curriculum cycle might you focus on the language of explanations?

REFERENCE

Lewin, M.Z. (1998). The Hand That Feeds Me. In *Rover's Tales.* New York: St Martin's Press.

WEBSITES

How Stuff Works

http://science.howstuffworks.com/nature/natural-disasters/volcano-explorer-game.htm

> There are many sites that provide animated explanations of scientific and natural phenomena. How Stuff Works, for example, has this explanation of a volcano erupting (Inside a Volcano).

YouTube

> There are many explanations available on YouTube as well, such as animated explanations of the digestive system.

Text Structure and Grammar

www.schools.nsw.edu.au/media/downloads/schoolsweb/studentsupport/programs/lrngdificulties/writespellsec5.pdf

> A resource from the NSW State Literacy and Numeracy Plan that deals with a number of matters canvassed in this chapter.

LANGUAGE FOR PERSUADING OTHERS

This chapter explores the language used for persuading. Learning to argue a point, to persuade someone to act and to recognise how texts position us to think and act in particular ways are important aspects of the school curriculum as well as life outside school. In this chapter we explore the key persuasive resources—the genres and language features—learners will develop as they advance through the compulsory years of schooling.

Learning objectives

In this chapter you will:

- become familiar with the genres for persuading or arguing and how they are structured to achieve their purposes
- consider how students learn to read and write persuasive texts across the years of schooling
- learn about the major language resources for arguing
- explore some curriculum contexts for persuasion
- acquire knowledge of some useful classroom strategies for teaching the language of persuasion.

Key terms and concepts

genres for arguing (expositions, discussions, challenges)

Mood system (imperatives, declaratives, interrogatives)

speech function system

Graduation

Engagement (attribution)

modality

text opener

paragraph opener

sentence opener

text connectives

Activities:

polarised debate

modality cline

INTRODUCTION

We admire political leaders who are able to persuade large numbers of individual citizens to act or believe in a particular cause or vision, as US President Obama has done. The following is an extract from a speech he delivered at the memorial service for the victims of a street shooting incident, in which six people were killed, including 9-year-old Christina Taylor Green.

> Imagine—imagine for a moment, here was a young girl who was just becoming aware of our democracy; just beginning to understand the obligations of citizenship; just starting to glimpse the fact that some day she, too, might play a part in shaping her nation's future. She had been elected to her student council. She saw public service as something exciting and hopeful. She was off to meet her congresswoman, someone she was sure was good and important and might be a role model. She saw all this through the eyes of a child, undimmed by the cynicism or vitriol that we adults all too often just take for granted.
>
> I want to live up to her expectations. I want our democracy to be as good as Christina imagined it. I want America to be as good as she imagined it. All of us—we should do everything we can to make sure this country lives up to our children's expectations.

Barack Obama, Memorial Service for the Victims of the Shooting in Tucson, Arizona, 12 January 2011

The tragedy occurred at a time of disenchantment and escalating extremism in American social and political life. Obama's purpose in the speech is probably twofold: to help American people make sense of this terrible event and to take charge of the divisive public discourse. At the time, the speech was widely held to have helped unify the country and to have changed the nature of political discourse. The speech achieves its purpose chiefly through a range of language choices commonly associated with successful rhetoric. A small sample of these evident in the extract above include appeals to empathy through the use of personal narrative as in the case of Christina and other victims, repetition (*Imagine—imagine*; *I want … I want … I want*), and construction of common goals through the use of plural personal pronouns (*our democracy, our children's*).

President Obama is an outstanding communicator who possesses an array of persuasive language skills. Most of us will not require such skills but we must all learn to deal with different points of view in family and community life as we go about living in a democracy. Stating an opinion, arguing a position, and negotiating an outcome are important aspects of life whether we are trying to improve the local streetscape, writing an expository essay, seeking permission to go to a party, or refuting a parking fine. Recognising how we can be influenced by the persuasive techniques of others is also an important skill to acquire if we are to be truly informed citizens.

Think about it

Consider the recent occasions at university, at work, at home, or in the community where you have engaged with persuasive texts. Someone may have tried to persuade you to a particular action or point of view or you may have attempted to convince another person of your argument. How effective were these attempts? What was the outcome and how did it affect you and others? What techniques were used? Why were some attempts more successful than others?

In the school curriculum, the genres most commonly associated with persuasive purposes are argumentative texts: expositions, discussions, challenges, and debates. In this chapter we examine these kinds of texts in detail to see how they are structured to meet their purposes and what language features are typically found in each.

Table 8.1   Genres for persuading: Arguing and responding

Genre	Social purpose	Sample curriculum contexts
Hortatory exposition	To persuade people to act in a particular way	Plastic bags should be banned Unflued gas heaters in schools Junk food in canteens Save our forests Water—a precious resource
Analytical exposition	To persuade people to a particular point of view	Should we welcome refugees? Raising the legal drinking age to 21 Sports stars as role models
Discussion	To discuss two or more sides of an issue	Superfoods — saving first world lives or disastrous for developing countries? Nuclear power—for and against
Challenge	To rebut a position on an issue	Graffiti is art of and for the people A response to the black armband view of Australian history

genres for arguing: genres used to argue a case, discuss an issue, or challenge a position (e.g. expositions, discussions, challenges).

GENRES FOR ARGUING

Persuasive texts can be found across the curriculum areas in a variety of **genres for arguing**. Students are expected to engage with spoken and written arguments around topics that vary in complexity and familiarity. Argument texts differ from the story genres and explanations discussed in previous chapters; they are structured around logical reasoning in support of a point of view or perspective rather than around time and events and their causes.

In learning to construct and interpret arguments, students learn to do the following things with language:

- express a point of view
- identify the issue and the writer's perspective in a text
- give reasons and evidence
- express positive and negative comments
- evaluate evidence provided by others
- say what is probable and what is usual
- say what should happen and what can happen
- adjust the intensity of their argument
- recognise the strengths and weaknesses in others' arguments
- craft a logical argument using textual evidence
- discuss how the audience can be positioned by the writer.

Expositions are an important example of argumentative genres. There are two forms of expositions: hortatory and analytical. *Hortatory expositions* (persuading to) put forward a point of view usually with the aim of persuading the audience to a particular line of action or belief. President Obama's speech is an example of this genre. In school, hortatory expositions may take the form of a letter to the editor to argue for more funding for public schools, a short documentary on endangered species, an anti-smoking poster, or a campaign speech for school captain. *Analytical expositions* (persuading that) adopt a position with respect to an issue or idea and provide evidence in support of that position. This genre is commonly found as essays in which writers are required to take up a stance on a particular topic, and then argue a case based on evidence (e.g. The Enduring Spirit of the ANZACs). Many students also encounter this kind of exposition in the assignments they write at university.

A hortatory exposition typically has the following structure.

- Statement of Position
  - issue and background information
  - appeal
  - preview of arguments (optional).
- Arguments
  - point
  - elaboration.
- Reiteration of appeal.

The text in Table 8.2 is an example of a hortatory exposition written by a Year 9 student following class discussions about the topic. The stages and phases of the text are identified. As you will notice, the text unfolds in a similar but not identical way to the pattern described above. For example, the student has presented the phases of the position statement in a different order. He has also included a summary of his arguments in the closing paragraph.

An *analytical exposition* is structured similarly, usually with the exception of the recommendation for action. The text in Table 8.5 on page 254 is an example of an analytical exposition. An analytical exposition typically has the following structure:

- Statement of position
  - issue and background information
  - thesis or position
  - preview of arguments (optional).
- Arguments
  - point
  - elaboration.

Table 8.2 *Should We Pay for Plastic Bags?*: A hortatory exposition

Stages and *phases*	
	Should We Pay for Plastic Bags?
Position statement *Issue* *Appeal* *Preview of arguments*	Plastic bags are disastrous for the environment. According to experts from Clean Up Australia, Australians are using over six million bags a year, part of the one trillion used annually in the world. People should pay for the plastic bags they use for their shopping. Making people pay for these plastic bags would encourage them to use reusable bags so that they don't have to keep on paying, and then the environment will benefit. Plastic bags might be cheaper initially but they do not last as long as the reusable bags. In the end, it is much more economical to buy the green bags. And as we all know, people love saving money.
Argument 1 *Point* *Elaboration*	Most plastic bags last in the environment for well over a few hundred years, even up to a thousand! Plastic bags are extremely deadly to wildlife, hurting, maiming, and, in most cases, killing animals on land and especially in the ocean. According to statistics, plastic bags were the most commonly collected items of rubbish in and around waterways and beaches on the recent Clean Up Australia Day. Unlike paper and other compostable materials, plastic simply does not break down in the environment.
Argument 2 *Point* *Elaboration*	When a plastic bag is made, poisonous and dangerous gases and other harmful by-products are produced. Air pollution results and with it come things such as acid rain; health problems for workers and those living close to plastic factories follow. The fewer bags we use, the less air pollution is made and the whole environment is better off.
Reiteration of appeal *Summarising argument* *Repetition of position*	We need to reduce the number of bags in not just our community, but also in the whole of Australia and even the whole world. We can achieve this by making people pay for the bags. Some will argue that such a fee is unfair but we all know that if people pay for something they will become more conscious of its cost. People will eventually move to reusable bags and this will make the whole of Australia a better place to live. Therefore, we need to make people pay for the bags they use. For the better of Australia.

Discussions present information about an issue from two or more perspectives, usually coming down in favour of one side based on the weight of evidence. Oral discussions often take the form of debates and classroom discussions. Students engage with discussions when they research topical issues (e.g. climate change, coal seam gas), study various levels of government, watch current affairs programs, follow popular social media sites, and participate in school politics.

A discussion in the primary school literacy classroom usually comprises a statement of the issue, then a consideration of different sides of the argument before a summarising recommendation. In secondary school, students are often expected to foreground points of the argument rather than positions in their discussion texts. A discussion typically has the following structure:

- Issue.
- Position A
  - points
  - evidence
  - identification and rebuttal of opposing positions.
- Position B
  - points
  - evidence
  - identification and rebuttal of opposing positions.
- Recommendation.

Table 8.3 *Is Graffiti Vandalism?* A discussion (a spoken presentation)

Stages and *phases*	
Issue	*Is Graffiti Vandalism?*
Background *Preview of stance*	Our class has been discussing the issue of graffiti. It is a hot topic in our school as our school fences are frequently covered in graffiti. So too are some of the fences in the streets of our suburb. There are also a number of graffiti-style artworks around the school and suburb that make our community a more attractive place. We think there is a difference between simply tagging and graffiti art.
Position A *Point 1* *Rebuttal* *Evidence* *Point 2* *Evidence*	Tagging is vandalism. It is simply someone putting their initials or name on somewhere to own it or to say 'I was here'. This cannot be called art because there is nothing attractive about it. The tags on the school fence spoil the look of the school. Further, when people try to tag in dangerous places, they run the risk of harming themselves or others. We often see these accidents on the television news.

(continued)

Table 8.3   *Is Graffiti Vandalism?* A discussion (a spoken presentation) *(continued)*

Stages and *phases*	
Position B *Point 1* *Evidence* *Point 2* *Evidence*	On the other hand, graffiti art is an artform. Graffiti art is not mindless; it usually has a message or story. The one on the neighbourhood centre, for example, celebrates our multicultural community. It is not a spontaneous act by vandals but something planned and carefully done as if our city walls and streets were canvases. Banksy's work is beautiful and original and now being shown in art galleries around the world.
Recommendation	In conclusion, let's all be clear about what kind of graffiti is vandalism and what kind is art. We urge people to stop vandalising the fences with their unimaginative tags. We also think it is time that serious attention be paid to helping more of these people become more imaginative and creative with their aerosols.

Formal debates are structured in a similar way to discussions, the important difference being that speakers in debates do not make a final recommendation. The preparation and drafting of texts for formal debates are similar to those of written discussions.

Challenges aim to argue against an accepted position, rebutting existing arguments and providing counterclaims. A challenge text usually describes the issue and the position that is to be argued against, and then systematically dismantles it through a series of counterarguments. The typical structure is:

1   Position

2   Rebuttal.

Challenges are complex texts for students and are more usually found in the senior secondary years where students will study them as the speeches of political activism and sometimes produce them as extended projects requiring extensive research and critical reflection on topics such as 'Breaker Morant: Patriot or murderer?' and 'Welcome to the death throes of journalism'.

Have a go!

Locate a copy of Noel Pearson's 1996 speech 'An Australian History for Us All'. It was studied as part of the New South Wales senior secondary English syllabus until 2008.

It is an example of a challenge, delivered at a time of considerable political debate over the historical experiences of Aboriginal Australians and their consequences. Pearson's purpose is to challenge the dominant conservative media and politicians.

As you read, try to identify the Position and the Rebuttal stages. Note that before these stages, Pearson's text has an Orientation stage in which he introduces the topic of the speech and establishes his credentials for choosing the stance he takes. How does knowledge of these stages assist you to understand the complexity of Pearson's text?

Think about it

What experience have you had with writing argumentative texts? How successful were you? What was difficult? What was easy? What topics were involved? What do you know about the functions, structures, and phases of these texts? How did you learn to write argumentative texts?

Locate the website of the learning support unit at your university and examine the resources available for helping students to write successful essays (i.e. analytical expositions). Note how the authors of those resources describe these texts. How do they describe the structure of the essay? Can you recognise the stages and phases? Are they labelled in similar ways to above? How might you use the information above and the resources you found in your own academic writing?

DEVELOPING CONTROL OVER ARGUMENTS

Students engage with increasingly complex argumentative texts about topics that become more abstract as they progress through the compulsory years of schooling. Students in the very early school years learn to argue by giving their opinions in brief spoken, written, and multimodal texts. They express simple likes and dislikes about familiar topics such as activities, food, and games. They are encouraged to give reasons for their opinions such as 'I like to go to the beach because …' and 'Everyone should wear hats because …'. Teachers assist by reading simple models of arguments, pointing out one or two obvious aspects of structure, such as the title and opinion or words such as 'favourite', 'should', and 'because'. Sometimes these are published texts; at other times the teacher and the students jointly construct them. Throughout, the emphasis is on class discussion about topics linked to curriculum areas such as Health and Personal Development, Science, and English.

These early opinion texts develop into simple arguments about familiar ideas and other topics that are jointly researched by the class. Teachers and students read brief argument texts and identify the issue, the writer's general stance with respect to the issue, and focus on how information is organised into chunks. Teachers continue to show students how to craft effective texts by jointly constructing models of the genre. Student writers at this stage show an awareness of how texts are structured to achieve their purposes.

From mid-primary onwards, emphasis shifts from the personal expression of opinion to a more impersonal, less subjective stance. Students begin to argue with justification so that the emphasis is on making a point and elaborating this with evidence. Opportunities to interact in productive small-group discussions are an important part of learning to compose lengthy written arguments later. Students also participate in debates, identifying different sides of an issue and weighing up the relative merits of evidence.

In later primary and early secondary school, students engage with more complex topics that require research. Teachers demonstrate how to construct sustained arguments using students' prior knowledge of the genre. Students construct independent arguments that become more complex. Attention is paid to how texts are structured clearly and logically through a range of language choices. Throughout this process, teachers and students examine models of argumentative texts from a range of community and institutional settings. They consider how these texts function inside and outside the classroom, identifying such factors as intended audiences and the kinds of persuasive techniques appropriate to the audience. Students in secondary school explore and develop letters to the editor on complex social issues, formal debates, essays, and speeches, showing increasingly sophisticated awareness of language choices. Importantly, older students must learn to rebut arguments as part of being able to take a critical stance.

Think about it

Have you observed teachers and students working with argumentative genres in your recent school experiences? What activities were evident? Did you notice explicit talk about the text? What kind of language was used? What are the benefits of having a shared language?

Have a go!

We described the stages of the teaching-learning cycle in Chapter 3.

Locate a number of examples of different kinds of argument texts suitable for use in the classroom, such as pamphlets, posters, advertising material, letters, and websites. Identify what is common about these texts in terms of structure, language features, and layout. Identify what is different. How might you use these texts to draw students' attention to the typical structure and language features of this genre in the classroom? What stage of the teaching-learning cycle is this activity most pertinent to?

WHAT ARE THE MAJOR LANGUAGE RESOURCES FOR ARGUING?

As students become increasingly accomplished with negotiating the genres of persuasion, they must also gain control over the language features of arguing and responding in a range of situations. Writers must express and elaborate ideas about a particular topic or issue clearly, engage and convince readers, and create a coherent text that makes sense in that situation.

Expressing and elaborating ideas: Developing control of field-related meanings

The following list summarises the language features that are important in persuading. Many of these features will be familiar from earlier chapters. Others are explained in more detail in the sections below and in later chapters.

- Generalised Participants ('Plastic bags can last in the environment for up to 1000 years'; 'Action must be taken to preserve endangered species')
- Processes:
  - sensing verbs, particularly thinking and feeling/wanting to express opinion and reaction ('I *believe* …'; 'I *consider* …'; 'I *like* …')
  - relating verbs, including '*is*' substitutes ('This *results* in …'; 'The large hand *symbolises* authority …')
- Complex noun groups ('the Grattan Institute's 2014 report into wealth across generations'; 'in light of such convincing evidence')
- Nominalisation where an idea or event usually represented by a verb group is transformed to a 'thing' represented by a noun group ('the residents' reaction …' rather than 'the residents tore up their rates notices and marched to the council offices').

> We introduced Participants and Processes—key language resources for expressing experiential meaning—in Chapter 2 and again in Chapters 4 and 5.

> Nominalisation is a process whereby an idea or event (represented by a clause or clauses) is transformed to a 'thing' (represented by a noun group). Nominalisation is often a feature of academic text and is discussed at length in Chapter 10.

Interacting with and convincing the reader: Developing control of tenor-related meanings

In this section we examine how interpersonal meanings contribute to persuading.

Figure 8.1   Choices from the language system involved in persuasion

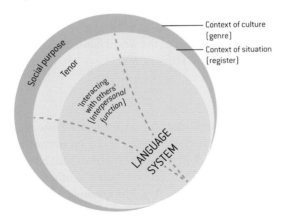

- Use of the **Mood system** to interact in dialogue and with readers
  - use of rhetorical questions as 'hooks' (Can you imagine your child walking around with a gun? Are you tired of sore feet or aching legs?)
  - use of commands to exhort the reader/viewer to action (Act now and save this magnificent species! See it before March 31st!)

> **Mood system:** the grammatical resources for making statements, asking questions, giving commands, and making offers.

*In Chapter 2
we introduced
language
for enacting
interpersonal
meanings such
as expressing
attitudes, for
adjusting the
strength and focus
of arguments, and
for expanding
and contracting
arguments.*

– use of a range of speech functions to participate productively in oral discussions (e.g. statements to initiate discussion: 'In my opinion …'; questions to encourage others to participate: 'What do you think, Luke?', 'Can you give me an example?'; commands to ensure order: 'Stay on task').

- Expressing attitudes (Attitude)
  – expressing feelings ('I am saddened by …')
  – evaluating qualities ('a convincing argument', 'the evidence is unequivocal')
  – judging people and behaviour ('Keeping children in detention is cruel', 'Those flat earthers who dismiss climate change …').
- Engaging with other voices, possibilities, and perspectives (Engagement)
  – attribution or reference to other individuals, statistics or research ('Some believe …', 'According to experts from Clean Up Australia …', 'Jones (2005) …')
  – modality in order to temper arguments ('It could be considered …', 'There is every likelihood that …')
  – aligning with audience ('As you imagine …', 'of course', 'naturally')
  – countering or challenging an alternative idea ('While it may be considered …', 'Although …')
  – negatives ('Animals should not be kept in cages').
- Adjusting the strength and focus of arguments (Graduation)
  – increasing and decreasing force ('I am extremely concerned …', 'Plastic bags last for a very long time')
  – sharpening and blurring focus ('Since 1980, the population of the world has increased by almost 30%', 'Residents have been lobbying for about 20 years now').

Mood and speech function

Persuasive language, because it involves negotiation between the speaker/writer and the listener/reader, is concerned with interpersonal meanings. The Mood system is the major grammatical resource for interacting in English. The basic Mood choices of imperatives (*Look at that hair!*), interrogatives (*Will you look at that hair?*) and declaratives (*We saw his hair the other day*) enable speakers and writers to interact for a range of different purposes. For example, if I want someone to do something, the most obvious Mood choice is an imperative (*Get a hair cut!*). However, such directness might not always work. I can use an interrogative (*Will you get your hair cut?*) or a declarative (*You need a hair cut*), both of which are less confrontational and more likely to achieve my purpose in most social settings. Such flexibility is captured in the closely related system of **speech function** where the relevant language features are commands, questions, statements, and offers.

The following table captures the relationship between speech function and Mood choices.

speech functions: a variety of language resources for interacting; they include resources for seeking information (questions), providing information (statements), asking someone to do or provide something (commands) and offering or giving something (offers).

*We introduced the
Mood system in
Chapter 2.*

Table 8.4   Different ways of interacting

Purpose of interacting	Speech function	Possible Mood choices
To get something done	Command	Imperative (*Get a hair cut!*) Interrogative (*Would you please get your hair cut?*) Declarative (*Your hair could do with a cut.*)
To give information	Statement	Declarative (*Sue is a great hairdresser.*)
To ask for information	Question	Interrogative (*Do you know a good hairdresser?*)
To offer something or to offer to do something	Offer	Interrogative (*Can I suggest a good hairdresser?*) Imperative (*Hey, check out my hairdresser's website.*) Declarative (*Here's my hairdresser's phone number.*)

Persuasive texts—particularly advertisements, public campaigns, and hortatory expositions—often feature a range of different speech functions as they endeavour to persuade readers and viewers to act in particular ways.

Similarly, because spoken discussions around issues of interest to the students are useful for preparing students to write persuasive texts, they are also good opportunities for students to learn about different ways of interacting and to consider the effects of different speech function choices. Talking about these language choices is a necessary part of supporting students to develop the metalinguistic understandings described in the current English curriculum. For example, students in Year 1 develop understandings 'that there are different ways of asking for information, making offers, and giving commands' (ACARA 2015). From here, students go on to learn about how effective discussion relies on successful cooperation with others through identifying and using language patterns for initiating a topic, building on others' comments, asking questions, disagreeing and encouraging others. In such activities, the students are using many of the language choices associated with building arguments (cause and effect, clarifying, adding information, etc.). Later, they will come to understand how language can both include and exclude by identifying language choices that align a listener/reader (*of course, obviously*) and include others by using pronouns (ACARA 2015).

However, the flexibility of the speech function system indicated in Table 8.4 can cause problems for students who may be unfamiliar with less direct uses of English. For example, EALD students may not recognise that an expression such as 'Would you like to pack up now?' is actually an indirect way of giving a command. Similarly, many students will not be experienced with using a full range of speech functions in group discussions, and thus they will need to be the focus of explicit instruction.

Have a go!

Identify the speech function choices in the text below. Are they direct or indirect? (Hint: consider the Mood choices.) How do these choices shape the relationship between the writer and the reader?

The Wollongong Herald

Marathon

Challenge yourself and join thousands of runners in the 10th annual Wollongong Herald Marathon. Crave the pursuit of 25 km through the Illawarra's most iconic sights. Push your mental and physical limits to the ultimate test. Are you up to it? Last year there were over 5000 runners from around the nation and overseas. This year we expect more so the competition will be tough!

Join us on Sunday April 1. Enter now. Claim the Run!

Now look through the persuasive texts you collected earlier. Can you identify a range of speech functions in the texts? Are these speech function choices direct or indirect? Do some texts favour some choices over others? Why?

Appraisal

We introduced the Appraisal system in Chapter 2 and develop it further in Chapter 9.

Persuasive language involves attitudes and opinions, making judgments, and exploring the perspectives of others. In reading persuasive texts, students will need to recognise how writers attempt to position them in particular ways through their interpersonal meaning choices. The *Appraisal system* describes the language resources for expressing attitudes, engaging listeners and readers, and adjusting the strength of our feelings and opinions. Of these, the latter two are particularly important to successful arguments. In arguing, students will need to express opinions with subtlety and with credibility. They will also need to manage a range of sources in order to use evidence in their arguments, to introduce other perspectives, and to lead the reader/listener along a carefully constructed line of argument.

Engagement: using language to engage with others or with alternative perspectives and possibilities.

Engaging with other voices, possibilities, and perspectives

Another important set of language resources for responding and arguing are those for engaging our listeners and readers (known as **Engagement**). We do this by introducing other points of view and voices, varying the spaces for negotiation and entertaining other possibilities. Attribution and modality are commonly used resources for achieving this.

attribution: the introduction of other perspectives into a text by explicitly referring to what others say or think about the topic.

Attribution

The term **attribution** refers to the introduction of other perspectives into a text by explicitly referring to what others say or think about the topic. Attribution can take the form of quoting others directly. For example, 'Lewin (1952, p. 169) has claimed, 'There is nothing so practical as a good theory''. Or it may report on what was written or said: 'Jones argues that primary teachers work as hard as their secondary colleagues.' Quoting and reporting are referred to as *projection*, which is another way of combining clauses. For example:

Projecting clause	Idea
Jones argues	that primary teachers work as hard as their secondary colleagues.

Projecting clause	Direct quote
Lewin has claimed,	'there is nothing so practical as a good theory'.

Projecting clauses include saying verbs: some that report information (Jones *argues* …, Lewin *has claimed*, Derewianka *points out*) and others that evaluate the idea or quote in some way (Abbott *claims* …, The World Bank *contends* …). Students will benefit from being shown a variety of saying verbs and discussing the range of meanings they construe as well as being encouraged to take up their use in their own writing.

We examined clause combination in Chapter 7.

Have a go!

Complete the following table as you work through your readings and construct your assignments. You'll find it useful for your own reference but you will also be able to transform it into a wall chart of saying verbs for your students as you read and construct model texts with them.

Saying verb	Meaning	Example
state	To present information as a fact	Keegal (2014) states that just three literacy projects were funded in 2016.
explain	To tell why or how something occurs	Martin (2009) explained what happens in the course of developing curriculum support materials.
argue	To present one side of an issue	Jones (2012) argues that despite their enthusiasm, teachers' knowledge about language is insufficient for new curriculum.
suggest		
point out		
conclude		
reveal		
imply		

As Derewianka (2011, p. 98) points out, students should be encouraged to discuss issues such as when it is appropriate to quote someone, how to select particular authorities to quote, how quoting can be used to add weight to an argument, how to cite the work of others, and how to paraphrase.

Have a go!

Read the paragraph below from an essay on scaffolding. Identify the language items through which voices or perspectives of individuals or sources other than the writer are introduced into the paragraph (hint: they are not always other writers). Note how they are introduced (hint: look for saying verbs, projecting clauses, pronouns). What contribution do these language resources make to the effectiveness of the writing?

Our understandings of scaffolding grow out of research into language and the role of language in learning. Bruner was influenced by Vygotsky, a psychologist working in post revolutionary Russia. Vygotsky sought to explain the influence of culture on the human mind. He argued that cognitive development is a result of learning which takes place in interaction with others in activities that are significant in the culture into which the child is being socialised (1986, p.98). This idea of learning preceding development was in contrast to Piagetian theory that argued learning takes place as a result of development. Vygotsky proposed the concept of the Zone of Proximal Development (ZPD) to describe the distance between what a learner can do by herself/himself and what s/he can do with the assistance of others (Love, Pidgon, Baker & Hamston, 2005, unit IB screen 36). Scaffolding is concerned with this mediating role of the adult or more expert other.

Attribution is particularly important for argument texts where evidence is carefully built from citations of reputable sources such as expert comment, research, and statistics. Secondary teachers will need to spend some time evaluating citation sources with students, assisting them to research widely and to locate authoritative sources. Students in primary school learn to record a range of information sources and begin to paraphrase and to take notes. Paraphrasing is also important to writing responses where students must summarise and describe the work under focus.

Modality

modality: language resources for expressing the degree of commitment, ranging from low (*maybe, might*) to high (*must, should*).

Modality is another important means by which persuasive texts can be opened up to other possibilities. In short, modality refers to the distance between yes and no; it is sometimes termed 'wriggle room' and can be expressed in varying degrees from low to high. For example, 'They may die in captivity' → 'They will probably die in captivity' → 'It seems likely they will die in captivity' → 'They will certainly die in captivity'.

Modality is expressed via a range of language resources, including modal auxiliaries.

Low	Medium	High
may, might, could, would	will, should, can, need to	must, shall, ought to, has to
'He could be angry'	'It will be acceptable'	'It must be right'
'Domesticated animals might die in the wilderness.'	'We need to care for sick animals.'	'Animals ought to be well cared for.'

Modality is also expressed through modal adjuncts:

Low	Medium	High
possibly, perhaps, maybe, arguably	probably, presumably, in all probability, apparently	definitely, absolutely, certainly, surely, undoubtedly
'Perhaps the animals died in captivity.'	'The animals probably died in captivity.'	'The animals undoubtedly died in captivity.'

Other grammatical resources through which modality is expressed include:

- nouns such as *possibility, probability, obligation, requirement*, for example 'It's a possibility that those who do graffiti are artists …'
- adjectives such as *possible, probable, obligatory, necessary*, for example 'That's a possible solution.'
- sensing processes such as *I think/reckon, bet, suppose, guess, imagine*, for example 'I imagine the animals would die if they are let loose in the wild.'

The choices writers make in terms of modality will either invite interaction with the readers or listeners or close it down. There will, though, be times when writers want to close down the spaces for dialogue with the reader, perhaps when setting up their position or making a summing-up argument. Young learners will often pick up obvious forms of modality quickly; more subtle uses can take time to acquire.

Think about it

Examine one of your recent assignments for your own use of attribution and modality. What do students need to know about these areas in order to write successfully in educational settings? How does university differ from high school?

Adjusting arguments

Graduation: using language to adjust the strength and focus of our utterances.

Writers can adjust the strengths and focus of their attitudes by using **Graduation**. The sentence 'Plastic bags are deadly to wildlife', for example, can be boosted by adding an intensifier, 'Plastic bags are *extremely* deadly to wildlife', or downplayed by using a different lexical item, 'Plastic bags are *dangerous* to wildlife'.

Graduation refers to two ways of adjusting our attitudes and opinions: force and focus. We grade our attitudes and opinions by using force and blur categories by using focus. These are useful language strategies for developing effective persuasive texts.

Force can be adjusted by intensifiers such as *terribly, extremely, utterly, absolutely, very, less, scarcely, somewhat, virtually, most, simply,* etc. These resources assist writers to drive home their point. Consider what they contribute in the following sentences: 'Unlike paper and other compostable materials, plastic simply does not break down in the environment.' The force of an argument can also be altered by changing the vocabulary item itself as we have seen above in the use of 'dangerous' instead of 'deadly'. Another example of this has become an accepted technical classification: *vulnerable—threatened—endangered—extinct*.

We can sharpen or soften the focus of our statements too, for example 'Take advantage of the *genuine* savings now!', 'The prospect of a very fast train from here to the city has created a *real* sense of optimism among the residents'.

Have a go!

The following sentences appeared in undergraduate essays.

'Oral language plays an incredibly important role.'

'Talking is an exceptionally important feature of language and this has been extensively recognised by many researchers.'

- What can you say about the use of Graduation resources?
- Adjust the Graduation used. What is the effect?
- What advice would you give these students about expressing their opinions or attitudes in analytical expositions?

FOCUS ON THE INTERPERSONAL: STRATEGIES FOR TEACHING AND ASSESSING

There are a number of strategies for teaching about the interpersonal language resources relevant to successful persuasion that can be adapted for use with students of different ages.

- Discussion cards can be used to foster students' participation in small-group discussions and to develop awareness of different ways of asking for information, seeking clarification, extending others' contributions, and disagreeing with others. For example, in a group discussion, students can be dealt three cards such as those shown below. During the discussion they should play all three cards, using one of the choices on the cards as most appropriate to the topic and stage of the discussion.

- Provide students with a range of persuasive texts suitable for classroom use. Ask the students to identify the interpersonal language they have in common. Make lists of what they always/usually/sometimes have.
- Vocabulary clines are useful to show relative strengths and weaknesses of expressions. A cline might focus on force through vocabulary such as *loved, liked, loathed, adored, hated, abhorred*, or it might focus on modal auxiliaries such as *might, may, should, must*, and *will*. Teachers should make sure there is a phrase or sentence to act as a scaffold for the students' contributions, for example 'I ... the book' or 'I ... make my bed'.
- Use cloze passages with modal words deleted and discuss different meanings made possible with different substitutions.
- Provide students with a 'closed text' (that is, one that has no attribution), perhaps one you have written yourself. Together, revise this to include other perspectives. Reflect on the effectiveness of each text.
- Demonstrate a range of ways to alter the modality of a text during joint constructions. Discuss the effects of these choices with students.
- Examine a number of published texts for a specific language feature, such as attribution. Record the type of attribution (statistics, general, specific, authoritative) and the publication

type (pamphlets, news stories, essays). Discuss the relationship between source and type of attribution.

- Collect and display a list of ways to introduce alternative points of view, including saying and thinking verbs to quote and report ('It is often *claimed* that …', 'He *said* …', 'She is *considered* among one of our finest artists yet many patrons are unaware of how many buildings are adorned with her street art'), nominalisations of these saying and thinking verbs ('It is our belief that …', 'That statement …'), and Circumstances of angle such as ('*According to Halliday* …', 'It is, *in our opinion*, a lot of rubbish').

In the classroom

Modality in Year 2–3

Louise teaches a combined Year 2–3 class. At the beginning of the school year, she wanted to get to know her students a little better and to consider with them the features of a positive, productive classroom environment. This was part of their human society and its environment topic of 'Needs and Wants', a topic that required students to state opinions and preferences as well as listen to those of others. Because of this, it was a suitable context for teaching students how to give opinions with some evidence and for learning about modality. The following sequence of activities describes how Louise went about doing this.

LESSON 1: BUILDING UP FIELD AND MODELLING THE LANGUAGE FOCUS

Engaging the students

Louise began by showing students images of three different teachers. The images were selected to suggest teachers who could be described as severe, friendly, and disorganised. Their purpose was to prompt student discussion of different teachers they knew. Together Louise and the children discussed the teachers represented and what their classrooms might be like.

Teaching about text

Louise then introduced some statements, such as 'We might get this finished before lunch' and 'You will finish these before lunch'. Students matched these to the images of different teachers. Then Louise highlighted the modality in the statements and discussed the effects of different modal auxiliaries, for example the difference between 'We must get this finished before lunch' and 'We might get this finished before lunch'. Together Louise and the students listed different modal auxiliaries on the whiteboard, such as, *will, may, might, should*, etc. Students then constructed their own statements for the different teachers by completing individual worksheets with cartoon-like images and speech bubbles.

LESSON 2: DEVELOPING THE FIELD AND LEARNING TO EXPRESS OPINIONS

Building the field further

In the following lesson, Louise displayed a number of images of different classrooms. These were selected to portray classroom environments that emphasised different aspects of student experience, such as a technology-rich classroom, an obviously artistic classroom, a traditional classroom, etc. Together Louise and the students discussed the classrooms represented. Students were encouraged to identify their preferred classroom and to give some evidence: 'I like this classroom because …'.

Justifying a position

Polarised debate

Louise drew a line in chalk on the floor of the classroom and labelled the ends with a ☺ and a ☹ so as to draw the children into a **polarised debate**. She selected one classroom picture and asked several students to take up a position on the line according to how they felt about the classroom. Each was encouraged to say why they did so in an attempt to persuade the others to join them on their position on the line. This proved challenging for the students but was nevertheless a useful strategy to demonstrate the range of opinions individuals have and that the justification or evidence can often sway people's opinions. For young children, it is also a powerful visual representation of different opinions.

Louise then showed a number of cardboard strips displaying statements with the modality highlighted in a different colour, for example 'I *must* be in this classroom', 'I *might* like this classroom' and 'I *probably would* like this classroom'—a **modality cline**. She also introduced an outsized cline on the classroom wall and identified the ends as 'strong' and 'weak'. The children then completed an individual worksheet on a large sheet of paper, cutting and pasting classroom images on a version of the cline according to how their opinions rated. As they did so, Louise moved around the classroom encouraging students to justify their opinions.

LESSON 3: FOCUS ON THE LANGUAGE OF MODALITY

Ordering modal auxiliaries

Louise briefly revisited the previous lesson's work using the classroom wall cline. She then introduced a number of coloured cards displaying modal auxiliaries. Together she and the children placed these on the cline according to whether they were considered weak, medium, or strong expressions of modality. Throughout this phase of the lesson, reference was made to the effects of different degrees of modality, for example 'Does that mean you have to do it?', and 'Does that leave any wriggle room?', and occasionally, 'Who might say that?'.

polarised debate: students take up a position on a line according to how they feel about an issue. Some students take turns to argue a position, while others are able to move if they are persuaded in a different direction. This is a key strategy for encouraging students to understand the importance of using evidence and other persuasive techniques.

modality cline: A continuum demonstrating relative strengths of different forms of modality (e.g. from *might/possibly* through to *must/definitely*).

The students were then given a list of modal auxiliaries to cut, sort, and paste onto the worksheets from the previous day. As they did so, Louise moved around encouraging the students to use the words in a sentence orally.

Joint construction

We described the joint construction stage of the teaching-learning cycle in Chapter 3.

This lesson concluded with a joint construction of a text entitled 'Our classroom', which comprised a number of sentences describing the kind of classroom collectively desired. Louise used prompts such as 'What must our classroom be like?' 'What might it have?', and 'What will it probably have?' As she did so her questions encouraged the children's use of modality. She was also able to shape the text according to her purpose. The completed text resembled this:

Our classroom

Our classroom should be a happy place to work.

We should learn in our classroom.

We must try to listen and respect each other in our classroom.

It probably should have lots of books and computers.

It may have some science and art equipment.

We might be able to play games here sometimes.

LESSON 4: INDIVIDUAL CONSTRUCTION OF TEXT

Justifying wants

In the final lesson, Louise returned to the issue of students' preferences for different kinds of classroom environments. Displaying the images of classrooms, she and the students discussed and described each. As students nominated their preferred classrooms, she prompted them for reasons and noted these under each so that each image was displayed with several reasons. Again, students were encouraged to support their opinions: 'I like the technology-rich classroom because I enjoy playing computer games'.

Introducing modal adjuncts

Louise then returned to the cline on the classroom wall and added modal adjuncts such as *definitely*, *probably, possibly*, etc. These were presented in a different-coloured card to distinguish them from the modal auxiliaries. Together she and the students orally constructed statements such as 'I definitely have to be in the artistic classroom because it looks like fun'. She also encouraged them to think of alternatives such as 'I would like to be in an artistic classroom but I would probably learn more in a traditional classroom'. This phase became an oral rehearsal for the individual written texts that students then constructed. As they did so, Louise encouraged them to use the words on the cline and other displayed texts to assist them.

While the written texts were necessarily brief, Louise was pleased with her students' accomplishments. Her goal was to encourage them to express their opinions and to give reasons, and in this she was successful. In order to do so, she had to give them access to the language resources through which this is accomplished. These language resources will continue to develop as students progress through schooling and encounter arguments and responses of increased complexity and abstraction.

Think about it

Examine the description of the lessons above and identify the various forms of scaffolding used. Think about the support Louise has built into the lessons in her planning (the designed-in scaffolding). What resources has she prepared? How does this set up situations for her to scaffold the students through their talk? Find points at which she explicitly teaches the students about the relationship between meaning and language.

We looked at types of scaffolding in Chapter 3.

CREATING COHERENT AND LOGICAL TEXTS: DEVELOPING CONTROL OF MODE-RELATED MEANINGS

In this section we look at a number of language features of persuasive texts that are important for creating cohesive texts.

- Text organisation
  - text openers
  - paragraph openers
  - sentence openers.
- Text connectives, which signpost the writer's developing argument (*First, On the other hand, Furthermore, To summarise*).
- Vocabulary is often abstract ('*Honesty* is important because …' , 'While both sides make *plausible points* …').
- Abstract terms, which often summarise a stretch of argument (such *actions*, the *main factors*, the *following arguments*).
- Reference, including pronouns, that summarises whole stretches of information ('As a consequence of *these* factors …').

We introduced key language resources for creating cohesive texts under the umbrella of textual meanings in Chapter 2. Reference is discussed in Chapter 5.

Organising information: Text, paragraph, and sentence

As students begin to write longer texts in the form of reviews and arguments, they need to gain control over information at the level of text, paragraph, and sentence.

Text openers

Argument texts, as we have seen, usually tell the reader how the text will develop in the position statement. The exposition in Table 8.5 was written by a Year 4 student in response to classroom discussions.

text opener: provides an overview of the text, guiding the reader by signalling its organisation and often the main themes or ideas. There is usually a relationship with paragraph openers in the remainder of the text.

Have a go!

Label the stages and phases of Table 8.5. You may need to refer to the information earlier in the chapter. Which language features can you identify? Think about interpersonal meanings (Mood, Graduation, attribution).

Table 8.5   *Guns aren't fun!* An analytical exposition

Stages and *phases*	*Guns aren't fun!*
	Guns have caused a lot of discussion in our school and community lately. People who are normally trying to stop these things sometimes talk to the government; however, the government doesn't always agree with them. I think guns should be banned **because children may get their hands on them and they are dangerous to people and to wildlife.**
	Can you imagine your child walking around with a gun? *The gun specialists are the people who make guns. They never agree with the government. They think if a child walks in and wants a gun they should give a gun to them.*
	About 50 000 people are accidentally killed by guns every year. *Children lose their parents and caregivers and need to be looked after by their grandparents. Honestly, think about what it would feel like to have your parent shot by a criminal.*
	A lot of our endangered species of animals are killed because of guns. *Also, guns are the reason why our animals are becoming extinct. Imagine all of our animals becoming extinct and we all will have to survive by eating trees.*
	So believe me, a lot of people think that guns aren't fun!!!

Our main purpose here is to examine how the information in the text is organised. In the first paragraph of her text, the student presents a preview of her argument in the sentence 'I think guns should be banned *because children may get their hands on them and they are dangerous to people and to wildlife*'. This is the text opener (sometimes called the *macroTheme*) and is an important signpost for the reader as it reveals what her arguments will be and the order in which they will unfold. Each of her subsequent paragraphs picks up on these three arguments: the problems of children getting access to guns ('I think guns should be banned because children may get their hands on them and they are dangerous to people and to wildlife'), the accidental killing of individuals ('About 50 000 people are accidently killed by guns every year'), and the danger to wildlife ('A lot of our endangered species of animals are killed because of guns').

Expositions and challenges typically feature text openers similar to that above. The text openers in discussions will usually provide a preview of the different perspectives on the issue.

Paragraph openers

Students must learn to organise arguments and responses into bundles of related information.

Paragraph openers in arguments must do two tasks. They must introduce a new argument and link back to the overarching argument or thesis of the writer. The writer of the exposition about guns examined above does this successfully. She previews her argument as we have seen above, and then proceeds in subsequent paragraphs to discuss the ways in which those elements are expressed in the texts. Each paragraph begins with a topic sentence or paragraph opener that links back to the text opener. In this way, the close relationship between the writer's thesis and the arguments through which the case is built is evident.

The paragraph openers or topic sentences (sometimes referred to as *hyperThemes*) are then elaborated through a number of sentences that may illustrate, explain, list, describe, or qualify the idea introduced in the paragraph opener. Paragraphs often conclude with a sentence that links to the following paragraph in some way.

Sentence openers

The **sentence opener** or Theme refers to the beginning of the sentence (more technically, the clause). The beginnings of the sentence are important for focusing the reader's attention on the developing argument or position.

The writer may, for example, choose to focus on the key points in an argument by using connectives such as 'First, there is the possibility that children may get their hands on guns'. In another example, the writer can opt for a direct appeal by inviting the reader to consider 'Can you imagine your child walking around with a gun?'

We have also seen how nominalisation enables the writer to change the focus of the message: 'When plastic bags are made ...' → 'The production of toxic gases ...'

And evidence can be foregrounded by including attribution as a sentence opener: '*According to experts from Clean Up Australia*, Australians use over six billion plastic bags each year.'

Think about it

Examine one of your recent university assignments for the patterns you have used for text openers, paragraph openers, and sentence openers. Can you improve your choices? Consider how knowledge of the genre and its conventions can assist students to monitor their organisation of arguments and responses.

---

paragraph opener (or topic sentence): occurs at the start of a paragraph and indicates its main idea. This idea is usually elaborated in various ways in the remainder of the paragraph. There is generally a close relationship to the text opener.

---

sentence opener: the starting point that gives prominence to the message, focusing attention on how the topic is being developed and enabling the reader to predict how the text will unfold.

We introduced Theme in Chapter 2.

Text connectives

Text connectives are signposts for the reader. They signal how the argument is developing and how different sentences and stretches of text are linked. In time-structured genres such as narratives, recounts, and instructions, text connectives are usually to do with linking events in time. In genres that are organised around ideas, and particularly arguments, they are more likely to do with reasoning and serve to sequence ideas, add information, clarify, etc. For example, in the following extract from a primary student's exposition arguing that children should not be able to pick their own teacher, *First* is used to signal the first argument and to introduce the point. *Also* is used to add extra information to the point about the problems of separating friends into different classes.

> *First*, if some child wants to be in a different class to his or her class that child will be left by themself. If a child gets left by themself they might start to feel lonely, and then when they go to recess or lunch they will not want to go sit with the others. *Also*, if a child makes a new friend, if the child and friend sit together at recess and lunch, the other friend might get jealous.

Table 8.6   Common text connectives and their functions

Clarifying	Cause/effect	Time	
for example	therefore	next	
in particular	then	then	
in other words	because of this	later	
namely	consequently	until then	
that is	as a result	previously	
to illustrate	for that reason	hitherto	
as a matter of fact	accordingly	then	
I mean	in that case	lastly	
Sequencing ideas	**Adding information**	**Condition/concession**	
firstly, first	in addition	on the other hand	
secondly, second, etc.	furthermore	otherwise	
in short	above all	if not	
to begin	likewise	on the contrary	
for a start	moreover	nevertheless	
at this point	similarly	instead	
finally	likewise	despite this	
to conclude	also	besides	

Students need to gain control over a range of text connectives in order to construct and interpret persuasive genres. They will need to understand the differences between their use in spoken and written arguments; connectives such as *and* and *but*, for example, are more frequently used in spoken texts than in written texts. Teachers will need to explicitly point out the differences in constructing written texts. They will also need to assist students to recognise the different meanings associated with particular words and phrases, such as the difference between connectives that add information (*also, and*) and those that introduce counter-arguments (*on the other hand, nevertheless*).

In Chapter 7, we examined how ideas or clauses are combined to form complex and compound sentences through the use of conjunctions. In this chapter, we have looked at how chunks of text are connected. It is important to point out to students that these conjunctions and text connectives signal particular kinds of meanings, such as those to do with adding ideas, cause and effect, time, contrast, and so on. Learning to recognise such meanings and to select conjunctions and connectives with precision are important skills in building effective and logical arguments in texts. The following chart was developed with an upper primary class who were examining how thoughts can be organised to form sentences and to link arguments across longer stretches of text.

Table 8.7   Connecting ideas through conjunctions and text connectives

	Coordinating conjunctions (creating compound sentences)	Subordinating conjunctions (creating complex sentences)	Text connectives (connecting sentences and stretches of text)
Addition	and	besides, as well as	in addition, also, apart from that, moreover, furthermore, and besides
Time Point in time Extent in time Frequency		after, before, when, just as, as, as long as, since, until, while, whenever, every time	then, just then, previously, after that, up till then, earlier, later, next, afterwards, after this, at once, soon, after a while, meanwhile, at this moment
Causality	so, for	because, since, so that, as, as a result of, in order to, so as	therefore, as a consequence, as a result, for that reason, because of this, consequently
Contrast/ concession	but/yet	although, though, even though, whereas, while, even if, despite, much as	however, by contrast, nevertheless, on the contrary, despite this, instead, on the one hand/on the other hand

(continued)

Table 8.7   Connecting ideas through conjunctions and text connectives *(continued)*

	Coordinating conjunctions (creating compound sentences)	Subordinating conjunctions (creating complex sentences)	Text connectives (connecting sentences and stretches of text)
Alternatives/ replacing	or, neither … nor	except for, other than, instead of, rather than	alternatively, or else, otherwise, on the other hand, instead, apart from that, except for that
Condition		if, as long as, in case, unless, on condition that, whether	in that case, if not
Sequencing ideas			in the first place, first of all, firstly, secondly, thirdly, in short, in summary, to summarise, briefly, in conclusion, to conclude, finally, in light of the above points
Clarifying			in other words, for example, in particular, that is
Manner/ comparison		by, through, as if, as though, like, as	likewise, similarly, in the same way

For further information about text connectives in a range of genres see Derewianka (2011), Humphrey, Love, and Droga (2011) and Humphrey, Droga, and Feez (2012).

Think about it

Return to your university essay and this time identify the text connectives you have used. How well have you made these choices? What kind of relationships are they signalling? How might your argument be strengthened by revisiting these connectives?

FOCUS ON TEXT ORGANISATION: STRATEGIES FOR TEACHING AND ASSESSING

Teachers draw learners' attention to how texts are organised by using a variety of strategies:

- Give students highlighters and provide them with models of effective arguments. Ask them to highlight the text openers, paragraph openers, and sentence openers, and in another colour show the links between these, using arrows to indicate links that point backwards and those that point forward. Encourage students to do the same with their own drafts.

- Give students practice at organising information for arguments. Provide them with paragraph openers or topic sentences on one set of cardboard strips and elaborating sentences on another set and ask them to match the elaborating sentences to the topic sentences. Different-coloured cards encourage students to notice the different functions of each sentence. This may be a group activity or a whole-class activity with an interactive whiteboard, tablet computer, or other mobile device.

- Provide students with paragraphs and ask them to identify the main idea or argument in the paragraph opener and the function of each of the subsequent sentences in the paragraph.

- Provide students with texts that have either the paragraph openers or the sentence openers removed. Ask them to construct suitable substitutes.

- Have students compare the sentence openers in different genres, such as information reports and expositions. Discuss the differences and explain why they are different with reference to their function.

- Provide students with sentence openers on one set of strips and the remainder of the sentence on another. Ask students to match them and read them to each other.

- Construct cloze passages, deleting the text connectives, and have students complete the passage. Discuss the functions of their choices.

- Jointly construct lists of text connectives for classroom display using shared texts. Organise them into their functions.

- Play the game 'Which text connective am I?' Give students clues and have them identify the text connective, for example *I am a text connective that clarifies. I am made up of three words. The first word is 'in'.* Encourage students to refer to the classroom chart for clues. Students can also be encouraged to write their own sets of clues.

CHAPTER SUMMARY

In this chapter we have identified the major genres for arguing in the school curriculum and described their structures and phases as well as how they become increasingly more complex and demanding over the years of schooling. We have introduced relevant interpersonal language features including Mood and speech function (for negotiating with listeners and readers), Engagement (attribution and modality for managing different perspectives) and Graduation (for adjusting opinions). An 'In the classroom' case study also described how one group of learners in a combined Year 2–3 were introduced to the concept of modality. The chapter also dealt with text organisation, knowledge of how persuasive texts are organised at the whole-text, paragraph, and sentence levels, and the relationship between these levels as a key resource for managing persuasive texts.

FOR FURTHER DISCUSSION

1 Survey the school-aged people you know about the issues that matter to them. Try to gather responses from various age groups. From this make a list of topics suitable for teaching argumentative texts in either early primary, middle to late primary, or early secondary contexts. Think about the curriculum contexts for such topics and try to link them with topics and tasks from these subjects.

2 How confident are you with respect to the language features discussed in this chapter? What do you need to know in order to teach these to students in your classes? How will you develop your knowledge?

3 Who has the responsibility for teaching students about arguing? How should primary teachers prepare students for high school? Who has responsibility once students arrive in secondary schools? Why?

4 Locate the NAPLAN marking guide for persuasive writing (www.nap.edu.au) and examine the criteria listed for persuasive texts. How confident are you with these criteria in terms of your own knowledge about language? What steps will you take to ensure you are equipped to prepare students for these tests?

REFERENCES

Australian Curriculum Assessment and Reporting Authority (ACARA). (2015). *The Australian Curriculum: English, version 8.1*. Sydney: ACARA.

Derewianka, B. (2011). *A New Grammar Companion for Teachers*. Sydney: PETAA.

Humphrey, S., Love, K., & Droga, L. (2011). *Working Grammar: An introduction for secondary English teachers*. Melbourne: Pearson.

Humphrey, S., Droga, L., & Feez, S. (2012). *Grammar and Meaning*. Sydney: PETAA.

Lewin, K. (1952). *Field Theory in Social Science: Selected theoretical papers by Kurt Lewin*. London: Tavistock.

Obama, B. (2011). Memorial Service for the Victims of the Shooting in Tucson, Arizona, 12 January

Pearson, N. (1996). An Australian History for Us All. Address to the Chancellor's Club Dinner, University of Western Sydney. In New South Wales Board of Studies (2000), *HSC English Prescriptions 2009–2014: Advanced Speeches*. Sydney: New South Wales Board of Studies.

WEBSITES

Australian Human Rights Commission: Face the facts
www.humanrights.gov.au

> The website for the Australian Human Rights Commission includes significant speeches, media releases, policy, and publications. The Commission regularly publishes *Face the Facts*, which contains accurate and accessible information relating to Indigenous peoples, migrants, refugees, and asylum seekers. The website provides useful teacher resources, including background readings, activities, and worksheets to support this information.

International Reading Association, and the National Council of Teachers of English: Readwritethink
www.readwritethink.org

> *Readwritethink* is a website dedicated to providing free resources to support K–12 teachers' literacy programs. These include interactives such as the persuasion map, which assists students to plan expository texts, worksheets such as the checklist for student self-evaluation, and lesson plans that cover both literary and factual texts from a range of media. Although the site is oriented towards teachers working in the USA, its resources are readily adaptable to other settings.

GetUp! Action for Australia
www.getup.org.au

> GetUp! is a community-based advocacy organisation that encourages individuals to become involved in issues of current concern. It provides a model for examining how social and political activism can operate and the forms of texts through which this occurs. The website also provides background information in a range of media suitable for developing students' field knowledge on current issues, such as refugees and asylum seekers, marriage equality, climate action, and coal seam gas.

NSW Department of Education and Training: Racism No Way: Anti-racism education for Australian schools
www.racismnoway.com.au

> The Racism No Way website has been developed to support anti-racism education. It provides accurate information regarding diversity, rights, and responsibilities to teachers and students as well as a large number of ongoing activities and good-quality resources.

LANGUAGE FOR RESPONDING

This chapter explores the language used for responding; that is, for analysing, interpreting, and evaluating. While the focus is on learning to respond to literary texts, responding is also an important part of Visual Arts and Drama as students engage with artworks, performances, and scripts. In this chapter we explore the key resources for analysing, interpreting, and evaluating literary texts—the genres and language features—that learners will develop as they advance through the compulsory years of schooling.

Learning objectives

In this chapter, you will:

- become familiar with genres for responding and how they are structured to achieve their purposes
- consider how students learn to read and write response texts over the years of schooling
- learn about the major language resources for responding
- explore some curriculum contexts for responding
- acquire knowledge of some useful classroom strategies for teaching the language of response.

Key terms and concepts

Genres for responding (personal responses, reviews, interpretations, critical responses)

Attitude (Affect, Judgment, Appreciation)

INTRODUCTION

When students respond to texts and other cultural media, they are required to analyse the elements of the text, to present their opinions and interpretations, and support these with convincing evidence from the text itself and from sources outside the text. The genres through which they do so include personal responses, reviews, interpretation, and critical responses.

Table 9.1   Genres for responding

Responding		
Personal response	To respond to a work in a personal way	My favourite movie *The Wiggles*
Review	To assess the value of a work	Reviews of books, films, games
Interpretation	To interpret messages in a work, usually a literary text or artform	What is the message of *The Book Thief*? Tragic elements in the works of William Shakespeare and related works
Critical response	To analyse and evaluate the themes, ideas, or messages in a work	Tarantino's film *Kill Bill*: a feminist manifesto?

GENRES FOR RESPONDING

Response genres function differently from the argumentative genres discussed in Chapter 8 in that their purpose is to describe, interpret, and often evaluate a work. However, learning to respond and evaluate places similar demands on students' language skills and understandings to what argument texts do. Many of the language features of persuasive texts are relevant to response genres. As students gain control of response genres, they must learn to:

- express a point of view
- give reasons and evidence (usually by providing an analysis or interpretation of the work and with reference to its qualities)
- express positive and negative comments
- adjust the intensity of their argument
- discuss the positioning of the audience
- build a logical argument.

genres for responding: genres used to respond to a work such as a literary text (e.g. personal responses, reviews, interpretation, critical responses).

Personal responses, which require students to react to a text or artform, are often triggered by teachers asking such questions as 'Did you like it? Why?' and 'Who was your favourite character?' They have a very simple structure:

1   summary or description (optional)

2   opinion/reaction.

The text in Table 9.2 is an example of a personal response to a book written by a student in Year 3. In the summary stage, this young student identifies the field of the text and briefly summarises its events, making a brief comment on the outcome. He concludes with his opinion of the book and a brief justification.

Table 9.2   *Fire:* A personal response

Stages and *phases*	
Title Description/summary Identifies field Events Comment	*Fire*, written by Dawn McMillan This book is about fire. At night a boy was in bed. He was worried. He looked in his mum's bedroom, but she was asleep. So he gently tapped her. She slowly woke up. The boy's dog was angry. The dog was barking over Mrs Brown's fence. He saw that there was a fire. Mum called the fire man/ladies. The boy got the dog and his brother Danny. He got Mrs Brown as well. The fire people put the fire out. Luckily none of them didn't get hurt or burnt.
Opinion	I thought my book was good because if you're deaf there are some actions that means there a fire somewhere.

Source: Lewis 2011

Reviews are an important way for students to demonstrate their knowledge of a text they have read or an artform they have seen in preparation for the more sophisticated responses required later in secondary school. Reviews summarise aspects of the work and evaluate these with reference to accepted conventions. A typical structure of a review is:

1   Context

2   Description

3   Evaluation.

This pattern is reflected in the Year 6 student's review in Table 9.3. The opening stage comprises two phases: a background giving details of the author and type of text, and a brief synopsis of the characters and events. It also leaves no doubt as to how the young writer feels about the book. The writer then describes three elements of the text—the plot, setting, and characters—demonstrating not only that he understands these are important elements of a story but also that he is able to organise his review around them. The final stage is a mixture of evaluation or judgment interspersed with some further information about the writer's style.

Table 9.3 Review of *Bridge to Terabithia*

Stages and *phases*	
Title	Review of the novel *Bridge to Terabithia*
Context *Background* *Type of work*	This novel, *Bridge to Terabithia*, is a passionate story written by an enthusiastic author, Katherine Paterson. The emotional story is based on a true story. The story is a fiction text about Jesse and Leslie who make an imaginary world, Terabithia.
Description of elements *Plot* *Setting* *Characters*	The plot is Jesse wants to be the fastest runner in 4th and 5th grades but is beaten by Leslie Burke who is a new girl who lives next to Jesse. They become great friends and make an imaginary place on a dried up creek bed called Terabithia. The setting on *Bridge to Terabithia* is in the middle states of USA. It is occasionally located at Terabithia, which is an island in a creek bed. The cubby is made of building scraps. The main characters in *Bridge to Terabithia* are Jesse and Leslie. Some other characters are the students at school, the teachers and Jesse's family. Jesse is artistic and he is proud of it. But his family isn't. He is also friendly and caring to his friends. Leslie is a tomboy and she is fast and rich but is very modest about it. They are excellent characters.
Evaluation *Opinion*	The book *Bridge to Terabithia* is written in the third person style. It is simple and straightforward. It is written in an old American English and spoken with a southern American drawl.

Source: Lewis 2011

Importantly, the student was assisted to organise his review in this way by the planning worksheet provided by the teacher. The worksheet included headings relating to the stages and phases of a review text, for example introduction (details of book, author, type of novel), plot, setting, characters, and style. This is an example of designed-in scaffolding.

We described designed-in and interactional scaffolding in Chapter 3.

Have a go!

Annotate the text overleaf, by a Year 7 student, with the stages typically found in reviews. What do you notice about the relationship between the stages and paragraphs? Can you identify any phases similar to those in Table 9.3? How might knowledge of these smaller 'chunks' of text assist you to scaffold your students as they learn to read and write reviews?

Stages and *phases*	
	Boy Overboard is a moving fictional novel written by the witty and popular Morris Gleitzman. The book was first published and became public in 2002. This gripping novel about a brother and his sister and their big dreams will surely keep you on the edge of your seat.
	In this moving tale, Jamal and his family live happily in one of the million villages in Afghanistan. But when the evil government find out Jamal's mother's secret school, the family are forced to desperately flee for their lives. They're going down under. Way down under. The story is set in a war-torn village in Afghanistan and then travels to the Pacific Ocean. On the way to Australia Jamal and BiBi meat Omar and Rashida. This is a well paced story and is told in first person by Jamal. Children can easily understand the language that is used. The moral of this story is always have hope.
	Boy Overboard will be loved by children of all ages. Some words may have to be looked up in the dictionary. This book is hard to put down and will always be keeping you in suspense. This book has believable characters and will teach you the lesson of always having hope and faith. I highly recommend this book for children aged 9–12 years old.

Source: http://boyoverboardteamb.blogspot.com.au

Interpretations require students to identify the themes or major ideas of a text or artwork and respond to its values. In doing so, students justify their interpretation by selectively referring to those elements that support their reading. In a sense, the textual references become the evidence to support the students' stance with respect to the theme. Students are often required to interpret more than one work in an interpretation; for example, they may respond to more than one related text dealing with a particular theme, genre, or issue or they may be asked to interpret several works from one artist. Interpretations are common in secondary school where they are typically found in the curriculum areas of English, visual arts, drama, and dance. The typical structure of an interpretation is:

1   Theme identification and preview of elements

2   Element evaluation

3   Theme reiteration.

Table 9.4 presents an interpretation produced by a Year 10 student in response to a task requiring students to explore how the themes of murder, deceit, betrayal, and revenge were treated in three texts, one of which was to be the set text, *Julius Caesar* (from which the themes were derived). The students could choose how they wished to present their assignment; some chose written essays, others PowerPoint presentations. The text here is the script for a speech presented by the student. Ridley Scott's film *Gladiator* and Bob Dylan's song 'Hurricane' were the related texts and the speech was accompanied by a still image from the film and a brief audio recorded extract from the song.

Table 9.4   Year 10 Interpretation (a speech)

Stages and *phases*	
Theme identification *Introduction to focus texts*	**Murder, Betrayal, Deceit, Revenge**. These so-called sins are as common in our stories or narratives now as they were in the 16th Century. Their continuity is evident in the play *Julius Caesar* by William Shakespeare, Ridley Scott's film *Gladiator* and Bob Dylan's song 'Hurricane'.
Preview of elements *Element and text 1* *Element and text 2* *Element and text 3*	What I hope to demonstrate to you is that in all three of these texts from very different periods of time, murder is intertwined with betrayal, deceit and revenge. These are the ingredients of tragedy. In *Julius Caesar* the murder of Caesar by the conspirators—Brutus and Cassius—is also the act of betrayal. In *Gladiator*, murder sets off a chain of events revolving around more murder and revenge as Maximus goes from general to slave and from slave to gladiator. The ballad 'Hurricane' tells the story of Ruben Carter, a boxer who was imprisoned by a crooked vengeful police officer for a murder he did not commit in the 1970s.
Element evaluation *Analysis of Murder in text 1* *Analysis of Murder in text 2* *Analysis of Murder in text 3* *Analysis of Deceit in text 3* *…* *Analysis of Betrayal in text 1* *…* *Analysis of Revenge in text 2* *…*	In Shakespeare's text, Caesar is murdered because he is a danger to democracy, thus setting off further murders. For example the death of Cinna the poet, killed in a case of mistaken identity. Murder is central to the film *Gladiator*. It begins with the murder of Marcus Aurelius, the attempted murder of Maximus our gladiator hero and the subsequent murder of his innocent wife and son. These murders set off Maximus' path of revenge. The story of 'Hurricane' begins with ordinary citizens being murdered in a bar. Deceit may lead to murder or may be an outcome of murder. For example in 'Hurricane', police falsified evidence to convict Ruben Carter and continued to deceive throughout a number of appeals in front of all white juries. … Another tragic element common to the texts is betrayal. Caesar believes Brutus is a close friend even though he's unaware Brutus is conspiring to kill him. In Scott's text, Caesar's failure to disclose Rome's rightful successor can also be seen as betrayal—betraying his father's wish for Rome's future. … Revenge too can be carried out by heroes as well as villains. Maximus set forth on a trail of revenge for the murder of Marcus Aurelius and his wife and son, yet the viewers are sympathetic and feel as though his revenge is justified. In this image the character played by Russell Crowe is shown middle distance, suggesting that we're not allowed to become as emotionally attached to him. …

Stages and *phases*	
Theme reiteration *Summary of analysis* *Reaffirmation of the evaluation*	To summarise, these tragic elements occur in different patterns. In the play, the acts of deceit and betrayal ultimately lead up to the murder of Caesar (act 3, scene 1). There is a pattern of deceit leading to murder leading to betrayal resulting in revenge, war and suicide. In *Gladiator* the pattern is: Betrayal plus deceit leads to murder leads to revenge leading to more murder (and so on). In 'Hurricane' the plot unfolds as a result of revenge then murder leading to deceit and betrayal. Although Shakespeare and Scott are dealing with the same historical settings for their texts, the three texts were composed in very different contexts—Shakespeare wrote *Julius Caesar* in the 16th century, Ridley Scott and Bob Dylan's texts are from the latter half of the 20th century. Those elements of drama are just as relevant to our stories now as they were in Shakespeare's day, they make us want to keep watching and reading to see how the tragedy unfolds and whether all will be well at the end.

Critical responses extend the interpretation genre by challenging the messages in a work. In writing a critical response, students must first identify the ideology behind the work in order to challenge it, and then deconstruct the elements through which the message or ideas are represented. Critical responses are highly valued in school yet are particularly difficult texts for students to produce because challenging a work's message usually requires them to read against dominant or conventional readings of it. For this reason they are typically found in late junior and senior high school, often in the form of major projects. The purpose of the critical response is reflected in the following typical structure:

1   Evaluation

2   Deconstruction

3   Challenge.

Space prevents us from presenting an example of a critical response here; they are explained more fully in Martin and Rose (2008), Christie and Derewianka (2008), and Humphrey, Love, and Droga (2011).

Think about it

Which of the response genres do you recall writing in school? How successful were you? How did you learn to write them? What might you as a teacher do to prepare your students to write response genres?

DEVELOPING CONTROL OF RESPONSE GENRES

It is important to note that learning to respond is a continuum from early personal responses that become reviews in the middle years to more complex interpretations and critical responses in secondary school. This is different from development in learning to argue because expositions feature throughout schooling, albeit with varying complexity and abstraction.

In the early years, students provide brief emotional responses to texts (including characters) and performances and are increasingly encouraged to give some extra details such as title and writer or artist. These responses are initially spoken but soon become multimodal as students are asked to respond by drawing as well as writing. Young learners are encouraged to give a reason for their opinions, for example 'My favourite character is the mouse because …'. Teachers explicitly model reviews for students, drawing their attention to aspects of the work such as characters or composition elements.

Learning to summarise events and to describe artworks succinctly are important steps in the middle primary years. Students begin to assess elements of a range of different works and to provide recommendations for particular audiences. Teacher and students jointly construct reviews about a shared book or artwork before students are expected to construct a review independently. By the end of primary school, students' texts may include critical responses to a work in terms of its composition and some exploration of its message and values.

In secondary school, responding entails increasing abstraction with more emphasis on reflecting on the values of the text or artwork. As with argumentative texts, these more mature response texts are complex, requiring skill in constructing logical arguments and control over an array of persuasive resources. Thematic interpretations and critical responses feature prominently in high school assessment, particularly in high-stakes examinations.

Think about it

Have you observed students learning about response genres in your recent school experiences? How closely do your observations reflect the developmental sequence proposed above?

WHAT ARE THE MAJOR LANGUAGE RESOURCES FOR RESPONDING?

As students become increasingly accomplished with negotiating the responding genres, they must also gain control over the language features for responding in a range of situations. The following list summarises important language features for responding. Many of these features will be familiar from earlier chapters. Others are explained in more detail in the 'Focus on' sections below.

Expressing and elaborating ideas: Developing control of field-related meanings

- Participants:
  - individual, referring to characters in the focus text (*'Jasper Jones was an* outsider') and composers of text (William Shakespeare, Ridley Scott)
  - abstract as ideas and themes are identified and discussed (*'Rural Australia's deep seated racism* is evident in this text', '*Their continuity* is evident')
- Processes:
  - Material verbs, to retell events and happenings in the focus text ('Charlie *jumped* out of his bedroom window and *ran* down to the river with Jasper Jones')
  - sensing verbs, particularly thinking to indicate reader–writer relationships ('We *know* these characters from To Kill a Mockingbird') and feeling/wanting to express opinion and reaction ('I *enjoyed…*'; '*I like …*')
  - relating verbs, to describe characters ('Jasper *is* worldly') and text ('Bridge to Terabithia *is* a passionate story'), themes, and symbols through use of 'is' substitutes ('The large hand *symbolises* authority …')
- Complex noun groups ('a heart wrenching film that leaves its viewers in despair at *institutional injustice*'; '*at the height of her powers as a writer*'; *Ruben Carter, a boxer who was imprisoned by a crooked vengeful police officer for a murder he did not commit in the 1970s*)
- Circumstances of manner, time, and place to summarise events of the focus text, often referring to a place in the text ('*in the final chapter*', '*in the opening scenes*').

We introduced Participants, Processes, and Circumstances— key language resources for expressing experiential meaning—in Chapter 2 and again in Chapters 4 and 5.

Engaging and convincing the reader: Developing control of tenor-related meanings

In this section we examine how interpersonal meanings contribute to the effectiveness of responding genres.

Figure 9.1   Choices from the language system involved in persuasion

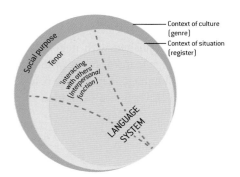

- Expressing attitudes (Attitude)
  - expressing feelings ('It made me cry', 'The audience loved it')
  - judging people and behaviour ('Tim Winton is one of our finest storytellers', 'She's *hysterical* and *aggressive*').
  - evaluating qualities ('her writing is *lyrical* and *powerful*', 'Silvey's voice is *distinctive*', '*career-best* guitar playing')
- Engaging with other voices, possibilities and perspectives (Engagement)
  - modality in order to temper opinion ('It *could* be considered …')
  - aligning with audience ('As you imagine …', 'They make us all want to keep watching …', 'naturally')
  - countering or challenging an alternative idea ('While it *may* be considered …', '*Although* …')
- Adjusting the strength and focus of arguments (Graduation)
  - increasing and decreasing force ('It's *impossible* to put down', 'Death is rendered *vividly*')
  - sharpening and blurring focus ('He is a *rather* pompous figure', 'I *sort of* liked it').

Modality was introduced in Chapter 2 and explained in detail in Chapter 8.

We introduced language for enacting interpersonal meanings such as attitude, for adjusting the strength and focus of arguments, and for expanding and contracting arguments in Chapter 2.

Appraisal

Language for responding, because it involves attitudes and opinions, making judgments, and exploring the perspectives of others, is particularly concerned with interpersonal meanings. In reading reviews and interpretations, students will need to recognise how writers attempt to position them through their language choices. Similarly, when composing reviews, interpretations, and critical responses, students will need to communicate their evaluations with credibility and subtlety. **Attitude** is the sub-system of Appraisal that describes the range of language resources through which we express attitudes and opinions about texts, characters, composers, and techniques.

Attitude: Using language to share feelings, express evaluations, and judge human behaviour.

We introduced the Appraisal system in Chapter 2.

Expressing Attitudes

Writers can express their Attitudes (negative and positive) in different ways: by expressing emotions directly (Affect), and by evaluating human behaviours (Judgment) and the qualities of things and processes (Appreciation). These language resources are critical to responding.

Expressing emotions through Affect

Expressions of Affect can be related to happiness or unhappiness ('I like that book', 'She hated it'), to satisfaction or dissatisfaction ('The children were bored by the film', 'They had a great time'), or to security/insecurity ('I'm feeling braver now').

Emotions may be those of the speaker or writer ('I'm so freaked out by that painting!') or those of another ('Matilda was scared of Ms Trunchbull'). We often use such affective language in our most immediate, informal responses to books, films, and performances ('I absolutely loved it'), often through forms of social media. Such language is also commonly found in the early personal responses and opinions described above ('I thought my book was good'). However, students must learn less subjective ways of expressing their attitudes and opinions.

Evaluating human behaviour through Judgment

Responding to texts frequently involves judging writers or characters and their behaviours from the perspective of social and ethical values rather than the direct feelings of the speaker or writer. We can do this in terms of personal and psychological attributes (social esteem) and in terms of moral, ethical, and legal factors (social sanction).

Table 9.5   Different types of Judgment

Social esteem	
Normality (is the person special? or not?) • delightful/weird, cheerful/unusual	'This is another excellent novel from the witty and popular Morris Gleitzman.' 'Jesse is artistic and he is proud of it.'
Capacity (is the person capable? or not?) • competent/incompetent, quick/slow	'Her productivity is outstanding: 10 novels in 6 years.'
Tenacity (is the person reliable? or not?) • careful/careless, diligent/lazy	'His character in that film was a salt of the earth type.'
Social sanction	
Veracity (is the person truthful? or not?) • honest/dishonest, open/sneaky	'She discussed her addictions openly during our interview.'
Propriety (is the person beyond reproach? or not?) • good/evil, just/cruel	'Lisbeth has a strong sense of morality.'

Expressing opinions about individuals in these terms rather than as mere likes or dislikes enables students to achieve a degree of objectivity and hence authority in their arguments and responses.

Have a go!

Return to the *Boy Overboard* review on page 266. Can you see any expressions of Affect or Judgment? Who or what is being evaluated in these language choices? Are they positive or negative?

Evaluating qualities of things and processes through Appreciation

When students respond to texts, artworks, and performances, they express their opinions about such aspects as composition or aesthetics, their social value or worth, and the reactions provoked. The language of appreciation is particularly pertinent to responses. The criteria used to appreciate works are shaped by the nature of the work and students will need to be taught explicitly about what counts with respect to the effectiveness of a cultural artefact, especially with respect to composing texts. The criteria for evaluating literary works will be different from those for evaluating artworks or performances.

Works and ideas can be evaluated according to:

- the *reaction* provoked in terms of impact (stunning/dull, absorbing/boring) and quality (beautiful/ugly, compelling/repulsive, impressive/disappointing)
- the *composition* in terms of balance (discordant/harmonious, well-shaped/distorted) and complexity (simple/extravagant, elegant/waffling)
- *value* (worthwhile/trivial, profound/shallow).

It is important to note that all the expressions of Attitude discussed above (Affect, Judgment, Appreciation) can be either explicit or implicit. We could say, for example, 'Markus Zusak is a very popular writer', thus making an explicit positive judgment of his capacity. On the other hand, we could say 'Tickets to the lunch with Markus Zusak sold out in a record-breaking one hour'. This latter sentence is not an explicit judgment of the writer, rather an implicit but nevertheless still positive judgment of his capacity. Learning to read such implicit or indirect expressions of Attitude requires knowledge of the context and text and is challenging for many students.

Have a go!

Locate a review of a film, concert, or book from popular media. Examine it for evidence of the writer's attitude. How is that expressed? How does the writer use Affect, Judgment, or appreciation? What is being evaluated and how? Is it direct or indirect? What assumptions does the writer make about the reader? What challenges does the review have for students or for those from language backgrounds other than English? What are the implications for your teaching?

FOCUS ON APPRAISAL: STRATEGIES FOR TEACHING AND ASSESSING

Appraisal system: the ways in which we use language to express feelings and opinions, to engage with other voices and perspectives, and to adjust the strength of our utterances.

There are a number of strategies for teaching **Appraisal** that can be adapted for use with students of different ages.

- Have students identify evaluative language in model reviews and interpretations. Ensure that they use evidence from the text and sort it into positive or negative; identify the target of evaluation (characters and behaviours or 'things'); say whether direct or indirect.

- Teach students from early in primary school to appreciate texts and other artefacts on the basis of what can be said about the form; for example, identify the elements (such as characterisation, setting, plot, pacing, camera shots) as well as discussing the big ideas or themes.

- Examine responses from a range of contexts—movie blogs, reader sites, newspapers as well as school assignments—and discuss how the evaluative language varies.

- Help students notice how experienced writers use attitude to develop characters—direct feelings (Affect); and more objective ways of talking about feelings and opinions (Judgment and Appreciation), using extracts of text or as texts are shared.

- Jointly construct reviews of texts that have been shared, focusing on Appraisal resources as relevant to instructional goals.

- Foster discussions as a whole class and in small groups around texts encouraging students to use the language of Judgment (characters and their behaviours) and Appreciation (Themes, techniques, structures)

- Examine 'impoverished' versions of reviews of shared texts with students and rewrite using Appraisal resources, initially in joint writing then in small groups. Include discussion of adjusting attitudes (see Chapter 8).

ORGANISING INFORMATION: TEXT, PARAGRAPH, AND SENTENCE

Students will need to gain control over information at the text, paragraph, and sentence levels as they write longer reviews and interpretations.

Text openers

Response genres vary in their use of text openers from other genres such as information reports. Reviews usually provide details of the text or work to be discussed and an indication of the writer's opinion; for example, 'This novel, *Bridge to Terabithia*, is a passionate story written by an enthusiastic author, Katherine Paterson'. Interpretations and critical responses, because they frequently deal with multiple works and themes, require more signposting for the reader. The text openers will preview the works to be discussed and the ideas to be explored or challenged. Table 9.6 revisits the interpretation presented earlier in the chapter to consider how the student has organised the information in the script for the speech. Through the text opener in the first paragraph, the themes or elements to be considered are introduced ('murder is intertwined with deceit, betrayal and revenge') as well as the texts through which she will do this. By previewing the elements in the order that they appear in the subsequent paragraphs, she is guiding the reader/listener as well as indicating how she will approach her interpretation (that they are entangled).

Table 9.6 Organising information in a Year 10 interpretation

Murder, deceit, betrayal, and revenge, these so-called sins are as common in our stories and narratives now as they were in the sixteenth century. Their continuity is evident in the play Julius Caesar *by William Shakespeare, Ridley Scott's film* Gladiator *and Bob Dylan's song 'Hurricane'. What I hope to demonstrate to you is that in all three of these texts from very different periods of time,* **murder is intertwined with deceit, betrayal, and revenge.** *These are the ingredients of tragedy. In* Julius Caesar *the murder of Caesar by the conspirators—Brutus and Cassius—is also the act of betrayal. In* Gladiator, *murder sets off a chain of events revolving around more murder and revenge as Maximus goes from general to slave and from slave to gladiator. The ballad 'Hurricane' tells the story of Ruben Carter, a black American boxer who was imprisoned by a crooked vengeful police officer for a murder he did not commit in the 1970s.*

In Shakespeare's text, Caesar is **murdered** because he is a danger to democracy, thus setting off further murders.

Deceit may lead to murder or may be an outcome of murder …

Another tragic element common to the texts is **betrayal** …

Revenge too can be carried out by heroes as well as villains …

The text then proceeds in subsequent paragraphs to discuss the ways in which those elements are expressed in the texts. Each paragraph begins with a topic sentence or paragraph opener that links back to the text opener, reminding us implicitly of the student's overarching goal. In this way, there is a close relationship between the writer's theme and the interpretation she is building through her analysis of the elements in each text.

In reviews, paragraph openers are somewhat less complicated because they are guided by the phase descriptions that are shaped by the nature of the work or artefact being evaluated. As we have seen, paragraphs in a review of a literary text will frequently be organised around elements such as plot summary, description of setting, character analysis, and message or central idea. Each paragraph should be introduced by a paragraph opener or topic sentence which introduces the general idea of the paragraph: 'The main characters in *Bridge to Terabithia* are Jessie and Leslie.'

FOCUS ON TEXT AND PARAGRAPH OPENERS: STRATEGIES FOR TEACHING AND ASSESSING

There are a number of strategies for teaching about text organisation of reviews and responses that can be adapted for use with students of different ages. Many have been introduced in earlier chapters and can be adapted.

- Label models of reviews and responses with paragraph and text openers.
- Focus on text organisation during joint construction.
- Provide students with jumbled texts and ask them to reassemble. Have them label the stages and phases of the particular genre under focus.
- Use cloze exercises in which students must complete the paragraph openers by drawing on the information provided in the text opener.
- Ask students to organise bundles of information under relevant paragraph openers. Then jointly construct the text opener.

CHAPTER SUMMARY

In this chapter we have identified the major genres for responding in the school curriculum and described their structures and phases as well as how they become increasingly more complex and demanding across the years of schooling. We have introduced relevant language features associated with evaluation. These begin with direct expressions of feelings and opinions which develop into more subtle and less subjective opinions drawing on analysis and interpretation according to social and cultural values. We have also described a number of practical activities aimed at developing students' skills in interpreting and constructing reviews and interpretations.

FOR FURTHER DISCUSSION

1   School book clubs are an increasingly popular phenomenon. They encourage dialogue about texts and help students to become discerning readers. Is there one at your school? If there isn't, how might you begin one?

2   Examine a selection of reviews written by professional reviewers—are these suitable models for students learning to write reviews? How does the context in which a review is published shape the language used?

3   Identify authentic audiences for student reviews; perhaps the local library or bookshop, displays in the classroom, the school newsletter or website. Encourage and support students to write for these audiences.

4   Develop some explicit criteria for the response texts the students are examining and constructing using the metalanguage developed during deconstruction and joint construction. Encourage the students to self-edit their own texts using these criteria.

5   Examine the portfolios of student work samples from the *Australian Curriculum: English* for response texts (www.australiancurriculum.edu.au/english/rationale) (ACARA 2015). Can you see a development from early primary school to lower secondary in the kinds of responses that students write?

REFERENCES

Australian Curriculum Assessment and Reporting Authority (ACARA). (2015). *The Australian Curriculum: English, version 8.1*. Sydney: ACARA.

Christie, F., & Derewianka, B. (2008). *School Discourse: Learning to write across the years of schooling*. London: Continuum.

Humphrey, S., Love, K., & Droga, L. (2011). *Working Grammar: An introduction for secondary English teachers*. Melbourne: Pearson.

Lewis, H. (2011). Mapping the development of children's writing: A functional perspective. Unpublished PhD corpus. Wollongong: Faculty of Education, University of Wollongong.

Martin, J.R., & Rose, D. (2008). *Genre Relations: Mapping culture*. London: Equinox.

··

WEBSITES

··

Start Your Own Bookclub

www.readwritethink.org/parent-afterschool-resources/activities-projects/start-your-book-club-30289.
html

This link contains some helpful hints for getting started.

Goodreads

www.goodreads.com

An excellent source for online reviews, often written by young people.

Australian Book Review

www.australianbookreview.com.au

A suitable website for older students developing their skills at interpretation.

Rotten Tomatoes

www.rottentomatoes.com

A website devoted to reviews of current films and television series. The short reviews offer models of
many of the language features of reviews and interpretations.

10

LANGUAGE FOR INQUIRING

Virtually all areas of the curriculum expect students to undertake inquiries. These generally include a variety of activities—observing, asking questions, hypothesising, conducting procedures, reporting on results, and so on. Inquiries generally produce texts that have multiple purposes, referred to as 'macrogenres'. In this chapter we will examine such texts and their language features.

Learning objectives

In this chapter you will:

- become familiar with macrogenres that arise from various types of inquiries
- consider how students learn to read and write inquiry macrogenres over the years of schooling
- learn about the major language resources for inquiring
- explore some curriculum contexts for conducting inquiries
- acquire knowledge of some useful classroom strategies for teaching the language of inquiry.

Key terms and concepts

macrogenres

genres for inquiring (fair tests, lab reports, investigation reports, design reports/portfolios, problem-solution reports)

Mood system

Attitude

Engagement

modality

language features

- related to field: everyday, academic, and discipline-specific language
- related to tenor: interpersonal meanings in inquiry genres
- related to mode: text organisation of inquiry genres
- density and abstraction (e.g. noun groups, nominalisation, abstract nouns)

INTRODUCTION

So far we have been concerned with ensuring that students have a solid grounding in the more common genres encountered in school contexts. Once they are familiar with the basic genres, however, they can combine them in various ways when appropriate. Here we will look at a range of extended tasks that involve a variety of 'mini-tasks' within the overall purpose of inquiring.

In the primary school, such inquiries tend to begin with *fair test reports*—simple experiments that involve changing one variable at a time while keeping all other conditions the same. In secondary school, fair tests evolve into more complex experiments, documented in *lab reports*. But not all inquiries involve experimentation. Some investigate a topic in some depth, resulting in an *investigation report*. Others involve the creation of a product or service, with the creation process recorded in a *design portfolio*. And finally, we will look at *problem-solution reports*, which are accounts of an inquiry involving the identification of a problem and its solution. A common thread linking these various inquiry reports is that they are typically project-based, involving a range of activities within an overarching inquiry task. Students need to capture the ongoing progress of the inquiry using such tools as process diaries, field notes, and rough drafts, recording each stage as it is completed, with constant revisions as the inquiry unfolds. The final product can take a range of formats: written, multimodal, digital, and performance.

Table 10.1   Genres for inquiring

Genre	Social purpose	Sample curriculum contexts
Fair test	To carry out and report on a basic experiment involving variables	Observing the effects of heat on solids and liquids in Chemistry
Lab report	To undertake a more complex experiment using the scientific method	Finding out how mixtures, including solutions, can be separated using a range of techniques in Science
Investigation report	To research a topic using a variety of sources	Examining how colonial settlement changed the environment in History Identifying the factors that influence the decisions people make about where to live in Geography
Design report	To design and create a product, service, performance or artwork	Planning, structuring, producing and presenting media artworks for specific audiences and purposes in Media Arts Designing and producing products and services in Design and Technology In English, constructing, editing, and publishing multimodal compositions using a range of software and visual, print and audio elements

Genre	Social purpose	Sample curriculum contexts
Problem-solution report	To devise a solution to a problem	Developing strategies to make the classroom and playground healthy, safe, and active spaces in Health and Physical Education In Digital Technologies, creating a range of digital solutions such as interactive adventures, implementing their solutions using appropriate software, and explaining how their solutions meet specific needs In Mathematics, formulating and solving authentic problems and creating financial plans Proposing entrepreneurial actions in response to identified work and community challenges in Work Studies

In this chapter, we are using the term 'report' in a different sense from 'information/descriptive report' (Chapter 6). Here we are using it to refer to an account of the investigation, while an information report is a description of a general class of things.

FAIR TEST

When an experiment involves variables it is called a '**fair test**'. Found mainly in primary school science, fair tests provide an opportunity for students to inquire into a scientific phenomenon using simple experiments. Fair tests change one factor at a time while keeping all other conditions the same. These represent the first steps into the scientific method.

fair test: an experiment where the variables are carefully controlled.

The report documenting a simple experiment (sometimes called a *procedural recount*) follows a number of basic, predictable stages:

1   The *aim* generally identifies a question to be answered by the experiment, setting out the purpose or goal to be achieved. This stage can also introduce the variables.

2   There is then a list of *equipment* and/or *materials* to be used, generally sequenced in order of use and specifying details such as quantity, length, number, size, and so on.

3   The *steps* (together with the materials) take the form of a *procedure* (see Chapter 3)—a set of steps to be followed.

4   The *results* take the form of a *recount* (Chapter 5), describing what happened or what the students observed.

5   The *discussion* is where students can summarise the results and reflect on the experiment, including problems encountered and suggestions for improvement. This stage is sometimes combined with the results stage.

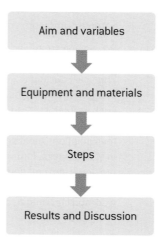

The stages of the report might differ slightly depending on the nature of the experiment, the age of the students, the focus of instruction, and so on. The report includes some 'embedded genres' such as a procedure and a recount as we can see above. These could be relatively free-standing and still make sense, but have been brought together to play a part in the fair test macrogenre.

Table 10.2 is an example of a fair test report looking at how the growth and survival of living things are affected by the physical conditions of their environment. Students in primary school were investigating how plants grow by planting seeds and observing their development. Rather than simply describing the plants' progress, the class identified a few variables that could affect their growth.

One group of students decided that they would keep constant the type of seed, the container, the use of fertiliser, and the amount of water, while the variable to be changed would be the amount of light. They placed one set of plant containers on the window sill in full sunlight, another set in the shade near the window, and another in a cupboard.

Other groups of students each changed a different variable and the class later compared the results of the various groups. They applied their findings to the growth of plants in their class vegetable garden.

In this chapter, we will use roman font for the stages, italics for the *phases* within the stages, and bold italics for any ***embedded genres***.

When designing a task, it is important to be very clear about the genre. A fair test differs from an explanation (Chapter 7). Finding out how an electrical circuit works, for example, results in an explanation. It would become a fair test if variables were introduced (e.g. the effect of different types of conductors). A fair test also differs from a procedure (Chapter 3). Creating a 'fantastic foamy fountain' from water, yeast, hydrogen peroxide, and soap is simply a demonstration or procedure. It would only be a fair test if a variable were changed such as the amount of yeast or the size of the bottle. A fair test will use words such as 'What is the effect of …?' or 'Which …?'. If you are clear about the purpose of the task (the genre), the students will be better able to recognise the expectations.

Table 10.2   Fair test report

Embedded genres			
Aim and variables	**WHAT IS TO BE INVESTIGATED?** How changes in light affect the growth of plants. **CAN YOU WRITE IT AS A QUESTION?** Which amount of light will make the plant grow the biggest?		
	TO KEEP THE TEST FAIR, WHICH THINGS (VARIABLES) WILL YOU …		
	CHANGE? The amount of light **(CHANGE ONLY ONE THING.)**	**MEASURE OR OBSERVE?** The height of the plant after three weeks **(WHAT WOULD THE CHANGE AFFECT?)**	**KEEP THE SAME?** • the type of seed • the container • the amount of water • the fertilizer **(WHICH VARIABLES WILL YOU CONTROL?)**
Procedure *Materials and equipment*	3 plastic cups 3 sticky labels Cotton wool 9 bean seeds Water (1/4 cup every third day) Measuring cup Centimetre ruler Notebook Digital camera		
Steps	1. Fill 3 plastic cups with cotton wool. 2. Plant 3 bean seeds around the sides of each of the containers. 3. Label the containers. 4. Place one container in direct sunlight, one in indirect sunlight, and one in the dark. 5. Water the plants with 1/4 cup of water every third day. 6. Record observations of growth every third day. 7. Take photos.		
Results *Recount*	**WHAT DID YOU DO? WHAT HAPPENED?** Our group planted 3 seeds in each container and placed one container in the full sun, one in the shade and one in the cupboard. We watered them and observed them every third day.		

(continued)

Table 10.2   Fair test report *(continued)*

Embedded genres	
Findings	**WHAT DID YOU OBSERVE?** Our results showed that most of the seeds germinated on day 3 or 4. The pot with no light had the tallest plants. The pot in the full sun had the next tallest plants. The pot in the shade had the smallest plants.
Discussion and conclusion	**WHAT DID YOUR RESULTS SHOW? COULD THE EXPERIMENT BE IMPROVED?** The results showed that all seeds could germinate, even in the cupboard. The plants without light grew tallest but they were thin and yellow and they died at the end of the experiment. This was because the energy in the seed helped them to germinate and grow but then they had no sunlight to make their own energy (food) using photosynthesis. They grew so tall because they were looking for sunlight. So our dependent variable should not have been the height of the plant but the health of the plant (bushy, green, strong). **WHAT DID YOU LEARN?** Our conclusion is that healthy plants need a lot of sunlight to grow strong and that when you do an experiment you have to change only one thing and keep all the others the same.

Think about it

Think back to your own science classes in primary school. Did you encounter fair tests? What was challenging about writing them up? What helped you? What does this suggest about teaching students to write fair test reports?

LAB REPORT

lab report: lab reports/prac reports describe and analyse an experiment (generally carried out in a laboratory).

Of all the school genres, the **lab report** is perhaps the one that has always been explicitly taught, with its predictable stages based on the scientific method. Its predictability is important as scientists need to be able to examine the procedure and results of other scientists' work in order to compare results and evaluate the reliability and validity of the experiment.

The lab report is similar to the fair test report. It includes, however, a number of additional stages, reflecting the greater complexity and rigour of the experiments in secondary school. The following are typical of the stages of a lab report:

1   *Abstract* (optional)—a brief paragraph summarising four essential aspects of the report: the purpose of the experiment (sometimes expressed as the purpose of the report), key findings, significance, and major conclusions.

2   *Introduction*—background to the experiment (e.g. why you are doing the experiment; identifying a question from observations or research; the significance of the question; what is already known; links to theory; definition of terms).

3   *Aim*—what are you trying to determine? Can be written as a question (e.g. How does packaging affect the ripening of fruit? How much energy is stored in different types of food? Which metal is the most resistant to corrosion?)

4   *Hypothesis*—an informed prediction of what will be found, based on background knowledge about the field and possibly on research already undertaken. Often presented as an 'if … then' statement. The experiment is set up to test the hypothesis.

5   *Materials and equipment*—specifying quantities, size, properties, etc. Can include a labelled diagram of specialised equipment.

6   *Method*—step-by-step, numbered instructions on how to carry out the experiment, sometimes including cautions (e.g. If the project takes you several days, try to run the tests at the same time of day in the same spot every time), alternative steps (e.g. If it doesn't work the first time …), specification of independent, dependent, and constant variables if appropriate (not all experiments involve variables), or variations (e.g. Now repeat the experiment using a different independent variable.).

All these steps should be written before the experiment. Sometimes, however, the method is written as a recount of the steps taken, rather than a set of instructions. In this case, it is written up after the experiment.

7   *Safety*—any precautions that might need to be taken.

8   *Results*—recording of observations/findings of the experiment, including quantitative/measurable raw data presented in the form of tables and graphs without any interpretation or comment.

9   *Discussion* (sometimes combined with the conclusion)—analysis and interpretation of the results: reflecting on and evaluating the experiment; reporting on any problems; perhaps proposing a new hypothesis; generalising from the results and explaining the results in light of any relevant scientific principle; assessing the validity and reliability of the experiment; interpreting the significance of the results.

10 *Conclusion*—summarising the findings, referring back to the purpose of the experiment: whether the hypothesis was confirmed and how well the results achieved the aim. States the most likely explanation and if necessary, what further work might be needed to validate this.

11 *References* (optional).

Lab reports are not necessarily related only to experiments carried out in a laboratory; they can include any inquiry that uses the scientific method.

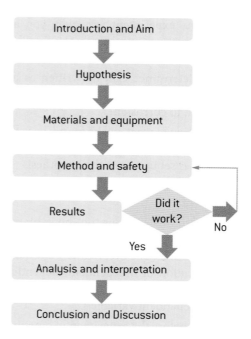

Table 10.3 is an example of a lab report. Students were asked to design and carry out an experiment, and to record the processes and the results.

Table 10.3   Lab report

Stages, *phases*, and **embedded genres**	
Introduction	When designing clothes, especially sleepwear and children's wear, it is important to use material that doesn't catch fire. Burns from clothing fires are a significant cause of serious injury and death. The information gained from this experiment will help people know which fabrics to avoid for clothes, curtains, bedding, and other things that involve cloth. It will also tell people which fabrics to keep away from heaters, matches, cigarettes, etc.
Aim	To determine whether some fabrics used for clothing burn more quickly than others.
Hypothesis	My hypothesis is that cotton will burn the fastest as it is loosely woven. I base my hypothesis on information that I collected stating that the weave of the material is a factor. Oxygen is needed in order for fabric to burn, and cotton lets a lot of air through the fibres.

Stages, *phases*, and **embedded genres**	
Equipment and materials	25 cm square of 7 different fabrics Scissors Tape measure A fireproof plate Long matches Stopwatch Metal tongs
Method (Procedure) *Equipment and materials*	The independent variable was: the type of fabric The dependent variable was: the speed that fire consumed the fabrics The constants in this study were: the size of fabrics used the way of lighting the fabrics the time that the fire is held to the fabric
Variables	The independent variable: the type of fabric The dependent variable: the speed that fire consumed the fabrics The constants in this study: the size of fabrics used the way of lighting the fabrics the time that the fire is held to the fabric
Steps	1. Cut out five 5 × 5 cm square pieces of each fabric. 2. Place a square of cotton on the fireproof plate. 3. Hold the cotton with the metal tongs in one corner and, using a match, light the square of fabric at the opposite corner. 4. Commence timing as soon as the flame touches the fabric. 5. Stop the stopwatch as soon as the fabric has completely burnt. 6. Repeat with the remaining 4 cotton squares. 7. Repeat with the remaining 6 fabrics, recording times and converting to a graph.
Safety	An adult should be present. Safety goggles should be worn. A fire extinguisher, fire blanket, or container of water should be available. Wear fire protective gloves. Roll up sleeves.
Results (recount)	The purpose of this experiment was to determine the burning rate of various types of cloth. The results of the experiment were polyester burned the fastest at an average of 61.97 seconds, cotton the second fastest at an average of 74.86 seconds, wool third fastest at an average of 116.80 seconds, linen fourth fastest at an average of 148.42 seconds, and rayon fifth at an average of 155.35 seconds. Silk and nylon just melted.

(continued)

Table 10.3   Lab report *(continued)*

Stages, *phases*, and **embedded genres**	
Graph	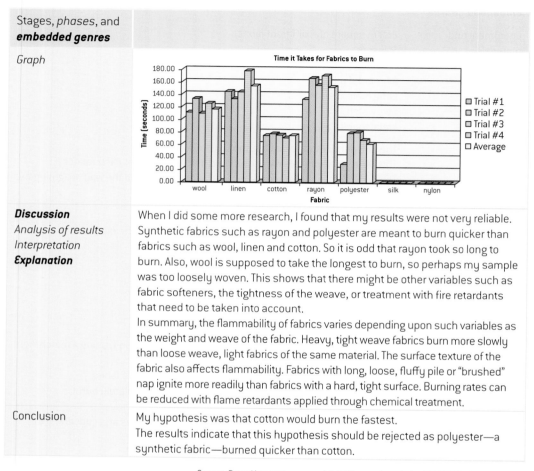
Discussion *Analysis of results* *Interpretation* **Explanation**	When I did some more research, I found that my results were not very reliable. Synthetic fabrics such as rayon and polyester are meant to burn quicker than fabrics such as wool, linen and cotton. So it is odd that rayon took so long to burn. Also, wool is supposed to take the longest to burn, so perhaps my sample was too loosely woven. This shows that there might be other variables such as fabric softeners, the tightness of the weave, or treatment with fire retardants that need to be taken into account. In summary, the flammability of fabrics varies depending upon such variables as the weight and weave of the fabric. Heavy, tight weave fabrics burn more slowly than loose weave, light fabrics of the same material. The surface texture of the fabric also affects flammability. Fabrics with long, loose, fluffy pile or "brushed" nap ignite more readily than fabrics with a hard, tight surface. Burning rates can be reduced with flame retardants applied through chemical treatment.
Conclusion	My hypothesis was that cotton would burn the fastest. The results indicate that this hypothesis should be rejected as polyester—a synthetic fabric—burned quicker than cotton.

Source: Based in part on www.selah.k12.wa.us/soar/sciproj2000/JZet.html#purpose

timeless present tense: a tense that is typically used to express general truths (*The flammability of materials varies*).

It is significant how the verb groups change in the different stages. In the procedure stage, for example, the verbs take the form of commands, telling the students what to do. In the recount of what happened, the verbs change to the past tense, referring to specific actions in the past. In the explanation stage, however, the verbs tend to be in the **timeless present tense** as the students are now making generalisations.

Have a go!

In many guidelines for writing lab reports, students are advised not to use the first person (e.g. I, we, my). Why do you think this is? Do you agree with it? Might it depend on the particular stage or embedded genre? Might it depend on the age of the students? Find any examples of first person pronouns in the report above. How might they be rewritten to make them more impersonal? (Hint: consider introducing students to the passive voice.)

INVESTIGATION REPORT

Across all years of schooling, students are asked to carry out investigations. Such investigations may take the form of a traditional project within a particular area of the curriculum, where students gather information about a topic or issue. Or they can take the form of a 'depth study': an intellectually challenging inquiry requiring rigour and deep learning. Such tasks are designed to prepare students for the complexity of modern life, dealing with new technologies, new economies and workplaces, and new identities in diverse communities and cultures.

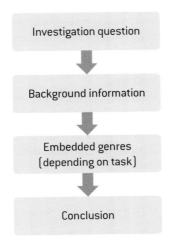

While fair test reports and lab reports are very predictable, **investigation reports** are less so as they depend on the nature of the investigation. Investigations are typically macrogenres— extended tasks involving a number of activities. The task provides the overarching purpose (macrogenre), while each activity represents a particular genre contributing to the overall purpose of the task. Such projects typically involve using both primary and secondary sources of information.

> **investigation report:** a report describing an investigation into a given topic.

In Year 6, for example, students conducted an investigation into the role of migration in developing Australian culture following Federation. Within this broad task, students needed to engage with a number of genres.

The students documented their research by compiling the various elements into a multimodal digital investigation report, including sources such as photographs, maps, diaries, newspaper articles, timelines, documents, letters, videos of interviews, and so on. For each of these genres in the investigation report above, the students were taught how to structure their texts into appropriate stages and, where appropriate, use the language features typical of the genre.

Table 10.4   Investigation report

OVERARCHING QUESTION (macrogenre): How did migration contribute to Australian culture following Federation?	
Embedded genres	Framework of investigation report
Waves of migration over time (***historical recount*** involving timelines and maps)	**EARLY 20TH CENTURY:** Assisted passages for British and Irish 'White Australia' policy introduced **POST-WWI:** Free passage for British ex-servicemen Migration from Southern Europe **1930s:** Jewish refugees escaping from Hitler's Germany **POST-WWII:** Department of Immigration established Refugees and displaced persons from Europe …
Reasons why people migrated to Australia (***factorial explanation***)	People migrate for many different reasons. These reasons can be classified as economic, social, political, or environmental. Economic migration is when people move to find work or follow a particular career path. … Social migration is when people move somewhere for a better quality of life or to be closer to family or friends. …
Stories of migrant groups (***interviews***)	**INTERVIEW QUESTIONS:** When did your family come to Australia? Why did they come? How was Australia different from your home country? How did you feel when you arrived in Australia? …
Understanding of different points of view (***empathetic autobiography*** seeing the world from the perspective of a migrant from another culture and in a different historical period)	A 'ten pound Pom' they call me. Escaped from dreary old London to the land of opportunity. After three months rolling around in the sea in a tiny cabin, I stepped ashore. Where would I go? What would I do? I had nothing and knew no one. No family, no money, no job, nowhere to live. Suddenly the big adventure started to look like a nightmare. …
Stories of individuals who have made a significant contribution to the development of Australian society (***biography***)	Vida Jane Mary Goldstein (1869–1949) fought her whole life for women's rights. She came from a family of Irish, Jewish, and Polish stock that migrated to Australia in 1868. In those days, a woman's place was in the home. They couldn't vote, they couldn't buy property, they could only get lowly jobs and their wages were much lower than men's. …
The benefits of migration to Australian society (***argument***)	Australia is one of the most multicultural countries in the world. Migration brings economic, social, and cultural benefits to Australia. …

DESIGN PORTFOLIO

In many subjects, students are required to conduct an inquiry with a view to creating something. These are usually authentic tasks that connect to the world beyond the classroom, often preparing students with relevant life skills. The creations can include products, services, artworks, and performances, and are aimed at:

- improving student engagement, innovation, and creativity
- enhancing the leadership, responsibility, and group work skills of students
- developing decision-making and project management skills
- broadening vocational options and entrepreneurial skills

The structure of **design portfolios** depends very much on the nature of the task. At its simplest, the design portfolio would include such stages as:

1   Design brief—outlining the outcome to be achieved
2   Project development and implementation—developing and implementing the production plan
3   Evaluation—assessing the outcome of the task
4   Production and marketing—an optional stage.

> **design portfolio:** a compilation of tasks contributing to the production of an object, service or performance.

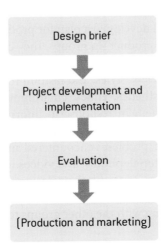

At the primary level, this might include making toys for the local preschool, or developing and implementing a service for the community such as organising a car wash for senior citizens, or participating in the production of the school play, where teams of students are responsible for organising rehearsals, creating the sets, printing programs, and designing the costumes. In one primary school where new classrooms were being built, students contributed to the design of the classrooms in response to the Geography curriculum topic of exploring the arrangement of space within places such as classrooms. They researched the advantages of different instructional spaces, created diagrams of preferred options along with the organisation of desks and classroom fittings, undertook surveys of teachers and students as to their preferences, and consulted with the building site manager about practical matters. They recorded their investigation in a classroom display comprising written texts, photographs, and diagrams, developing the linguistic resources needed to describe, recount, explain, interview, make decisions, express opinions, and evaluate. At the end of the year, they shared their experiences at the school's Festival of Learning.

At secondary level, students are supported to take greater responsibility for the production process. This might include learning the skills of curating and marketing student artworks at a local gallery. Or creating picturebooks in English or a language other than English for younger students. Or developing leadership skills through Student Action Teams, targeting a real-world issue in the school or community. At one school, the students were involved in a commercial bakery partnership, combining their understanding of economics and business skills, health education, hospitality, and food technologies. In different groups, they had to develop a business plan, undertake market research, do a risk analysis, contribute to the design of the kitchen, create, test, and sell a range of products, maintain the herb garden, and develop book-keeping skills.

One curriculum area involving the production process is Technology and Design. In the following example, students in lower secondary were guided through the task of designing and creating sleepwear for teenagers. The project folio in which they documented their progress took the form of a macrogenre, incorporating a number of minor genres. Together with the teacher, they jointly constructed a design brief for the product, similar to one that a client might propose. They surveyed students in other classes to identify likes and dislikes, outlined the specifications of the sleepwear, and developed a plan for producing the sleepwear together with a list of criteria for evaluating the product. In groups, they carefully analysed the design brief with a view to designing their own distinctive sleepwear. They brainstormed lots of ideas based on their research of possible materials, styles, and fashion trends. They conducted a Consider All Factors exercise: function, aesthetics, ethics, environment, and safety. They made a few different prototypes, modifying them in response to informal market research among their peers. Throughout the process, they evaluated the implementation and documented in their production log any decisions made, problems encountered and modifications introduced. They included sketches, swatches of material, photos, and videos in their portfolio. When they were satisfied with the final product, they wrote up their design portfolio, including material from the design brief and production log. They then drew on the report to pitch their sleepwear to students in another class, competing with the other groups to 'win the contract'.

The following provides an idea of typical components of such a report.

Table 10.5   Design portfolio

TASK (macrogenre): Design and produce sleepwear for the teenage market	
Embedded genres	
Design brief • *Survey, interviews* • *Specifications* • *Production plan* • *Flowchart* • *Budget*	• identifying a need for the product (e.g. existing products, market research, client identification, customer profile) • stating the specifications for the product • developing a production plan specifying actions, timeframe, costings, constraints, and considerations • developing a list of criteria for success (e.g. functionality, durability, aesthetic qualities, ethical issues, cost-effectiveness, environmental factors, ergonomics, market appeal and demand)
Project development and implementation • *Mind-map* • *Procedure* • *Recount/Production log*	• brainstorming ideas and researching (e.g. properties of materials, production processes, equipment) • developing a production plan • considering design factors (e.g. aesthetic, practical, safety) • deciding on techniques to be learnt and practised • selecting materials • making prototype/s, experimenting and testing of materials, tools, techniques • modifications and improvements • decision-making and justification of decisions • reference to relevant theory • quality control at every stage • producing a finished product • regularly documenting the process, decision points, problems encountered
Evaluation • *Criteria* **Reflection journal**	• ongoing evaluation of functional and aesthetic aspects of design, typically recorded in a reflection journal • problems encountered and how they were overcome, improvements made, safety issues, etc. • final evaluation of success with regard to the learning outcomes and success criteria in the design brief • recommendations for future production • reflections on personal learning
Production and marketing (optional) • *Business plan* • *Posters, advertisement, social media campaigns* **The pitch presentation**	• business plan • developing marketing strategies • pitching the product to a potential client or customer

As with investigation reports, the nature of the design portfolio will differ somewhat depending on the task. In primary schools, for example, the report might not be as rigorous or involve as many stages and phases. With reports documenting the production of artworks or performances, there might not be such an emphasis on the market, though many of the stages will be similar. In each case, however, the task is concerned not simply with the product, but with documenting the process and instilling in students the need for accountability and providing evidence. For many students, it's not so much the creation of the product that poses problems but the language challenges in writing up the report. It is therefore important that teachers provide models of the various stages of the production log and final report, jointly construct critical parts of the brief or report, and teach students the language needed for successful documentation of each stage.

Have a go!

Have you compiled an e-Portfolio during your studies? If so, can you see the potential for using such tools to showcase evidence of learning for production tasks? If not, find out about e-Portfolios online from sites such as those mentioned at the end of this chapter. E-Portfolios provide a workspace where students can collect a variety of artefacts such as images (photos, drawings, artworks, diagrams); audio (voice and music); reflective journal; digital stories; blogs; Excel, PDF and Word documents. Tools such as Google Docs and OneNote can be used when jointly developing group reports. Work created with tools such as Glogster, Animoto, and YouTube can be inserted in spaces such as Weebly, Wikispaces, and Blogger.

PROBLEM-SOLVING

Finding innovative solutions to problems is one of the most important 21st-century skills. Problems can be personal, social, environmental, practical, or technical. Problem-solving in schools should deal with authentic, challenging problems that matter to the students and that have no easy solution. This often takes place in the context of rich tasks that require students to be critical and analytical thinkers. Rich tasks involve real, substantive problems to solve and engage students in social actions that have value in their world, community, school, or new worlds of work. Such inquiries often involve various disciplines contributing different perspectives on the problem and the solution.

Students are expected to be creative, innovative, and entrepreneurial as they engage in problem-solving tasks in most areas of the curriculum. In technologies subjects, for example, students create designed solutions in response to needs. They are expected to:

- investigate, design, manage, create, and evaluate solutions
- responsibly select and manipulate appropriate technologies—materials, data, systems, components, tools, equipment—when designing and creating solutions

- critique, analyse, and evaluate problems, needs, or opportunities to identify and create solutions.

Similarly, in Humanities and Social Sciences, students develop the ability to question, think critically, solve problems, communicate effectively, make decisions, and adapt to change.

In one primary school, students identified bullying as a problem in the school. It was decided that the students would lead change, becoming the experts and coming up with credible strategies. In cross-grade groupings, they researched possible solutions. They began by contacting an authority in the field (e.g. from Kids Helpline) to explain the reasons for bullying and its effects on the victims. They watched videos of victims' stories and investigated actions taken by other schools. They then went online to a number of websites dealing with bullying and made notes of solutions that were recommended, e.g.:

- make a banner displaying an anti-bullying slogan
- read blogs written by bullying victims to understand the impact of bullying behaviour
- develop a school culture of inclusivity where difference is celebrated
- write a song about bullying, record it, and ask the local radio station to play it
- role-play scenarios that represent bullying situations and different ways of responding
- write an anti-bullying rap, e.g. 'Be a buddy not a bully'
- model and practise positive social skills
- create a class dance to represent the emotions involved in bullying
- based on a particular scenario, write an email to the bully suggesting different ways of behaving.

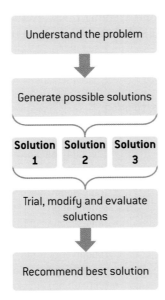

In their groups they discussed the strategies and placed them in order of priority, justifying their decisions. Each group selected their three most effective strategies, trialled them in the group, and evaluated them against a list of criteria. The groups came together and shared their listed priorities. They decided which ones they would recommend for implementation and prepared a **problem-solution report** for the principal.

At secondary level, students grapple with significant social, economic, and technological problems. In Tasmania, for example, the Nextgen Challenge has motivated over a thousand students in teams to identify a problem facing the business community and to devise a solution. To convince the judges of the effectiveness of their solution, they design a business plan, deliver a sales pitch, and create a marketing plan (product, price, place, promotion, packaging). They are supported in this by a number of mentors from the business and educational community who provide students with real-world advice. In response to an identified problem of youth unemployment, for example, a team of students drew up a business plan to export Tasmanian products overseas. Another team worked on boosting tourism by producing a travelling cultural festival. And another identified the limited use of technology by businesses and proposed a plan to use the online retail environment to attract and benefit customers.

There is a degree of overlap between design portfolios and problem-solution reports. The design portfolio is generally more vocationally oriented, with an emphasis on the development of lifelong skills in the process of designing and producing a product. Problem-solution reports, on the other hand, don't necessarily create a product. They are more concerned with researching possible solutions to a problem without necessarily implementing the solution. As with production projects, problem-solving is typically user-oriented: there is a genuine audience for the solution.

Generally, we solve problems by identifying the problem, researching and listing its possible solutions, weighing them one by one, trialling them, evaluating them, and selecting the best solution. Table 10.6 gives an example of some of the typical stages of a problem-solution report.

Table 10.6   Problem-solution report

TASK: Identify a problem and design a solution	
Potential stages	
Problem identification	• defining the problem and its significance • background to the problem (context, need, urgency)
Research methods	• researching secondary sources for background information • investigating primary sources for empirical evidence (e.g. trialling of possible solutions, interviews, observations, surveys) • assessing the reliability of information sources • consulting with experts where possible

TASK: Identify a problem and design a solution	
Findings	• presentation of data from research • solutions arising from research data
Recommendations	• evaluation of different solutions • justification for preferred solution and how it addresses the problem, anticipating any objections • what will need to be done to address the problem and how (e.g. timeline, budget, resources, education)
Conclusion	• restatement of problem and preferred solution
References	• list all material referred to using citation conventions
Appendices (optional)	• detailed information that is important but would disrupt the flow of the report can be included in appendices

Problem-based projects are often 'messy' and don't follow a linear sequence. Similarly, the reports don't necessarily follow the model above, but will generally include many of the elements of this macrogenre.

Have a go!

Drawing on a school context with which you are familiar, design an outline for a problem-solving task that fulfils the following criteria:

• responds to an authentic problem in the school, neighbourhood, or beyond

• addresses a particular audience

• involves deep learning

• draws on various disciplinary knowledge and skills in resolving the problem

• preferably involves working in groups

• is age-appropriate but challenging.

How will you assess the final report, particularly if group work is involved?

How would you scaffold the students in the process of compiling the report?

DEVELOPING CONTROL OF INQUIRY GENRES

Students in the early primary years learn to inquire by asking questions, observing, predicting, and describing, primarily through oral interaction and using their senses. Their investigations generally involve hands-on activity with concrete objects. They might, for example, explore the different properties of materials by looking at them, touching them, smelling them, listening to them, even tasting them. Or they might carefully observe and compare a range of 'minibeasts' and draw their features, such as the number of legs, wings, body segments, and so on. Such activities are heavily scaffolded by the teacher. Their observations are often recorded using drawings and brief multimodal texts.

In the mid- to later primary years, students are moving beyond observations and basic experiments to undertake fair tests, to investigate topics in greater depth, to create simple products and services, and to design solutions to problems. They learn how to document and evaluate their inquiries in line with relevant success criteria.

In secondary school, students engage with more technical and abstract inquiries, often involving an understanding of theory. They conduct research, locating and evaluating relevant texts, judging their trustworthiness, and differentiating between primary and secondary sources. The texts they have to read are often dense and challenging, and organised differently from those they have encountered in primary school. This requires explicit teaching in terms of how to tackle such texts. While still needing support in interpreting and composing texts, the students are becoming much more independent and taking on greater responsibility. Their investigations are recorded in extended, multi-stage texts. Such texts are typically digital and multimodal, containing sophisticated diagrams and tables. They are often collected in a portfolio representing a macrogenre containing a number of embedded genres.

WHAT ARE THE MAJOR LANGUAGE RESOURCES FOR INQUIRING?

Expressing and elaborating ideas: Developing control of field-related meanings

Field knowledge can be represented as three language tiers:

Tier 1: everyday, conversational language that students tend to 'pick up'.

Tier 2: high-utility language related to school contexts across all subjects, including Processes such as *evaluate, interpret, analyse, classify, summarise,* and *predict*, and abstract Participants such as *point of view, concept, consequence,* and *problem*.

Tier 3: technical and specialised language specific to particular disciplines. In Mathematics, for example, they will need to know the meaning of Processes such as *multiply, divide, partition, solve,* and *calculate*; Participants associated with *two-dimensional shapes, grid maps, simple* *column graphs, digits, odd and even numbers*, and *data displays*; and Circumstances such as *in sequence, accurately, to the nearest five cents*, and *into equal sets*.

In most cases, Tier 1 words don't need to be explicitly taught as students will encounter them frequently in their reading and conversations and can easily infer them from context (though EALD students will need more support with these words in English). Tier 2 words should receive a great deal of attention as they are critical to academic learning across all areas of the curriculum. Tier 3 words need to be taught in the context of tasks that are specific to a particular topic in a learning area.

When we look at the field of inquiring and consider the language choices students make, we could refer to the lab report above (Table 10.3). There are a number of Tier 1 words, such as *fire, clothes, death, cigarettes*. We can also find Tier 2 words that represent general academic concepts and are found across most learning areas: *hypothesis, components, cause, information, determine, factor, purpose, experiment, researched*. And there are many Tier 3 specialised words that are specific to that task in that particular discipline: *oxygen, independent variable, constant variable, graph, the burning rate, flammability, combustible, ignite, fibres*.

Inquiry tasks involve active learning and the teaching of a range of skills. Looking at the Tier 2 Processes in the *Australian Curriculum* for Humanities and Social Sciences, for example, students are required to:

- *Question*: Develop appropriate questions to frame an investigation.
- *Research*: Locate and collect relevant information and data from primary and secondary sources.

Tiered Vocabulary

Tier 3
Domain-specific academic vocabulary

Tier 2
High-utility academic vocabulary found in many content texts, cross-curricular terms

Tier 1
Everyday words familiar to most students primarily learned through conversation

- *Analyse*: Examine primary and secondary sources to determine their origin and purpose.
- *Examine*: Examine different viewpoints in the past and present.
- *Interpret*: Interpret data and information displayed in a range of formats.
- *Sequence*: Arrange events in chronological order.
- *Evaluate*: Use criteria to make decisions and judgments and consider advantages and disadvantages of preferring one decision over others.
- *Reflect*: Reflect on learning to propose personal and/or collective action in response to an issue or challenge.

- *Communicate*: Present ideas, findings, viewpoints, and conclusions in a range of communication forms.

Tier 2 Participants are often fairly abstract. Again, in the History curriculum, we find such Tier 2 Participants as:

- the *theory* that people moved out of Africa around 60 000 BC
- the *evidence* for the emergence and establishment of ancient societies
- *key features* of ancient societies
- the *analysis* of unidentified human remains
- the use of *resources*
- significant *beliefs, values, and practices* of the ancient Egyptians
- *reasons* for change and continuity over time
- the *effects* of *change* on societies.

Here we are concerned not only with vocabulary items but with how they work together in sentences to express and connect ideas.

All these skills require high levels of language and literacy that can benefit from explicit teaching. When setting a task, for example, the teacher needs to carefully consider the choice of Process. Are the students expected to justify? Evaluate? Analyse? Explain? Speculate? It can't be assumed that students know what is intended by such terms. The teacher might need to explain or model what is meant by such Processes so that students are clear about the requirements.

Have a go!

Go to the *Australian Curriculum* website and create a list of Tier 2 Processes and Participants by scanning the content descriptions and achievement standards of a range of subjects in various grades. Then create a list of Tier 3 Processes and Participants relevant to particular subjects such as Digital Technologies and Science.

Engaging the reader: Developing control of tenor-related meanings

It is often thought that to be convincing it is necessary to use persuasive devices such as rhetorical questions, emotive statements, hyperbole, and so on. With inquiry genres, however, the use of interpersonal resources is more subtle. With most inquiries, the student is asked to take on roles such as apprentice scientist, designer, entrepreneur, or problem-solver, shaping the tenor of the context. When they see themselves in these roles, students are more likely to approach the inquiry as investigators who ask relevant questions and who pursue deeper understandings. Inquiry tasks also tend to assume a real audience: a customer needing a product or service, a client after a solution, or a community of inquiry interested in the outcome of an experiment.

In relation to tenor, when students take on the role of inquirer, preferably with a genuine audience, there is a greater degree of authenticity in the task, which results in spoken and written interactions that promote a more authoritative voice. It is the logical reasoning, the evidence, and the robustness of the inquiry that are convincing rather than any rhetorical flourishes.

Even though inquiry genres can look 'interpersonally neutral', in fact there can be several interpersonal 'hot spots'.

Mood refers to how we use speech functions such as commands, questions, statements, and offers to interact with others. As we have seen above, inquiries can often involve interviews. In one class, the students had been taken to visit the local aged care facility. The visit was a disaster with the students tongue-tied, not knowing how to engage with the residents. For their next visit, the teacher decided to give the interaction an end-product—a memory book documenting the childhoods of the senior citizens. The interactions now had a purpose. But the students still needed support if they were going to collect the information needed. The class discussed how the level of formality would change depending on who you were interacting with and decided that they would need to use a respectful tenor with this audience. They then considered the types of questions they could use:

> **Mood system:** the grammatical resources for making statements, asking questions, giving commands, and making offers.

- yes/no questions which are closed and would elicit a succinct, narrow answer
- wh- questions which would be more open-ended and elicit expanded information.

They played around with the questions, changing yes/no ones to wh- ones and vice-versa to see the effect on the type of response. In groups, they developed questions, trialled them on their classmates, and adjusted them as necessary. They learned that they needed to listen to the answers carefully and follow up with relevant comments or questions rather than just continue with their pre-prepared list. They researched childhood toys and games of the early 20th century and asked relatives for copies of childhood photos before making a presentation of the memory books.

Attitude. As we saw in Chapter 9, we can express attitudes in three important ways: by sharing feelings, by appreciating the qualities of something, or by judging human behaviour. In the case of inquiry genres, there is not so much emphasis on feelings or judgment, but more on appreciation. This is particularly the case when students are asked to use appreciation in evaluating various aspects of the inquiry. In academic contexts, evaluation generally involves the development of criteria. In curriculum tasks, teachers typically make the learning intention of the task explicit to the class, often writing it on the board as a constant point of reference. The teacher and students then negotiate a small set of criteria that would demonstrate that the task objective has been met (or not). The students constantly refer to the success criteria as they carry out the task, jotting down notes during the task to provide as evidence. If, for example, the learning intention were 'to evaluate the success of the inquiry', then the types of criteria might include (depending on the type of inquiry):

> **Attitude:** using language to share feelings, express evaluations, and judge human behaviour.

- Were the results useful?
- Was the product innovative?
- Did the solution work?
- Did the service meet expectations?
- What could have been improved?
- Were the results valid? (Did they achieve the objective?)

- Were the results reliable? (Could they be repeated with similar results?)
- Did your insight into the topic of investigation increase? In what ways?

Students thus learn what characteristics of an inquiry are valued and the kind of language used to assess them.

Engagement. In most areas of the curriculum, students are asked to consider 'point of view'. This often refers to the ability to 'step inside another's shoes' and see a situation from the other's perspective. This is important in inquiry tasks where the inquirer needs to determine the requirements of the task from the point of view of the consumer or client, convincing them that you understand the situation well enough to be able to provide realistic solutions. An example of this is the 'pitch', which is common in production and problem-solving tasks where the student has to persuade an audience of the benefits of a particular product, service, or solution. Engagement involves not only understanding the point of view of the audience but also opening up space for alternative possibilities, typically through the use of modality. In inquiry tasks, students are encouraged to speculate, hypothesise, view things from different angles, and consider other possible solutions. The language of low **modality** is used:

> *Maybe* we *could* …
> This is one *possible* answer …
> *Perhaps* we *should* …
> It *might* work better if …
> It's *not certain* whether …

A secondary science teacher taught low modality to the students as a way of making the point that such language is at the core of inquiry—not necessarily 'finding the correct answer' but exploring various possibilities.

> **Engagement:** using language to engage with others or with alternative perspectives and possibilities.

> **modality:** language resources for expressing the degree of commitment, ranging from low (maybe, might) to high (must, should).

Have a go!

Design an inquiry task using one of the inquiry genres in this chapter. Identify any points in the inquiry that involve the use of Mood, Attitude, or Engagement resources. Detail examples of the interpersonal resources that you would teach the students to use at these points. Discuss how these might be taught.

Creating coherent and logical texts: Developing control of mode-related meanings

Inquiry texts need careful crafting to remain concise and coherent, especially when controlling the abundant material collected along the way that contributes to the final product. The problem-solution report opposite, for example, demonstrates the level of design involved in organising the flow of information through the text.

The enormous growth in the use of internet over the last decade has led to radical changes to the way that people consume and share information.

Although **serious problems** have arisen as a result of this, there are **solutions.**

One of the major problems of the internet	is the ease with which children can access *potentially dangerous sites.*
• For example, **pornography sites**	are easily accessible to them because they can register with a site and claim to be an adult.
• **Exposure to pornography**	affects their thoughts and development, which is a negative impact for the children and for society.
Another major problem	is the growth of online fraud and *hacking.*
• **Hacking of government and company websites**	results in sensitive information falling into the hands of criminals.

These problems require *an urgent solution*.

• **Governments**	should ensure that **adequate legislation and controls** are in place that will prevent young people from accessing dangerous sites ...
• **Parents**	also have a part to play. They need to **closely monitor the activities of their children** and restrict their access to certain sites ...
• **Companies**	must also **improve their onsite IT security systems** to make fraud and hacking much more difficult by undertaking thorough reviews of their current systems for weaknesses.

To conclude, the internet is an amazing technological innovation that has transformed people's lives, but it brings with it **serious problems such as pornography and hacking.** However, with the right action by **governments, parents and businesses,** it can be made a safe place for everyone.

Source: Adapted from www.ieltsbuddy.com/problem-solution-essays.html

Have a go!

Here you are invited to interact with the text by doing a close reading. Close reading is a strategy where students are guided to examine a text in detail and annotate the text with notes indicating points of confusion, points of particular interest, questions, links to other texts, and so on. With the text on page 303, some annotations have already been done for you. Quickly skim the text to get the gist and then reread the text, following the instructions below.

1   Trace over the arrows
   •   that introduce the problems
   •   that introduce the solutions
   •   that spell out the solutions
   •   that refer back to the problems of pornography and hacking
   •   that refer back to the main problems in the conclusion
   •   that link 'dangerous sites' introduced in the second half of the sentence as 'new information' (Rheme) to make it the focus of the next sentence—'pornography sites'
   •   that link 'hacking' introduced in the second half of the sentence to make it the focus of the next sentence.

2   Find three examples of text connectives. What is each one doing?

3   Pronouns are used to make a text cohesive (see Chapter 5). Find pronouns in the text and draw arrows back to the thing that they refer to.

4   What does 'as a result of *this*' refer to? Do you remember what we call this type of reference? Why might it make reading difficult for some students? (see Chapter 5).

We could also consider the mode demands in terms of multimodal texts. In many of these inquiry genres, for example, students need to deal with graphs that enable them to compare and contrast results.

Have a go!

We can't always assume that students know how to read diagrams such as graphs. One way to check their understanding is to ask them to orally explain the graph. See how you go with explaining the graph on p. 288. And in terms of constructing graphs, how would you teach students about their function and how to create them, either by hand or electronically?

FOCUS ON DENSITY AND ABSTRACTION

Reader alert! You might find the following section quite challenging. It is technical, abstract, and dense. It is the key, however, to understanding why many students hit a brick wall as they progress from upper primary into secondary school. The language of the texts that they read and write becomes increasingly complex—often to the point where they give up. So if you want to better understand the demands of academic texts, keep on reading. (You might even gain insights into your own reading and writing of such texts.)

As students move into secondary school, they need to read and write texts that are increasingly dense and abstract. Compared to the free-flowing nature of casual conversation, written academic texts try to be concise and efficient, packing a lot of information into every sentence. Key resources to package information are the noun group, nominalisation, and abstraction. As we explore these, we will look at examples from a problem-solution report by a Year 10 Geography student (ACARA website) on the problem of river bank erosion and possible solutions.

The noun group

As we have seen earlier, the noun group can be stretched to fit in various kinds of descriptive information. We can add information in front of ('pre') and behind ('post') the main noun:

... the environmental	changes	occurring on the river bank at Bicentennial Park ...
pre-modifiers	head noun	post-modifier

Notice that the post-modifier often contains another noun group (e.g. *the river bank at Bicentennial Park*), which allows for even further expansion of the information.

Have a go!

Look at the following noun group and circle the head noun. Then underline the pre-modifiers and post-modifiers. Can you see another noun group inside the post-modifier? Does it also have pre-modifiers and a postmodifier?

... several large, layered, various-sized rocks placed along a sloping or angled bank ...

The terms *pre-modifiers* and *post-modifiers* simply tell us about the structure of the noun group, e.g.:

... one simple construction	method	of building a fence and planting native plants ...
pre-modifiers	head noun	post-modifiers

We can also look at the *function* of each part of a noun group. As we have seen in previous chapters, pre-modifiers can answer questions such as:

- how many? (Quantifier, e.g. *one*)
- like what? (Describer, e.g. *simple*)
- what type? (Classifier, e.g. *construction*).

And post-modifiers provide additional information about the thing in question, typically specifying 'which one?'. Their function is to qualify, so they are called 'Qualifiers'. In the above noun group, the post-modifier tells us which method.

Have a go!

Look back at the previous noun group (... *several large, layered, various-sized rocks placed along a sloping or angled bank* ...). Which word is quantifying the rocks? Which word/s are classifying the rocks? Are there any words that describe the rocks? What is the post-modifier doing?

(Clue: if a word is a Describer, you can usually put an Intensifier such as 'very' in front of it. If it's a Classifier, you can't.)

The noun group is a key resource in written academic language for compacting various types of meanings around the head noun, thus increasing the density of the text, as in the following noun group:

... the most effective strategy to manage change and reduce erosion on the outer bend of the river at the Bicentennial Park site ...

Structure	pre-modifier				head noun	post-modifier
	... the	most	effective	management	strategy	to produce change // and reduce erosion on the outer bend of the river at the Bicentennial Park site ...
Function	Pointer	Intensifier	Describer	Classifier	Thing	Qualifier

Notice how, in this case, the Qualifier takes the grammatical form of two embedded clauses. The second clause contains a further noun group: *erosion on the outer bend of the river at the*

Bicentennial Park site—which in turn contains other noun groups (*the outer bend*, *the river*, *the Bicentennial Park site*). When we have noun groups inside noun groups inside noun groups, you can see how the noun group can become extremely dense.

The point of this is not to simply label parts of the noun group. Rather, it is to consider how the noun group can include a number of meaning-making resources, though in doing so they can make a text very information-dense. When we are doing inquiry tasks, we need to specify, quantify, describe, and classify the things we are investigating. We also need to provide further information, qualifying the thing in question and making it more specific. One of our main devices for doing this kind of work is the noun group.

Nominalisation

Nominalisation is a typical feature of academic written texts. It is a crucial language resource in science and technology and social science texts, and one that is important in successful writing in the secondary years. It is the reason many texts are difficult for students to read because it enables writers to construct worlds of logic and abstraction rather than the events and happenings of more everyday texts. Students encounter nominalisation in texts they read from middle to upper primary years, but they are not expected to control it consciously in their written texts until the secondary years.

At a very basic level, nominalisation is thought of as 'changing verbs into nouns', such as turning the verb *explode* into the noun *explosion*.

> **nominalisation:** a process in which an idea or event (represented by a clause or clauses) is downgraded to a 'thing' (represented by a noun group). It is a language resource for creating more compact text, and is often a feature of academic and bureaucratic texts.

Have a go!

Try doing this exercise on nominalisation from the internet:

Change these verbs into nouns:

    invest

    reject

    analyse

    participate

    illustrate.

Nouns can also be created from other words, such as adjectives. Change these adjectives into nouns:

    careless

    difficult

    intense.

You probably found it quite easy. But did it actually reveal anything about the nature and role of nominalisation in academic texts?

Turning verbs into nouns isn't the full story. Rather than thinking at the level of the single word, we need to move to the level of the clause. In spoken language we might represent an event with a clause such as *the bomb exploded loudly*. In written language, however, we often represent an event as a 'thing'—a noun group that is part of a larger clause: <u>*the loud explosion of the bomb*</u> *startled us*. So now the grammar has changed, compacting the original clause into a noun group that is part of a larger clause.

Conversational spoken language is usually relatively devoid of nominalisation. The first complex sentence below is typical of spoken language produced during class discussion:

When plastic bags are made // toxic gases and other dangerous substances are released into the air // and these by-products pollute the atmosphere // and ruin water supplies.

Compare the first sentence with the following more written-like sentence:

<u>The production of toxic gases during the manufacture of plastic bags</u> causes <u>air and water pollution.</u>

Notice that the first sentence contains four verb groups (*are made, are released, pollute, ruin*) and hence comprises four clauses (as marked). In contrast, the second sentence contains one verb group (*causes*) and comprises one clause. So four clauses have been collapsed into a single clause containing two nominalisations. This increases the density of the text by compacting the information. More importantly, however, it has created two 'things' (*production of toxic gases* and *air and water pollution*) that can now be brought into an explicit relationship with each other. In this case, it is a causal relationship ('*this* causes *that*'). This is an important resource for the kind of reasoning and building of logical relationships that are characteristic of academic writing.

Have a go!

Just for practice, without assuming that it is necessarily 'better', have a go at nominalising the following clauses to create a single clause (i.e. a simple sentence with one verb), maintaining the same information:

If we don't manage the river bank better, it will continue to erode and further pollute the river with chemicals, sediment, nutrients, and rubbish and in the longer term, the aquatic habitat will be lost.

Now see if you can unpack the following nominalised sentences (e.g. by inserting verbs):

The increased rate of river bank erosion is a result of the human destruction of vegetation on the river bank.

The reshaping of river banks can result in erosion reduction and an increase in public accessibility to the river.

You would probably agree that the nominalised sentences are less clear than the 'un-nominalised' ones. So why does nominalisation exist? It must have a function, or else it would disappear.

If we return to the problem-solution report above, we can see how the student has used nominalisation in various ways. It is common, for example, to introduce an event in a more spoken-like way and then to nominalise the event as the text moves on:

The purpose of this report is to investigate how a local environment changes. →
<u>The environmental change that is being investigated</u> is located at Bicentennial Park …

Grammatically, the verb (*changes*) has now become a noun (*change*). (Or more technically, the Process meaning is no longer expressed through the verb group but is now realised by a noun group.) But this has implications for other parts of the sentence. *Environment* now gets dragged into the noun group (underlined) as an adjective (*environmental*) and the verb group (*to investigate*) also becomes part of the noun group (as a Qualifier—*that is being investigated*). This is an efficient way of accumulating meanings as the text progresses: 'I have spelt it out, now I'm going to compact it into a thing'. Such a strategy contributes towards the cohesion and flow of the text. It also, however, increases the density of the text.

Notice how the author later compacts information from the two clauses in the first sentence into a nominalisation in the second.

Erosion is causing the exposure of rubbish and pollutants and these **are being released** into the river.

The **release** <u>of rubbish and pollutants into the river</u> is reducing water quality and is threatening aquatic ecosystems.

This has the effect not only of making the text flow coherently from one point to another, it also allows the noun group to be positioned at the beginning of the sentence (in Theme position)—a place of prominence. Verb groups (e.g. *are being released*) typically come in the middle of the sentence—the place of least prominence. But noun groups can be positioned either at the beginning or end of the sentence, both of which are places that draw the reader's attention. Having introduced the idea in the first sentence above, the writer is now packaging it up as the point of departure for the ensuing text, alerting the reader that this is now the focus.

The writer continues this strategy in the subsequent sentences.

Theme (sentence opener) is discussed in Chapters 2 and 8.

The release of rubbish and pollutants into the water **is reducing** water quality and **is threatening** aquatic ecosystems.
The **reduction** in water quality …
The **threat** to aquatic systems …

Having introduced the problem in spoken-like verb form (*is reducing* and *is threatening*), the writer now nominalises the verb groups to provide the focus for the following paragraphs dealing with *the reduction in water quality* and *the threat to aquatic systems*. In this way, he is making clear to the reader how the text is unfolding.

As you can see, nominalisation isn't simply 'changing a verb into a noun'. It is a text-level strategy for crafting the packaging and flow of information. Once you have a noun group:

- You can keep extending it to include further descriptive information, as in the noun group pyramid on page 315. You can't do this with a verb group.
- You can bring it into a relationship with other things—relationships of cause and effect, of comparison and contrast, of parts of whole, of classification. It is less easy to do this with verb groups.
- You can move it to the beginning or end of the sentence, giving it greater prominence. Verb groups are typically stuck in the middle.
- You can use it as a summarising move to organise the structure of the text, keeping your reader focused on how the text is developing.

Nominalisation isn't, however, necessarily 'better'. On the negative side, it allows you:

- to create texts that are overly dense. There needs to be a balance between 'spelling it out' and 'compacting'.
- to sound 'sophisticated', often when you don't know what you're talking about. Using full sentences rather than nominalisations forces you to demonstrate your understanding of a topic.
- to eliminate human responsibility and create ambiguity. Rather than saying 'humans are destroying the environment', you can simply refer to 'the destruction of the environment'. This is a strategy commonly employed by politicians and journalists.

Students need to understand that nominalisation is a strategic choice they can make when composing texts. Used with discernment, it can result in a coherent, compact text that is well-structured and logically organised.

Abstraction

Abstract nouns are usually compared to concrete nouns such as *table*, *flower*, and *pencil*—things we can see and touch. There are certain abstract nouns that have a function similar to nominalisation in that they can be used to capture a stretch of surrounding text, compacting it into a single term. Abstract nouns such as *problem*, *idea*, *fact*, *concept*, *issue*, *result*, *process*, *cause*, and *reason* are often used in this way. These are sometimes referred to as 'shell nouns', 'catch-all nouns' or 'summarising nouns'. While their dictionary meaning can be defined in a general way, their specific meaning can only really be interpreted in relation to the surrounding text. If I refer to an *issue*, for example, I would need to clarify the nature of the issue by referring to the particular context. In the problem-solution Geography report above, for example, the author has written:

The *issue* at this location is that <u>when the river is in full flow during the wet season, the outer bank erodes at a greater rate</u>.

Having specified the meaning (underlined above) of *issue* in this context, the author can now move on and simply use the term *issue* rather than continually restating *when the river is in full flow during the wet season, the outer bank erodes at a greater rate*.

Such terms can be used to create cohesion in texts. In this case, for example, *issue* can be used to constantly refer to the matter outlined, e.g.:

The *issue* at this location is that

when the river is in full flow during the wet season, the outer bank erodes at a greater rate.

This *issue* has caused concern …

The *issue* with the river bank …

We can see from this example that such abstract nouns can be used as cohesive devices, constantly referring back and forth to the point in the text where the issue has been elaborated.

Think about it

Abstract nouns such as these can cause problems with reading academic texts. Let's imagine that the reader has skimmed the explanation of the issue, perhaps without fully understanding it. From then on, whenever the word 'issue' is used, the writer assumes that the reader knows what is being referred to, while the reader might in fact become increasingly lost.

Here are some more examples from the problem-solution text:

The *problem* with this site is	that the rate of erosion has been increased by human activity. The river bank vegetation that once stemmed the rate of erosion at this site has been destroyed by human activity; that is, by use of the land as a landfill site and a recreational park.
A further *problem* with this site is	that it was once a waste landfill site and the increased rate of erosion is causing rubbish and pollutants to be released into the water.
The *problem* of increased erosion	is due to the human use of the land …

Notice how the abstract noun *problem* is summarising the information provided in the second column. Now let's look at how the author uses the abstract noun *strategy* in the Recommendation stage of the report, where he is evaluating the various solutions to the problem:

After evaluating both *strategies* to reduce erosion at the study site, it is recommended that Option B be implemented. While this *strategy* is more expensive than revegetating the bank, it would be more effective in stemming erosion and stopping the flow of pollutants into the river. Furthermore, this *strategy* will not affect the recreational use of Bicentennial Park. This *strategy* will improve the water quality of the river and prevent damage to aquatic ecosystems. Survey results also revealed that Option B was the management *strategy* favoured by the general public … I therefore conclude that the most effective *strategy* to manage change and reduce erosion on the outer bend of the river at the Bicentennial Park site is Option B.

Have a go!

Now read the paragraph above carefully. Do you have any idea what the preferred strategy actually was? Most probably not, because you weren't able to read that section of the text where Option B was described in some detail. (In fact, Option B was something called 'riprap revetment'—a wonderful term referring to the use of paving stones or rocks to protect the river bank.) So while the use of the term *strategy* can be very effective in terms of creating cohesion in the text, it can also lead to confusion if the reader has not fully understood what is meant by *strategy* in this context.

The problem-solution report above contains several examples of similar abstract nouns:

Abstract term	Interpretation of the abstract term
Erosion on the north bank is causing more damaging environmental **effects**, including	the exposure of rubbish and pollutants being released into the river. The release of toxins and chemicals and rubbish into the water is reducing water quality and threatening aquatic ecosystems.
Erosion at the study site is having an **impact** on aquatic ecosystems in the Great Barrier Reef.	The rubbish, chemicals, sediments, and nutrients leaching from the former landfill site threatens this internationally significant reef system including its rich biodiversity.
Therefore, the environmental changes occurring on the river bank at Bicentennial Park may have far reaching **consequences** in the long term.	If left unmanaged, the river bank will continue to erode and further pollute the river and Great Barrier Reef with chemicals, sediment, nutrients, and rubbish. In the longer term, this will result in a loss of aquatic habitat and will have consequences for the functioning of ecosystem services we depend on.
Advantages of revegetation are	that it enhances biodiversity, reduces erosion, improves the look of the area and provides wildlife corridors. This option is environmentally sound because the river would be restored to its natural state before human intervention. It also has low start-up costs because of the simple construction method of building a fence and planting native plants.
The **disadvantages** are	that it incurs costs in the long term for maintenance and upkeep of the site. It will most likely not stop the leaching of chemicals and rubbish into the river and will impact the local community by restricting the access that residents have to the river. This will mean that people will no longer be able to fish from the banks, or on rocks in the river itself.

In each case, the author has used an abstract term—*effects, impact, consequences, advantages, disadvantages*—to distil the information in the second column. In fact, the verb 'to abstract' means to rise above specific instances to a higher level of generalisation—an important higher-order thinking skill in educational contexts.

The use of abstract summarising nouns is not restricted to inquiry reports. They are also commonly found in explanations, reviews, and arguments. The *Australian Curriculum: English* requires that students understand how certain abstract nouns can be used to summarise preceding or subsequent stretches of text by exploring the use of such nouns to compact and distil information, structure argument, and summarise preceding explanations.

Table 10.7   Types of abstract nouns

Abstract nouns that encapsulate stretches of discourse	Abstract nouns that encapsulate mental processes	Abstract nouns that encapsulate causal relationships	Abstract nouns encapsulating general concepts
account	analysis	consequence	advantage
accusation	assumption	effect	approach
argument	belief	factor	disadvantage
assertion	concept	purpose	fact
claim	conviction	reason	issue
comment	expectation	result	process
conclusion	idea		proposition
debate	notion		strategy
discussion	opinion		system
evidence	perspective		task
point	prediction		topic
question	thesis		trend
statement	thought		
suggestion	view		
	viewpoint		

Many of these words belong in the Tier 2 category of academic words that are frequently used in all areas of the curriculum.

FOCUS ON DENSITY AND ABSTRACTION: STRATEGIES FOR TEACHING AND ASSESSMENT

One of the major implications for teaching is simply that teachers of subjects in all curriculum areas need to be aware of the challenges posed by texts that are increasingly dense and abstract as students move through upper primary and secondary education. This doesn't mean that dense, abstract texts should be avoided or 'dumbed down', because students will eventually need to deal with them. Rather it means that teachers need to provide explicit support to students in reading and writing such texts through activities such as close reading, shared reading, and joint construction.

Any assessment of students' comprehension and composition of dense, abstract texts should not take the form of a test. Rather the emphasis should be on monitoring and observing any difficulties that students are experiencing with such texts. This can best be done in the context of activities such as guided reading and guided writing, where the teacher has the opportunity to work with small groups of students or with individual students, focusing on specific literacy features in context.

Dense noun groups

Consider the implications of dense noun groups for listening, reading, and writing.

- Have you ever listened to a lecture that sounded as if it were a textbook being read aloud? Did you find it difficult to follow? When we listen to texts that are dense with information, our brain doesn't have time to process all the content being thrown at us. In more informal spoken language, noun groups are typically shorter and there are fewer content words per clause, so we find it easier to keep up. Is this something you might need to be aware of when reading informative texts to your students, when providing complex explanations, or when preparing students for their oral presentations?

- When we read, we are able to take the time to peruse dense texts carefully and to reread if necessary, so there is not the same pressure as in listening to such texts. Even so, many students have trouble reading the academic texts of secondary school. It is not just a matter of some technical terms or 'hard' words. The grammar of written texts is different from the grammar of spoken language, and dense noun groups can cause reading problems. It is important that students are able to see these as 'chunks of meaning' rather than as a string of unrelated words. It is a revealing activity to colour-code the noun groups in an academic text. As in the History investigation report below, the text often becomes a sea of highlighting, indicating that there is a density of information to process.

> The peak of the campaign by the Axis powers (Germany, Italy and Japan) in Europe was the 1941 Blitzkrieg invasion of the Soviet Union (USSR) code-named Operation Barbarossa. It is still the largest military operation—in terms of manpower, area covered and casualties—in human history. The Axis force was made up of more than three million troops, / 3600 tanks and / 4300 aircraft. In 1939, Germany and the Soviet Union had signed a political and economic pact that agreed not to attack each other. Germany's invasion of the USSR in 1941 broke this agreement. The Germans won resounding victories and occupied some of the most important economic areas of the Soviet Union, mainly in Ukraine. The Eastern Front became the site of some of the largest battles, / most horrific atrocities, / and highest casualties for Soviets and Germans alike. These influenced the course of both World War II / and the subsequent history of the 20th century. The German forces captured millions of Soviet prisoners who were not granted protections stipulated in the Geneva Conventions.

During shared reading sessions with the class, draw students' attention to lengthy noun groups in the text being discussed. Highlight the noun group so that students can see that it is a single unit of meaning. Show them how to identify the head noun in the noun group. Discuss the function of any pre-modifiers and post-modifiers. In close reading activities, get them to highlight examples of extended noun groups. In guided reading sessions, work with groups of struggling readers to ensure that they are able to interpret the meaning of lengthy noun groups.

- When students write inquiry reports, they need to be able use noun groups to package the information in various ways. Often this causes no particular problems. There is nothing wrong with well-chosen, brief noun groups. They can be quite effective and can decrease the density. If, however, students are writing rambling, 'spoken-like' texts, they could benefit from support in how to compact the information. In a Geography inquiry into the liveability of different places, the student might have started by describing one street simply as a cul-de-sac. With questioning from the teacher, however, the student is able to provide a much richer description of the street by extending the noun group. This can be represented visually as a 'noun group pyramid' as below:

| | | | | street | | |
| | | | | What? | | |

| | | | cul-de-sac | street | | |
| | | | What type? | What? | | |

| | | peaceful | cul-de-sac | street | | |
| | | What like? | What type? | What? | | |

| | very | peaceful | cul-de-sac | street | | |
| | Intensify? | What like? | What type? | What? | | |

| this | very | peaceful | cul-de-sac | street | | |
| Which? | Intensify? | What like? | What type? | What? | | |

| this | very | peaceful | cul-de-sac | street | with well-kept gardens | |
| Which? | Intensify? | What like? | What type? | What? | Tell me more | |

| this | very | peaceful | cul-de-sac | street | with well-kept gardens | that would be a desirable place to live. |
| Which? | Intensify? | What like? | What type? | What? | Tell me more | Tell me more |

Nominalisations

As we have seen above, it is simplistic to teach nominalisation as 'changing verbs into nouns'. There are a number of useful strategies for highlighting nominalisation with students from the upper primary years onwards.

- Students from upper primary onwards should be encountering nominalisations in texts they are reading.

- Practise unpacking nominalisations by asking your students to put the nominalised sentence into a more spoken form, as if talking with a young child. This typically involves inserting a verb.

- Focus on nominalisation during joint construction of texts with students, as in the following vignette.

  A Year 3 class in Queensland was learning to nominalise when writing up an inquiry report into the construction of a motorway in the neighbourhood and possible consequences. In jointly constructing the report, the teacher provided two 'spoken-like' simple sentences (single clauses): *Motorways will be constructed* and *Animal habitats will be destroyed*. She asked the students to identify the verb group in each sentence. Then they had to identify the 'content' part of the verb group: *constructed* and *destroyed*. The teacher asked them to change these into nouns, giving the clue that you could put 'the' in front: *the construction* and *the destruction*. They then considered what else would change because of the nominalisation and decided that *motorways* and *animal habitats* would also become part of the noun group: *the construction of motorways* and *the destruction of animal habitats*. Now that they had constructed two 'things', they were now able to bring them into a causal relationship: *The construction of motorways* _will result in_ *the destruction of animal habitats*. The children were thus being inducted into the language of the written mode.

Abstraction

- Provide students with a text extract that contains an abstract noun encapsulating something mentioned previously in the text. Ask them to circle or highlight the abstract noun and to underline the stretch of text being referred to, as in the following excerpt from a problem-solution report on the problem of drugs and alcohol among Year 10 students:

  We have decided to use *posters, brochures and information in the school notices regarding the dangers of alcohol, tobacco and marijuana and promote safe use by giving them information such as a standard drinks guide in order the guide them in the right or safe use or abstinence and create a supportive environment*. It targets Year 10 students; however, the whole student body can also receive the information. Year 10 students are focused on because they are mature enough to understand the information provided. These strategies aim not to shock or scold but rather inform students.

Note: these abstract nouns are often accompanied by words such as 'this …', 'such a …' or 'the previous …'.

- As above, but this time delete the abstract noun and ask students to select an appropriate one from a provided list (e.g. Table 10.7).

> One of the main _____ raised by farmers against organic practices is *the cost of implementing alternative procedures*. However, *these expenses are quickly recoverable because of the higher prices that organically farmed produce can command. Case studies have shown that the expense of implementing humble, old-fashioned organic methods have been recovered within a single growing season*. This is a convincing _____ that paying upfront for the change to organic farming is well worth it.

CHAPTER SUMMARY

In this chapter we have explored a number of genres related to inquiry tasks: fair tests, lab reports, investigation reports, design portfolios, and problem-solution reports. These genres typically arise out of tasks that involve a number of activities that are documented over time and that accumulate into a multi-stage report. Many of these reports are macrogenres, involving the embedding of supporting genres within the body of the overall text. As our language focus we have looked at those features that contribute towards the density and abstraction of academic texts, including lengthy noun groups, nominalisation, and abstract nouns.

FOR FURTHER DISCUSSION

1   During your school education, did you produce any of the inquiry genres in this chapter? Which one/s? Were you provided with the kind of support outlined here in writing up the inquiry? Would you have benefited from such support?

2   Much of this chapter appears more relevant for secondary students, but there are many potential insights for teachers of primary students. What would you see as the main implications for primary-level schooling?

3   Imagine that you are the curriculum leader in a secondary school. Who would you see as responsible for teaching inquiry genres? What might this look like in practice? How would you ensure that all teachers have similar understandings of what these genres involve? And who would be responsible for supporting students with reading dense, abstract texts and writing cohesive texts? How would you explain to a colleague the significance of extended noun groups, nominalisation, or abstract nouns in relation to students' literacy?

4   What are the main understandings that you would take away from this chapter? What do you know now that you didn't know before? What would you feel confident to try in the classroom?

REFERENCES

Australian Curriculum Assessment and Reporting Authority (ACARA) (2012). *National Assessment Program (NAP)*: www.nap.edu.au.

WEBSITES

Problem-based learning
www.innovationunit.org/sites/default/files/Teacher%27s%20Guide%20to%20Project-based%20Learning.pdf

ePortfolios

Using ePortfolios in the Classroom (Edutopia)
www.edutopia.org/blog/e-portfolios-in-the-classroom-mary-beth-hertz

Using Google apps to create ePortfolios
https://sites.google.com/site/eportfolioapps/overview/examples

Using Weebly to create ePortfolios
www.smore.com/b5x5-weebly-com-for-eportfolios

Nextgen Problem-solving Challenge
http://illuminate.education/wp-content/uploads/2015/03/nextgen-Curriculum-Links.pdf

Fair tests

The following resources were found to be very useful in learning about variables and basic photosynthesis:
http://splash.abc.net.au/home#!/media/1390357/fair-test

APPENDIX 1   A FUNCTIONAL MODEL OF LANGUAGE

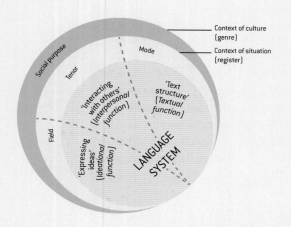

- the tenor ('who is involved'—roles and relationships)
- the mode ('the channel of communication'— spoken, written, multimodal, digital).

These three factors together reflect and create the register of that situation. In a particular science lesson, for example, the register might reflect a combination of the field (e.g. the water cycle), the tenor (e.g. peers working on a small group activity), and the mode (e.g. a multimodal interactive model).

Depending on the genre and register, we will make choices from certain areas of the language system that have evolved to serve certain functions in our lives:

- Given a particular *field*, we will make choices from the *Ideational* resources of the language system, enabling us to express and combine our ideas.
- Given a particular *tenor*, we will make choices from the *Interpersonal* resources of the language system, enabling us to create and maintain certain roles and relationships.
- Given a particular *mode*, we will make choices from the *Textual* resources of the language system, enabling us to shape texts that are coherent and cohesive.

A functional model thus allows us to identify the language demands over which our students will need to gain control in order to succeed in the various contexts of schooling.

Appendix 2 will provide a map describing where these various language resources are dealt with in the chapters of this book.

A functional model sees language as a resource for making meaning—a system of choices that vary depending on the context. Our language choices are both influenced by the context and help to construe the context.

At the broad level of the cultural context, our language choices reflect factors such as the values, social behaviours, customs, and beliefs of the various discourse communities that make up the culture. In particular, we are concerned with the discourse community of schooling and the social purposes for which we use language in educational contexts. We refer to these social purposes as genres.

At the level of particular situations within the culture, we can identify three main factors that impact on our language choices in any specific situation:

- the field ('what's going on'—the subject matter or topic)

Language function:	Text level	Sentence and clause level	Group/phrase and word level
... to achieve a particular social purpose (genre)	**Stages** (how the text moves through predictable stages to achieve its goal, e.g. *to explain, describe, recount, instruct, entertain, argue*) **Phases** (less predictable phases within each stage)		
... to express ideas (field) e.g. *to represent understandings and experience— from the everyday, specific and concrete to the technical, abstract, generalised knowledge of school subjects*	• Building up and organising field knowledge across the text • Patterns of Processes, Participants and Circumstances (e.g. taxonomies, event sequences)	Combinations of Processes, Participants and Circumstances to create clauses, e.g. • do-er + action verb + done-to *(Kirsty grabbed her bag.)* • sayer + saying verb + 'what is said' *(The old woman whispered her secret.)* • senser + sensing verb + 'what is sensed' *(We saw a rainbow.)* • 'thing being described' + relating verb + 'description' *(A koala is a furry creature with a pouch.)*	• Various types of Processes (e.g. action, sensing, saying, relating) expressed through verb groups (including tense) • Various types of Participants (e.g. everyday, abstract, technical, nominalised, specific) expressed through e.g. noun groups • Various types of Circumstances (e.g. time, place, manner, reason) expressed through adverbials (e.g. adverb groups, prepositional phrases)
... to connect ideas (field) e.g. *to create relationships between ideas*	Developing logical relationships between stretches of text (e.g. time, cause, consequence, comparison, concession)	• Creating relationships between ideas in the form of simple, compound and complex sentences • Independent and dependent clauses • Sentence punctuation	Conjunctions (coordinating and subordinating)
... to interact with others (tenor) e.g. *to develop roles and relationships depending on such factors as age, expertise, status, authority, familiarity, contact*	Developing the interpersonal 'tone' of the text (e.g. degree of objectivity, authoritative voice, 'pulses' of emotion, humour, sarcasm)	• Using rhetorical strategies (e.g. making concessions, rebutting, justifying, speculating, amplifying, citing others) and devices (e.g. 'rule of three', rhetorical questions, parallelism) • Using questions, statements, commands, and offers to negotiate meanings interactively. • Quoting and reporting speech/thought (e.g. in dialogue)	Using evaluative vocabulary for: • Expressing attitudes (e.g. sharing feelings; appreciating qualities; making moral judgments) • Engaging e.g. with the reader, with the discourse community, with other possibilities, with alternative perspectives, with 'layers of meaning' (through resources such as modality, citation practices, metaphor, simile, personification) • Adjusting the strength (e.g. of attitude, probability)

(continued)

(continued)

Language function:	Text level	Sentence and clause level	Group/phrase and word level
... to structure and organize texts (mode) e.g. *to create texts that are cohesive and coherent*	• Cohesive devices (e.g. repetition, reference, synonyms, antonyms, collocation, substitution, ellipsis, summarising nouns) • Managing the flow of information (e.g. previewing and reviewing through text openers and closers and paragraph openers and closers; paragraph development)	• Guiding the reader through the text, e.g. sentence openers/topic sentences/Theme and Rheme • Nominalisations to compact ideas by recasting 'events' as 'things' • Using active or passive voice to adjust information focus	• Text connectives e.g. to sequence ideas *(firstly, finally),* to express causality *(therefore, as a result),* to clarify *(for example, that is),* to express condition *(if, in that case)* and to express concession and contrast *(however, though, alternatively)* • Using correct spelling and punctuation to assist meaning in written texts

APPENDIX 2   A MAP OF LANGUAGE FEATURES IN THIS BOOK

Context of culture (genre)

- how genres enable us to achieve our social purposes

Chapter 1 Introduction to genre	Chapter 3 Procedures	Chapter 4 Stories	Chapter 5 Recounts	Chapter 6 Information reports
PURPOSE				
	To tell someone how to do something	To explore the human condition through entertainment	To tell what happened	To observe and describe a general class of things
EXAMPLES				
	• Simple procedure • Directions • Conditional procedures • Procedural recount	• Narrative • Anecdote • Fables	• Personal recount • Autobiography • Empathetic autobiography • Memoir • Biography • Historical recount • Historical account • Literary recount	• Descriptive • Classifying • Compositional • Contrastive • Historical

Chapter 7 Explanations	Chapter 8 Arguments	Chapter 9 Analysis and response	Chapter 10 Inquiry
PURPOSE			
To explain how or why, including reasons and consequences	To argue a case or to discuss an issue	To analyse a text or a topic	To investigate, create and evaluate
EXAMPLES			
• Sequential • Cyclical • Causal • System • Factorial • Consequential	• Hortatory exposition • Analytical exposition • Discussion	• Personal response • Review • Interpretation • Critical response	• Macrogenres • Fair tests • Lab reports • Design portfolios • Investigation reports • Problem-solution reports

Context of situation (register)

- how a combination of field, tenor, and mode create a particular register
- the relationship between the register and our language choices in any particular situation

Field (subject matter/topic/'what's going on?')

Function	Using language to represent an event or idea (Ideational function)					
Form	A clause					
		Chapter		Chapter		Chapter
Function	**Process** to represent doings, happenings and states of being/having • action • sensing (thinking, feeling, perceiving) • saying • relating (being and having)	1 (Introduction), 2, 4, 6, 10	**Participant** to represent the participants in a process • human and non-human • concrete and abstract • specific and generalised	1 (Introduction), 2, 10	**Circumstance** to represent the details surrounding a process • where? • when? • how? • why? • etc.	1 (Introduction), 2, 10
These functions are typically expressed by the following grammatical choices …						
Resources	• verb groups (action verbs, sensing verbs, saying verbs, relating verbs) • nominalisations • tense/aspect	4, 6, 7, 10	noun groups pronouns adjectives/ adjective groups	4, 5	adverbials • adverbs/ adverb groups • prepositional phrases • noun group (uncommon)	4, 5

Function	Using language to make connections between events or ideas					
Form	Sentences (combinations of clauses)					
		Chapter		Chapter		Chapter
Function	to represent a single event/idea	1 (Introduction), 2, 7	to connect two or more events/ ideas of equal status	1 (Introduction), 2, 7	to connect two or more events/ideas of unequal status	1 (Introduction), 2, 7
These functions are typically expressed by the following grammatical choices …						
Form	simple sentence (a single clause)	4	compound sentence (two or more independent clauses typically joined by a coordinating conjunction)	5, 7	complex sentence (an independent clause typically joined to one or more dependent clauses using a subordinating conjunction)	7
	Patterns of choices at the level of the text					

Tenor (roles and relationships/'who's involved?')

Function	Using language to interact with others (Interpersonal function)							
Form	Various interpersonal resources							
	Chapter			Chapter		Chapter		Chapter
Function	to enable the exchange of information and goods/ services	1 (Intro-duction), 2	**Attitude** to express attitudes • feelings (Affect) • evaluation of qualities (Appreciation) • judgment of human behavior (Judgment)	1 (Intro-duction), 2, 8, 9	**Engagement** to promote engagement • with other points of view/ perspectives • with other possibilities • with the audience	1 (Intro-duction), 2, 9	**Graduation** • to strengthen or weaken commitment to a proposition • to sharpen or blur the focus	1 (Intro-duction), 2
These functions are typically expressed by the following linguistic choices …								
Resources	• the Mood system • speech functions (questions, statements, commands, offers) • patterns of speech functions	2, 8	• vocabulary items and expressions that express attitudes (attitudinal noun groups, verb groups, adjective groups, adverb groups) • patterns of attitudinal resources across a text	8, 9, 10	• modality • rhetorical devices (e.g. rhetorical questions, 'rule of three') • patterns of engagement across a text	8, 9	• boosting or lowering the strength of nouns, verbs, adjectives or adverbs • using intensifying adverbs (*very, extremely*)	8
			Appraisal					

Mode (channel of communication / 'organising coherent texts')

Function	Using language to organise and structure texts			
Form	Cohesive devices			
	Chapter			Chapter
Function	to create cohesion	1 (Introduction), 2	to guide the reader through the text	1 (Introduction), 2, 8, 9
These functions are typically expressed by the following linguistic choices …				
Resources	• reference items (e.g. pronouns) • substitution • ellipsis • text connectives • vocabulary patterns across the text (lexical cohesion)	2, 5	• Theme and Rheme • Thematic patterns • Text openers • Paragraph openers • Sentence openers	2, 8, 9 -

GLOSSARY

action Process

Expresses meanings about doings or events, for example *chasing*, *racing*, *burns*, *builds*. (More technically referred to as a material Process.)

action verb

A verb or verb group expressing a material Process of doing or happening.

adverb or adverb group

A grammatical form that has a number of functions. One of the main functions is to modify a verb (he ran *fast*, it flowed *very smoothly*).

Appraisal system

The ways in which we use language to express feelings and opinions, to engage with other voices and perspectives, and to adjust the strength of our utterances.

Attitude

Using language to share feelings, express evaluations, and judge human behaviour. (See **Appraisal**.)

Attribution

The introduction of other perspectives into a text by explicitly referring to what others say or think about the topic. (See **Appraisal; Engagement**.)

auxiliary verbs

Parts of the verb group that modify the main verb in a range of ways such as tense (e.g. she *was* eating) and modality (she *might* leave).

brainstorming

Encourages students to make links between their previous learning and new information. For example, students may be asked to list features of a character in a particular text or what they know about a topic such as Weather. **Floorstorming** is a variation of brainstorming in which students respond to visual stimuli such as a montage of images related to the focus topic. Floorstorming often involves students seated in a circle on the floor.

bundling or categorising information

Activities that require students to group or categorise information (images, sentences or parts of sentences, words, or even whole texts). In the building the field stage of the teaching learning cycle, this usually involves organising information into 'chunks' that anticipate the genre to be studied. For example, students are asked to sort cards containing information about an animal into categories such as Classification, Habitat, Diet, Appearance, and Reproduction. Bundling activities encourage collaboration and interaction.

causal explanation

Explains a phenomenon in terms of a time sequence that includes an element of cause and effect.

Circumstance

The details surrounding an activity—Where? When? How?, and so on. In grammar, the Circumstance is the part of the clause that provides these details, for example: he ran *up the hill*, she came back *yesterday*, they played *happily*.

Classifier

That part of the noun group that answers the question 'What type?', expressed through such grammatical forms as adjectives (an *electric* train), nouns (the *weather* forecast), or verbs (the *dining* room).

clause

In terms of its grammatical form, a clause can be described as a group of words containing a verb. In terms of its meaning, however, one way of thinking about a clause is that it represents a slice of experience involving a Process, Participant/s in that Process, and any Circumstances surrounding the Process.

cloze exercise

A variation on traditional cloze exercises in that the teacher selects the particular language feature under focus to be deleted. For example, for a class studying procedures in an instructional text, it would be appropriate to delete the action verbs occurring at the beginning of the commands. Students must then supply the missing verb from either their own knowledge or a list. Further support can be provided by the addition of an initial letter to match one of the items on the list. The aim is to highlight the language feature relevant to the genre and to provide students with practice in recognising it and supplying an appropriate language item.

cohesion

The ways in which certain language features are used to make links between items in a text.

cohesive devices

Language features that create cohesion in a text.

complex sentence

A sentence consisting of an independent clause and at least one dependent clause.

compound sentence

A sentence consisting of two or more independent clauses joined by a coordinating conjunction.

consequential explanation

Explains a phenomenon that involves an input and the consequences of that input.

context of culture

The broad cultural context within which we use language for purposes such as explaining, recounting, describing, and so on, depending on the discourse community—in our case, the discourse community of schooling.

context of situation

A specific situation within a culture that gives rise to a particular register.

collaborative writing

Students work together to construct a text, to provide feedback to each other such as they respond to the meanings of the text, or to edit according to the language focus of the task.

coordinating conjunctions

Words such as *and*, *but*, *so*, *yet*, *or*, and *for* that link two independent clauses. They can also link words or word groups.

cyclical explanation

Explains a phenomenon that involves a cycle of events.

dependent clause

A clause that depends on another clause for its meaning. Sometimes called a subordinate clause.

Describer

That part of the noun group that answers the question 'What like?', expressed through the grammatical form of adjectives (*red*, *beautiful*) and sometimes verbs (the *wrecked* car, a *bellowing* bull).

design portfolio

A compilation of tasks contributing to the production of an object, service or performance.

designed-in scaffolding

The support consciously planned by teachers that takes in account students' prior knowledge and experience, the selection and sequencing of tasks, a range of student groupings, use of a focus text, use of multiple information systems such as image, colour, sound etc., and metalinguistic and metacognitive awareness. Importantly, designed-in scaffolding provides the environment for interactional scaffolding.

EALD

Stands for English as an Additional Language or Dialect (formerly ESL).

ellipsis

Cohesion can be created by leaving words out, forcing the reader to retrieve the meaning from the preceding text.

embedded clause

A clause that is embedded inside a noun group (e.g. 'the old man *who gave me meat*'; 'the first step *in making honey*'; 'the bees *that guard the queen*'). An embedded clause can also be used to realise a Participant (e.g. '*Going to the dentist* makes me nervous'.)

Engagement

Using language to engage with others or with alternative perspectives and possibilities. (See **Appraisal**.)

existing verb

A verb or verb group expressing a process of simply existing, usually preceded by 'there' (e.g. *there is* a hole in the bucket).

extended reference

When a word such as *this* or *that* or *it* refers back to a stretch of text. (See **Cohesion**.)

factorial explanation

Explains a phenomenon in terms of the factors that contribute towards a particular outcome.

fair test

A basic experiment where the variables are carefully controlled.

field

The subject matter or topic being developed in a particular situation.

genres

The ways in which we achieve our social purposes through language.

genres for arguing

Genres used to argue a case, discuss an issue, or challenge a position (e.g. expositions, discussions, challenges).

genres for entertaining

Genres used to entertain and reflect on life through the telling of stories (e.g. narratives, anecdotes, fables).

genres for explaining

Genres used to explain a phenomenon (e.g. sequential, causal, cyclical, factorial, and consequential explanations).

genres for instructing

Genres used to tell someone how to do something (e.g. simple procedures, directions, procedural recounts, conditional procedures and protocols).

genres for recounting

Genres used to tell what happened (e.g. recounts of personal experience, biographies, autobiographies, memoirs, literary recounts, historical recounts and accounts).

genres for responding

Genres used to respond to a work such as a literary text (e.g. personal responses, reviews, interpretation, critical responses).

genres for inquiring

Genres associated with extended tasks requiring students to observe, hypothesise, ask questions, conduct procedures, report on results etc. Because the tasks tend to have multiple purposes, the texts are often macrogenres; that is, comprise more than one genre.

Graduation

Using language to adjust the strength and focus of our utterances. (See **Appraisal**.)

ideational function

Language resources for expressing ideas ('What's happening?'; 'Who/What's involved?'; 'How? When? Where? Why?') and connecting ideas.

independent clause

A clause that is not dependent on another clause for its meaning. Sometimes called a main or principal clause.

infographics

Hybrid texts that combine image and language to convey information (usually factual) quickly and succinctly. Examples of infographics include transport maps, site plans, and graphs that summarise data.

interactional scaffolding

Support provided by teachers to students in dialogue. It includes such strategies as recasting, recapping, making links to prior experience, and pointing forward. Interactional scaffolding is crucial to students' cognitive and linguistic development.

Interpersonal function

Language resources for creating interpersonal meanings (interacting with others, expressing feelings, taking a stance, making judgments, etc.).

investigation report

A report describing an investigation into a given topic.

jigsaw task

An information gap activity which boosts talk opportunities in the classroom. Students are organised into groups and provided with information on a particular aspect of a topic. They become experts in that particular aspect, then form different groups comprising experts from each aspect to pool information and build common understandings of the topic from these various aspects.

jumbled text

Stages and phases of an example of the target genre are cut and mixed up, which students must reassemble using their knowledge of the stages of the genre. They can also be asked to label the stages and phases using functional labels.

lab report

Lab reports/prac reports describe and analyse an experiment (generally carried out in a laboratory).

lexical cohesion

Cohesion between content words through word associations such as repetition, synonyms, antonyms, collocation and word patterns (class—subclass, whole—part).

macrogenres

Texts comprising a number of elemental, shorter genres that are organised and related in particular ways. Macrogenres are commonly found in textbooks and on websites.

metalanguage

A shared language for talking about language.

modality

Language resources for expressing the degree of commitment, ranging from low (*maybe, might*) to high (*must, should*).

modality cline

A continuum demonstrating relative strengths of different forms of modality (e.g. from *might/possibly* through to *must/definitely*).

mode

The channel of communication being used in a particular situation (e.g. oral, written, visual).

mode continuum

A way of thinking about texts in terms of whether they have more 'spoken' language features or more 'written' ones.

mood system

The grammatical resources for making statements, asking questions, giving commands, and making offers.

nominalisation

A process in which an idea or event (represented by a clause or clauses) is downgraded to a 'thing' (represented by a noun group). It is a language resource for creating more compact text, and is often a feature of academic and bureaucratic texts.

non-finite clause

A dependent clause that has no subject and is not marked for tense (e.g. *Crossing the road,* she was struck by a car).

noun group

A word or group of words consisting of a head noun plus modifying words that can come before or after the head noun.

paragraph opener

A paragraph opener (or topic sentence) occurs at the start of a paragraph and indicates its main idea. This idea is usually elaborated in various ways in the remainder of the paragraph. There is generally a close relationship to the text opener.

participants

People, animals, objects, and abstract things that participate in Processes.

passive voice

A structure in which the subject of the verb is the recipient of the action (e.g. *the thief was caught by the police*), as opposed to the active voice, in which the subject of the verb is the source of the action (e.g. *the police caught the thief*).

past simple tense

Used to talk about actions and states that we see as completed in the past.

Pointer

That part of the noun group that answers the question 'Which?', expressed through the grammatical form of determiners such as articles (*a, an, the*), demonstratives (*this, that, these, those*), and possessives (*his, her, their, my, Ben's*).

polarised debate

Students take up a position on a line according to how they feel about an issue. Some students take turns to argue a position, while others are able to move in a different direction if they are persuaded. This is a key strategy for encouraging students to understand the importance of using evidence and other persuasive techniques.

prepositional phrase

A group of words beginning with a preposition. It can function as a Circumstance telling more about the Process (e.g. walked—they <u>walked</u> *up the hill*) or a Qualifier in the noun group telling more about the Thing (e.g. house—the <u>house</u> *on the hill*).

present simple tense

Used to talk about actions and states that are true in the present, that occur regularly, or that reflect universal truths.

problem-solution report

A report identifying a problem and proposing an effective solution.

procedural recount

A text that recounts or retells a procedure, often a simple experiment. Procedural recounts are often found embedded in more elaborate genres.

procedure

A text that enables people to do or make something, such as recipes and craft activities. It typically comprises stages such as a goal or outcome, a list of materials and equipment, and a series of steps.

process

A doing, happening, or state.

projection

A way of combining clauses in which one clause projects an idea or a direct quote (e.g. *The challenger promised to resign if he lost the ballot*; *'Mind the step!' she warned*).

protolanguage

An infant's idiosyncratic system of meanings and sounds.

Quantifier

That part of the noun group that answers the question 'How much?' or 'How many?', typically expressed through numerals (number words).

recount

A text with the purpose of telling what happened.

reference

The use of language resources to make a text cohesive by referring back (or forward) to something or someone mentioned elsewhere in the text.

register

A combination of the field, tenor, and mode in a particular situation.

relating processes

Processes of *being* and *having*. They are important in identifying and describing phenomena.

relating verb

A verb or verb group expressing a process of creating a relationship between two pieces of information (e.g. between a thing being described and its description: Her dress *was* dirty and torn).

Rheme

The part of a clause that generally follows the Theme (**'sentence opener'**) and introduces new information.

saying verb

A verb or verb group expressing a Process of saying (e.g. reporting or quoting: They *said* nothing.).

sensing verb

A verb or verb group expressing an inner mental process of feeling, thinking, or perceiving (She *wanted* a hug; Mario *thought* of his old mates; They *saw* his frightened face.).

scaffolding

Support provided to learners from a more experienced other in order to achieve outcomes that they would otherwise not be able to achieve on their own.

scanning

The reader looks through the text for particular pieces of information, playing close attention to sections. To do this, knowledge of the stages and phases of the genre is particularly useful.

sentence opener

The starting point that gives prominence to the message, focusing attention on how the topic is being developed and enabling the reader to predict how the text will unfold. (More technically referred to as **Theme**.)

sequential explanation

Typically uses a linear sequence to explain how something works.

simple sentence

A sentence that consists of a single independent clause.

skim-reading

Designed for quickly gaining general information about a whole text. The reader skims over the surface to get a general sense of the content or its main points.

speech functions

A variety of language resources for interacting; they include resources for seeking information (questions), providing information (statements), asking someone to do or provide something (commands) and offering or giving something (offers).

subject and object pronouns

Subject pronouns come before the verb (*we* like chocolate) while object pronouns come after the verb (chocolate doesn't like *us*) or a preposition (for *us*, to *me*, behind *him*).

subordinating conjunction

Joins a dependent clause to an independent clause (e.g. *when*, *because*, *unless*, *although*).

substitution

Cohesion can be created by substituting an all-purpose, general word such as *do*, *one*, *some*, or *so* for a word met previously.

system explanation

Explains how a system works in terms of the relationships between its parts.

teaching-learning cycle

A framework for planning and teaching language and literacy in different curriculum fields. Based on the principle of 'guidance through interaction in the context of shared experience' (Rose & Martin 2012, p. 58), the cycle scaffolds students as they gain increasing control of the curriculum topic as well as language choices in the written mode. The teaching-learning cycle requires teachers to develop students' explicit knowledge about language.

tenor

The roles and relationships being enacted in a particular situation.

text connective

A word or phrase that signals a connection between sentences and paragraphs or sections of text by clarifying (*for example, that is*), showing cause or result (*therefore, as a consequence*), indicating time (*then, next*), sequencing ideas (*first, in conclusion*), adding information (*and, as well*), or expressing condition or concession (*on the other hand, despite this*).

text opener

Provides an overview of the text, guiding the reader by signalling its organisation and often the main themes or ideas. There is usually a relationship with paragraph openers in the remainder of the text.

textual function

Language resources for shaping texts that are coherent and cohesive.

Theme

The first part of the clause that signals how the topic is being developed. (Also referred to as '**sentence opener**'.)

Thing

That part of the noun group that answers the question 'Who or What?', typically expressed through the grammatical form of common nouns (*house, dog*), proper nouns (*Mrs Brown, Green Park*), or personal pronouns (*she, it*).

think-pair-share

A strategy designed to foster student talk. Students are given a short period of time to marshal their thoughts individually before working with another on a task, then the results are shared with a larger group. **Pair-share** is a variation in which students work in pairs initially to talk through a problem before sharing with a larger group.

timeless present tense

A tense that is typically used to express general truths (*The flammability of materials varies*).

vector

A vector connects one element in an image with another element through the use of a line or arrow, pointed finger, or extended arm.

verb group

A word or group of words expressing a Process meaning.

viewing angle

The angle from which the viewer perceives an image can convey different relationships. A high angle means that the viewer is looking down on characters or subjects, suggesting a sense of power or dominance; low-angle shots make characters and objects seem more powerful than the viewer; eye-level angles are relatively neutral and suggest an equivalent relationship between the viewer and the characters or subjects in the image.

visual metalanguage

An explicit, shared language for talking about the meanings of image, for example placement, salience, viewing angle, and composition.

FURTHER READING

Aktas, R. N. (2005). Functions of 'shell nouns' as cohesive devices in academic writing: A comparative corpus-based study. University of Iowa, Retrospective Theses and Dissertations. Paper 16168: http://lib.dr.iastate.edu/cgi/viewcontent.cgi?article=17167&context=rtd

Australian Children's Television Foundation (2011). *Persuasive Text: An introduction to using persuasive language in the classroom* (DVD-ROM). Melbourne: Australian Children's Television Foundation.

Burridge, K., Clyne, M., & de Laps, D. (2009). *Living Lingo*. Melbourne: Victorian Association of Teachers of English, Unit 4.

Callow, J. (2013). *The Shape of Texts to Come: How image and texts work*. Sydney: PETAA.

Christie, F., & Derewianka, B. (2008). *School Discourse: Learning to write across the years of schooling*. London: Continuum.

Christie, F., & Martin, J.R. (eds) (1997). *Genre and Institutions: Social processes in the workplace and school*. London: Cassell.

Coffin, C., Hewings, A., & O'Halloran, K. (eds) (2004). *Applied English Grammar: Functional and corpus approaches*. London: Hodder-Arnold.

De Silva Joyce, H., & Feez, S. (2012). *Text-based language and literacy education: Programming and methodology*. Sydney: Phoenix.

De Silva Joyce, H., & Gaudin, J. (2007). *Interpreting the Visual: A resource book for teachers*. Sydney: Phoenix.

Derewianka, B. (2011). *A New Grammar Companion for Teachers*. Sydney: PETAA.

Derewianka, B. (1990). *Exploring How Texts Work*. Sydney: PETAA.

Fang, Z., & Schleppegrell, M. (2008). *Reading in the Secondary Content Areas. A language-based pedagogy*. Ann Arbor, MI: University of Michigan Press.

Gibbons, P. (2006). *Bridging Discourses in the ESL Classroom*. London: Continuum.

Gleeson, L. (2014). *Writing Like a Writer*. Sydney: PETAA.

Green, B., & Beavis, C. (2012). *Literacy in 3D*. Sydney: PETAA.

Humphrey, S., Droga, L., & Feez, S. (2012). *Grammar and Meaning*. Sydney: PETAA.

Humphrey, S., Love, K., & Droga, L. (2011). *Working Grammar: An introduction for secondary English teachers*. Melbourne: Pearson.

Hutton, P. (2011). *Writing Persuasive Texts*. Sydney: e:lit (PETAA).

Macken, M. (1996). Literacy and learning across the curriculum: Towards a model of register for secondary teachers. In R. Hasan & G. Williams (eds), *Literacy in Society*. London: Longman, pp. 232–78.

McDonald, L. (2012). *A Literature Companion for Teachers*. Sydney: PETAA.

Mallan, K. (2014). *Picture Books and Beyond*. Sydney: PETAA.

Martin, J.R., & Rose, D. (2009). *Genre Relations: Mapping culture*. London: Equinox.

Martin, J.R., & Rose, D. (2003). *Working with Discourse: Meaning beyond the clause*. London: Equinox.

Oxford University Press (2011). *Yarning Strong Land Anthology*. Melbourne: Oxford University Press.

Polias, J. (2010). Pedagogic resonance: Improving teaching and learning. *NALDIC Quarterly, 8*(1), 6–17.

Rose, D., & Acevedo, C. (2006). Closing the gap and accelerating learning in the middle years of schooling. *Literacy Learning: The Middle Years, 14*, 32–45.

Rose, D., & Martin, J.R. (2012). *Learning to Write, Reading to Learn: Genre, knowledge and pedagogy in the Sydney School*. London: Equinox.

Rossbridge, J. & Rushton, K. (2015). *Put it in Writing: Context, text and language*. Sydney: PETAA.

Rossbridge, J., & Rushton, K. (2010). *Conversations about Text 1: Teaching grammar using literary texts*. Sydney: PETAA.

Rossbridge, J., & Rushton, K. (2010). *Conversations about Text 2: Teaching grammar using factual texts*. Sydney: PETAA.

Schleppegrell, M.J. (2004). *The Language of Schooling: A functional linguistics perspective*. Mahwah, NJ, and London: Erlbaum.

Tan, S., Marissa, K.L.E., & O'Halloran, K. (2012). *Multimodal Analysis: Image*. Singapore: Multimodal Analysis Company. http://multimodal-analysis.com/products/multimodal-analysis-image.

Williams, G. (1994). *Using Systemic Grammar in Teaching Young Learners: An introduction*. Melbourne: Macmillan.

INDEX